Create Your Best Future

Chicken Soup for the Soul: Create Your Best Future
Inspiring Stories for Teens and Young Adults about Making the Right Decisions
Amy Newmark, Dr. Milton Boniuk. Foreword by David Leebron.

Published by CSS Boniuk, an imprint of Chicken Soup for the Soul Publishing, LLC.
www.chickensoup.com.

Front cover photo courtesy of iStockphoto.com/ChristopherFutcher (© CEFutcher)
Back cover and interior compass courtesy of iStockphoto.com/13goat (© 13goat)
Photo of Amy Newmark courtesy of Susan Morrow at SwickPix.

Design by Brian Taylor, Pneuma Books, LLC
Layout by Marie Killoran

Distributed to the booktrade by Simon & Schuster. SAN: 200-2442

Publisher's Cataloging-In-Publication Data
(*Prepared by The Donohue Group, Inc.*)

Chicken soup for the soul : create your best future : inspiring stories for teens and
   young adults about making the right decisions / [compiled by] Amy Newmark [and]
   Dr. Milton Boniuk.

      pages ; cm

   ISBN: 978-1-942649-02-1

   1. Teenagers--Conduct of life--Literary collections. 2. Teenagers--Conduct of life-
-Anecdotes. 3. Young adults--Conduct of life--Literary collections. 4. Young adults-
-Conduct of life--Anecdotes. 5. Anecdotes. I. Newmark, Amy. II. Boniuk, Milton.
III. Title: Create your best future : inspiring stories for teens and young adults about
making the right decisions

BF637.C5 C45 2015
158.10835   2015938136

PRINTED IN THE UNITED STATES OF AMERICA
on acid∞free paper

25 24 23 22 21 20 19 18 17 16 15   01 02 03 04 05 06 07 08 09 10 11

Create Your Best Future

Inspiring Stories for Teens
and Young Adults about
Making the Right Decisions

Amy Newmark & Dr. Milton Boniuk
Foreword by David W. Leebron

Chicken Soup for the Soul Publishing, LLC
Cos Cob, CT

The Boniuk Foundation

www.theboniukfoundation.org

Chicken Soup for the Soul

For moments that become stories™
www.chickensoup.com

Contents

❶

~Standing Up for What's Right~

❷

~Choosing to Be Your Very Best~

❸
~Looking Past Stereotypes~

❹
~Developing Self-Esteem~

❺
~Volunteering and Giving~

❻
~Embracing Differences~

❼
~Accepting and Asking for Help~

8

~Powering Through Challenges~

9

~Reaching Out to Others~

➓
~Counting Your Blessings~

Foreword

The education of young people occurs in varied ways and for many purposes. We educate to impart knowledge, to develop skills, to inculcate values, and to foster good character. We use many different means to achieve these goals, from the examples adults set to traditional classroom instruction to the use of the newest digital technologies. But from the beginning of human history, one of the most common ways we learn is through stories.

Such stories can teach us and inspire us along many dimensions. They can teach us to be strong and confident in the face of adversity. They can teach us to be kind, generous and forgiving to others, and to be grateful for those who seek to help us. They can inspire us to be bold enough to change what is wrong in our lives or wrong in the world we see.

Small children make few decisions, and it falls on parents and teachers to make decisions for those children and begin to prepare them for their future. Teenagers and young adults are still learning also, but at the same time they are beginning to make an increasing number of decisions of ever greater importance. They will undoubtedly make mistakes, and some of those mistakes will be with them for a long time. But they will also make some great decisions, and learn from some extraordinary people, and those decisions and that learning may influence the entire course of their lives.

The subtitle of this book reminds me of one of my favorite jokes. A journalist interviews a very successful person. He asks: "How did you get to be so successful?" After the pondering the question for a few moments, the successful person responds, "Making the right decisions." The journalist follows up with another question: "Yes, but how were you able to make such good decisions?" The response after a bit of thought: "experience." The journalist, being a very probing journalist, asks a further follow-up: "And how were you able to accumulate that experience?" Without hesitation, the interviewee responds, "By making the wrong decisions."

The stories in this volume were selected by Dr. Milton Boniuk and the team listed in his introduction to assist you in making the right decisions. Dr. Boniuk and his wife Laurie are two of the most remarkable people I have met. They have generously devoted substantial resources to fostering religious tolerance in particular, but also improving the education of young people to instill broad values of tolerance and appreciation for diversity of all kinds. They believe that such education is the foundation of a better society.

This work takes place not only in the publication of this book through the efforts of The Boniuk Foundation, but also through an allied endeavor at Rice University, The Boniuk Institute for the Study and Advancement of Religious Tolerance (www.boniuk.rice.edu). The mission of the institute, founded in 2013, is "to understand and promote religious tolerance by using innovative methods to" undertake research, produce educational programming, and foster dialogue. It identifies religious intolerance as one of the root causes of war, discrimination, and violence in our world, and is committed to undertake those educational and research activities that will begin to eliminate such intolerance.

While the goal of this volume is much broader, and it illustrates many of the values and good behaviors we hope you aspire to, almost all of them also affect the degree to which we practice and foster tolerant, welcoming and supportive attitudes toward the differences we see in others. The Boniuks sincerely hope, as do so many of us, that through such efforts we can raise new generations that will end the hatred and violence that has ruined so many lives. This volume of brief stories celebrates the very best in the human spirit, and although aimed at teenagers and young adults, it is worth reading for all of us.

~David W. Leebron, President, Rice University

Introduction

Life is a journey where you build on experiences within your family, community, and the world at large. We access information and ideas through schooling and other extracurricular activities, including sports, music, arts as well as various types of entertainment, such as radio, TV, movies, and the Internet. Finding part-time or summer jobs helps us learn to interact with strangers, develop business skills, and achieve some financial independence that will help us plan for our future.

My father, who came from Poland, and my mother, who came from Russia, immigrated to Canada in the early 1920s. I was one of five children born and raised in Glace Bay, Nova Scotia. My parents had limited formal education, and my siblings and I witnessed the hardships our family and others endured during those difficult times. Providing a good education for their children was extremely important to our parents. They could not help us with our scholastic studies, but they taught us to be honest, respectful, caring, and kind to others. We were extremely fortunate to have excellent, dedicated teachers in the local schools. With our parents' ability to provide the direction we needed, and sufficient financial support to further our education, all five siblings graduated from Dalhousie University in Halifax, Nova Scotia: three physicians (all ophthalmologists), one dentist, and one schoolteacher.

Ideally, all children need a strong family unit with two parents and/

or grandparents, who can play a significant role if they are allowed to do so. Good schools and good teachers are extremely important, and friends may have a positive effect, too. But they can have a negative effect if they influence others to use alcohol and drugs. Technology has added new hazards for children and adults alike, when texting on cell phones while driving can lead to tragedy and death. Individuals targeted by bullies not only in our school hallways, but in cyber-space, have committed suicide. Video game addiction, both in children and adults, has ruined families financially and destroyed the lives of teenagers and young adults who otherwise had a promising future.

I hope that the stories in this second book, for teenagers and young adults, will help the readers make the right decisions toward a healthy, productive, and fulfilling life. Tragedies may happen or be avoided because of fate. Those we cannot change. In my practice as an ophthalmologist, I have seen many such cases. I recall, in particular, treating a ten-year-old boy who happened to be riding a bike, and while riding sustained an injury to his only good eye when a firecracker exploded just as he was passing by. He happened to be in the wrong place at the wrong time. I continue to see this patient forty-five years later, and even though he is gainfully employed, I often think how his life could have been so different if his encounter had been one or two seconds earlier or later. This type of tragedy we chalk up to fate, but there are many tragedies that can be avoided by living right and making good decisions. I hope that the stories in this book help with those decisions.

Reading Chicken Soup for the Soul stories has been uplifting for me, and reading them allows me to relax and sleep peacefully when I realize how lucky I am compared to others who have had such difficult times. I hope you and your family members enjoy reading these stories, and I am confident that exposure to these stories and the lessons contained within them will help us all become part of a more tolerant, respectful, caring, and passionate society.

My wife Laurie and I have been very fortunate to have accumulated a large estate by investments, primarily in real estate. Approximately twenty years ago, we decided to contribute one-half of our estate to charity. We are both excited about having the opportunity to use these funds to implement programs developed at The Boniuk Institute at Rice University and The Boniuk Foundation. These programs include education of our children, parenting programs, and the promotion of religious tolerance.

I am very grateful to Bill Rouhana, CEO, and Amy Newmark, Publisher, of Chicken Soup for the Soul, for allowing us to develop these educational programs with them. Bill and Amy share our commitment and dedication to these projects.

I would like to acknowledge the assistance of the following individuals who helped select the stories for inclusion in this book: my wife Laurie, my son David Boniuk and his wife Kelli, my grandsons Justin Sable and Ryan Sable, Yan Digilov, Dr. Silvia Orengo-Nania and her daughter Julia Nania, her nieces Anna Hanel and Marisa Rao, Lee Pelton, a freshman at Rice University, and Gaby Barrios, Natalie Danckers, and Anjale Raghuran, all juniors at Rice University.

I would also like to thank David Leebron, president of Rice University for his continued support. I also thank the following members of the advisory board of The Boniuk Institute at Rice University for their unwavering support: Charley Landgraf, member of the board of trustees and current chairman of the advisory board; Malcolm Gillis, former president of Rice; and Bill Barnett and James Crownover, former chairmen of the board at Rice University.

~Dr. Milton Boniuk

Chapter 1

Create Your Best Future

Standing Up for What's Right

Without Prejudice

When you teach your son, you teach your son's son.
~The Talmud

I f my mom had followed the pattern of her mother and grand-mother, she probably would have been a racist. A kind and loving racist with gracious manners and Southern hospitality, but a racist nonetheless. And I might have been a racist, too.

My mom experienced the typical racial prejudice and segregated lifestyle of white families in Jackson, Mississippi long before that segregation was portrayed in the book and movie, *The Help*. She found the same culture of segregation and discrimination when she moved to Louisiana in her early teens. But at some point on the road to adulthood, my mom decided not to share that culture with her children.

Though few black families lived in our Houston neighborhood in the 1960s, my mom was determined to help her girls embrace racial equality. When Alabama's governor tried to prevent the desegregation of the state's public schools in 1963 and state troopers were called to block elementary school doorways, my mom grabbed our hands and lined us up in front of the family television to watch the grainy black and white images. Mom cried as black children were turned away, clinging to their parents' hands. My sisters and I were young—just three, five and seven. We were far too young to understand the issues and emotions behind Mom's tears or the battle over integration. But our age didn't matter to Mom. She wanted us to share the history-making moment with her.

Mom followed the news of the civil rights movement and talked about it at the dinner table. When Dr. Martin Luther King, Jr. was jailed in Birmingham in 1963, my mom sent him a letter. She didn't know Dr. King, but she wanted to assure him of her prayers. He was changing the world her girls would live in.

On those weekends when we visited my mom's dad and step-mom, stepping back into the world of white prejudice, Mom showed us how to respect her dad's black employees. My grandfather may have called the lawn man "boy," but my mom introduced him to us as Mr. William. She took time to visit with Mr. William during each visit and ask about his family. She taught us the same respect for the women who cooked and cleaned at my grandparents' house.

Once my youngest sister started school, Mom put feet to our dinner table discussions about racial discrimination. She began volunteering once a week at a Baptist ministry center in one of Houston's poorest neighborhoods. There she talked with young black and Hispanic moms who came for sewing classes and food distributions. She cuddled their babies and joked with their children. And she encouraged us to volunteer with her during school breaks once we were old enough.

As I approached ninth grade, Houston's school district was pressured to rezone the schools to speed up integration. I wasn't excited about switching to a new school—a school four miles farther from my home—or the prospect of leaving my friends behind. For weeks after school started, I came home with stories about knifings and fights between black and white students. I worried that I might get caught in the middle of one of those fights. But my mom encouraged me to plow through fear and discomfort, keep the big goal in sight, and make new friends with students of other races.

Mom's lessons stuck. Today my husband pastors a multi-ethnic church congregation in Nevada. If you scan the crowd on a Sunday morning, you'll see people from almost a dozen ethnic heritages. Funny, but I rarely notice the diversity until a newcomer or friend comments on it.

I think my mom notices the diversity though. When she visits our church, she smiles at the rainbow of races. After the worship service is over, Mom shakes hands and greets people without any hint of prejudice. I see her joy as she talks to my wide array of friends, and I know she is pleased. This is the life Mom always had in mind for her girls.

~Donna Finlay Savage

Speaking Up

A time comes when silence is betrayal.
~Dr. Martin Luther King, Jr.

never looked up when my friends were talking and joking about the "Retarded Boy" (as they referred to him) a few tables away. It didn't even cross my mind that he might feel bad when people whispered about him, or that he might be hurt when he saw the weird, disgusted looks from his peers. So I just let them talk, and I never intervened.

Then came the day I was standing in the kitchen helping with dinner, asking my mom about my brother's doctor's appointment. They were testing him for autism. My parents had told me there was a huge chance of it coming out positive, but I had never thought about him like that. My brother, Captain, four years old at the time, had always been my best friend. We would wrestle, play games and have the best of times together, even though we were far apart in age. My mom told me about the appointment, and when she got to the point about the test, she stopped. I turned around and she had tears in her eyes. I stared at her, wishing she would say something, when I realized what that silence meant. My eyes got blurry and my breathing got very ragged. "The test came out positive, sweetheart," she said with a calm voice. I broke down, crying and asking why it had happened to Captain.

My mom was trying to pull me together, saying that Captain

couldn't see me like this and I had to be a big girl, when the front door opened, and Captain, our three-year-old sister Cali, and my father came in. I walked out of the kitchen. Captain was talking to our dad and then stopped, switching his attention to me. As he looked up at me with those huge blue eyes, I had to look away. I couldn't look at him. Everything had just changed. He was no longer that little baby brother who was just a normal little boy anymore. He was a little boy with a disease who didn't deserve anything that was going to come with it.

Over time, I was able to accept his disease a little more. We had to move a while later because Captain needed treatment and where we lived at the time didn't have the type he needed. So we moved to Maryland. Time passed and Captain and I both started at a new school. One day, I was standing in the bus line waiting when the "short bus" came and picked some kids up. The children in the other line started making jokes about the "retards" on that bus and I felt a strange feeling in my stomach. One that I had never felt before. As the other kids laughed about the cruel jokes, I said, quietly, that those comments weren't very nice. No one listened and I went on my way. I regretted it immediately, and wished I had said something else.

My family moved once more to a new school and I was given my chance to speak up pretty quickly. During band class, my teacher, Mrs. Young, stopped our playing to give us some feedback.

"Guys, we're playing like the kids on the short bus! Come on!" I felt that same feeling I had on the bus line, except worse. This was an adult, and I thought adults would be more careful about what they said. Apparently, ignorance comes in all different ages. The entire room was laughing when I raised my hand. I wasn't sure what I was going to say but I wanted to be heard.

"Yes, Alexis?" Mrs. Young asked. The class quieted down because the new girl was about to talk for the first time. I could feel my face getting red and was about to just say never mind, when my mouth opened and this came out:

"I don't think we should make fun of the short bus, because there are a lot of people on that bus who have great personalities and have the same feelings we do." I could feel my voice getting louder. "And also, I know some people on those buses and they are some of the most caring, sweetest, and smartest people so I would appreciate it if you didn't make fun of them."

The room was very quiet and everyone stared at me. Mrs. Young apologized for the comment and then started the song again. Everyone was a little on edge. At the end of the class, everyone was giving me weird looks and sizing me up. They looked like they were labeling me a nerd right off the bat, but I didn't care, because I knew three things: I had spoken the truth and what others in the class were probably thinking, I had taught everyone something, and while everyone in the classroom was being a follower, I had decided to take a different path. I want to become a leader and a positive role model and go on to teach others about people on the "short bus." I want to teach people about my brother Captain, who doesn't know that he's different. And really, he's not. He's just a five-year-old who loves baseball and eating cookies, and I never want to hear anybody make fun of him.

~Alexis Streb

A Flower for Leourn

We can do no great things, only small things with great love.
~Mother Teresa

We were out to change the world. This was our time, our senior year. My best friend Beth and I had big dreams and big hopes for our last year at high school. We were ready for a miracle we knew we would see. With great anticipation, we started the year with my senior quote in mind: "But God and I have big dreams, and with big dreams you can't give up, you have to keep pressing on."

I would like to say that I was the first to notice her, but in my world of "big dreams," this one small, quiet freshman did not appear on my radar. My sensitive best friend Beth was the first to notice her.

"Kristi, did you see the girl standing by us in the lunch line? She looks so lost, so out of place," Beth said to me. We had heard of a family that had just moved to our town from Cambodia. We knew there was supposed to be a new girl at school from that family, but we had yet to meet her... until now.

Leourn was a small, dark-haired beauty. She was thrust into a new country where she struggled with the little English she knew, and it made it very hard for her to get to know people in our small town. She was starting her freshman year and was trying her best to blend in without attracting any attention.

We watched in the lunchroom at our "Senior Table." This table was reserved for our senior sport jock friends, and no one else. Leourn would get her lunch tray with the rest of the students, but she always kept her head down with her eyes focused on the floor. She would then head to the only table of girls she recognized. Unfortunately, it was the table for the most popular girls in the freshman class. Every single day, Leourn would sit at the very edge of her seat and eat as fast as she could. She kept her eyes fixed on her food and we never, ever saw her look up. We would watch in dismay at the interaction of the other girls at her table. They would make gestures to one another and laugh at Leourn while she ate.

As we paid attention over the next week, we never heard anyone so much as say "Hi" to Leourn.

We watched as Leourn walked, with her head always down, through the halls of a high school where most didn't even acknowledge her existence. She was a girl invisible.

Beth and I prayed and talked — what could we do to help Leourn? With love and faith, we decided to try our hardest to let one lonely girl know that there were people who knew she existed and, more importantly, that there was a God who knew and loved her.

As the weeks and months passed, Beth and I made an effort to let Leourn know that we cared. We sat with Leourn at the freshman girls' table. The other freshman girls tried to let us in on the joke that "nobody talks to Leourn." Their lofty glances and laughs were met with death stares from two upperclassmen.

We sought out Leourn in the halls and said "Hi" and tried to continue to engage her in conversation. I would like to say that, at this point, Leourn responded to us with smiles and small talk. But she didn't — Leourn still kept her head down and responded very little. We were okay with that, because we knew that God wanted us to keep trying to spend time with Leourn, regardless of her response.

When February rolled around, our school sold carnations that we could send to one another for Valentine's Day. I immediately thought of Leourn and decided I would send her a flower for the holiday. When I thought about what to write, it occurred to me that keeping it simple would be the best for someone just learning our language and customs.

So I just simply wrote:

> *Happy Valentine's Day, Leourn —*
> *I want you to know how much God loves you.*
> *Your friend, Kristi*

I will never forget that Valentine's Day.

For the first time, Leourn was the one who sought me out. She found me in the hall with the carnation clutched tightly in her hands. Then she did something amazing. She looked up.

She actually took her eyes off the floor, looked up at me with beautiful beaming eyes, and in a low choked whisper said two words: "Thank You."

It was a life-changing moment for me.

You see, Beth and I were out to change the world, but instead God was changing me. I learned that I may never be president, be famous, or have a million dollars to my name. But I learned that what Christ wanted from me was for me to love Him with all my heart and all my soul so that I could spread that love to everyone around me — one flower at a time.

It's like walking out to a pond and throwing in one tiny pebble. Though that pebble is incredibly small compared to the pond, it still creates ripples that affect the water around it. As I learned my senior year, every word that comes from our mouths and every action we carry out affects the people around us, whether we realize it or not.

We ended our senior year not knowing how many people's lives we touched. However, Beth and I knew that our two lives were changed. Leourn went on to graduate from our small high school three years after us, and I went back for her graduation. As Leourn walked out of the gymnasium after the ceremony, I gave her a big hug and told her congratulations. As she looked up at me, the tears streamed down her face. I asked her if the tears were happy ones or sad ones, and she said they were both. I gave her another hug before she walked off into the crowd.

As I look back, I hope in my own small way that we helped to make her first year in a new country easier, and that we brought a little light into her world.

~Kristi Powers

Chicken Soup for the Soul.

Small Girl Learns a Big Lesson

The test of courage comes when we are in the minority.
The test of tolerance comes when we are in the majority.
~Ralph W. Sockman

Auden, my dear grandmother, passed away in 1992. I was only five years old, too young to remember enough about her. But one important life lesson she taught me remains unforgettable.

When Auden was a high school senior in 1940s Chicago, there was a "must-go-to" party after the prom. My grandmother was invited and was eagerly anticipating the big event. That is, until a few days later when she found out that Jennifer, one of her best friends, hadn't received an invitation. Auden's excitement quickly turned to anger when she discovered the reason for the exclusion.

Jennifer wasn't invited because she was Jewish.

Understand, this wasn't just a big party, it was *the* party of this senior class's high school *lives.*

No matter. My grandmother didn't take this sitting down.

"I didn't want Jennifer, or anyone, to feel left out," Auden said. If Jennifer wasn't welcome, then Auden wouldn't go either. Instead, she invited Jennifer over for their own small party. A two-person party... that turned out to be *the* party of the Class of 1940s young lives as more and more classmates decided to do the right thing.

"Injustice," I remember Auden telling me more than once, "is everyone's battle."

I was only a kindergartner, but I listened, I learned and I remembered.

As I have grown up, racism is something I have read about in history textbooks, something that happens to other people, in other times, in other places. Certainly I never thought I would witness something so ugly in my small hometown in Southern California. My middle school was largely white, but with a healthy minority mix of Hispanic, Asian and a few African-American students. I have been brought up to notice skin color only the way I might notice someone's red hair or freckles or dimples. I just see people. Human beings. My classmates. My friends.

But one morning I arrived at school to find out my friend Damien had been suspended for getting into a fight with another student. I was shocked. Damien was a kindhearted, gentle person, an honors student, even voted "friendliest" by his eighth-grade classmates. He always smiled and said "hello" when you passed him in the hallways. He was popular with the cool kids and also with the less-cool kids because he was nice to everybody. Damien was the last person I would suspect of being suspended.

Throughout the day, the details of Damien's suspension leaked out. At first I was shocked, then perplexed, then, as I gradually pieced together the whole story, furious.

This is what happened. Damien was waiting for his ride home after school when the school troublemaker, a white kid who had already been suspended numerous times and was just a few missteps away from juvenile hall, sauntered up to him, sneered a racial slur (Damien, I should mention, is African-American) and began to push him around. Damien first tried to walk away, then tried to defend himself. When an administrator finally noticed the scuffle and rushed over to tear them apart, it looked as if both boys had been involved in the fight. Both were suspended immediately. Even when the few witnesses said that Damien was just defending himself, school administrators remained firm. Damien had been involved in a fight with another student, and therefore he was suspended.

"Zero tolerance," they said, unaware of the irony. "No ifs, ands or buts about it."

Not only did Damien have to miss school for a few days, as a student who had been suspended he was also barred from any of the remaining school functions: dances, the end-of-the-year field trip to the beach, even the eighth-grade graduation ceremony. To me, this seemed unbearably unfair, especially since Damien had merely been defending himself.

I talked to the principal. She remained steadfast in her stance. I passed around a petition at school and drummed up support from more than 400 students, nearly the entire eighth-grade class. The administration remained stubbornly firm behind the suspension.

On the day of graduation, Damien sat in the audience instead of onstage with the other graduates. As class president, I was allowed to give a speech at the ceremony. I stood at the podium, tears welling up in my eyes at the sight of Damien sitting amid the crowd of parents instead of onstage with his classmates and friends.

I cleared my throat.

"When I was very young," I began, "an incredibly wise lady, my grandmother Auden, taught me a valuable lesson. 'Injustice is every-one's battle,' she used to say. And I say that it is an injustice that Damien is not up here onstage with us today…"

I wish I could tell you that our principal was affected by the ovation Damien received and invited him up with us. But she didn't. This battle against injustice was lost.

Or maybe not. The smile on Damien's face told me he didn't feel completely left out.

It is now four years later. When I see Damien in the high school halls, he still sometimes thanks me for what I did.

In truth, he should thank my Grandma Auden.

~Dallas Woodburn

The Fat Kid

If we really want to love, we must learn to forgive.
~Mother Teresa

"Recess!" one boy yelled. Lines formed quickly, but I stayed at the end. Looking down, hands in my pockets, I kicked rocks across the blacktop. I watched the boys play basketball as the girls looked on. They did not know who I was. I wondered whether I should ask to play, but just then Joe hit the ground. He limped to the side of the court with help from a teammate.

"Hey, you want to play?" asked John, his team now short a man. John was a tall, skinny boy everyone liked. He was one of the most athletic kids in my grade.

"Umm, I'll play the next game," I said as I sat watching. That's all I ever did — watch.

The next day, science, math, social studies, and English passed as usual, and I sat with friends eating lunch.

"Are you going to play basketball with us today?" asked John. "Joe is still hurt."

"Yeah, I'll try it today," I said nervously, knowing what would happen.

Lunch ended, and the lines to go outside formed even faster than the day before. John called me to the hoop, and I walked over slowly, peering out of the corner of my eye at the girls watching. I saw one of them point at me, but I kept walking.

The game started, and everything was okay. I made a few baskets, and, as one of the tallest kids, I got a lot of rebounds. Although this was only recess basketball, I felt like I could play for the New York Knicks. The day was perfect, and after watching for all those hours, I was glad to finally play.

The girls came over. I tried not to make eye contact, but it was difficult not to. A group of them chanted "Fat @$$" and "Lard @$$," but I kept playing.

During the next period, I sat with my head on the desk. I didn't want those girls to know they'd gotten to me. I would laugh at anything just to put it out of my head. I kept hearing their words, though, and felt myself shatter completely.

I went home on the bus that day with my head leaning against the window. My mom was waiting at my stop. I walked to her and gave her a hug, sobbing. I told her they'd made fun of me again. I told her I wished I was thin, and that kids weren't so mean to me. Even though I did have friends, I felt like I didn't and never would because people saw me as fat before they got to know me.

I fell asleep that night wondering what it would be like if I were a skinny, handsome boy. I was jealous of all the kids who were never teased and had everything easy. No one I knew got teased the way I did. Maybe it was a good thing. *Maybe*, I thought, *maybe it will make me mellow when I grow up.* But now, I was the boy no girls ever looked at.

A few years later, I went to a sports camp with activities every second we were awake. In the beginning, I was the same "fat kid" I was at school. But, week by week, the pounds came off. When my mom visited after five weeks, she couldn't get over how I looked and told me I must have dropped at least fifteen pounds. I felt great. Three years of camp passed, and I dropped more and more weight. Each summer I came home a different person.

One day at school, I saw an overweight boy walking through the hall with his head down, trying not to make eye contact. I thought that maybe he had been teased like I had been and just couldn't take it. I wondered if he was crying like I once had.

The next day, I saw him again. "You're so fat!" yelled a boy. "You're the fattest kid I've ever seen!" taunted another as he shoved him against the locker. My good friends, ones I had known since I was little, were teasing this boy and calling him the same names that had traumatized me through the years. Upset, I went over to them.

"Get away from him!" I screamed. "What did he ever do to you?"

Although they walked away, I didn't think they got the message that words hurt. The boy looked at me, smiled, and said thanks, and then walked to his next class. He never looked back; he just kept walking through the hallway. This time, though, he walked with his head up.

~David Gelbard

The Boldest Girl in Class

Courage is what it takes to stand up and speak; courage is also what it takes to sit down and listen.
~Winston Churchill

'll never forget the first time I heard my English teacher, Mr. Barnes, make an inappropriate comment in class. He'd just handed out our first assignment and someone asked how long it should be. "Like the length of a lady's skirt," he said. "Long enough to cover everything, but short enough to keep it interesting." The guys howled and gave each other high fives. Mr. Barnes just sat there and smiled with an annoying little smirk on his face. It made my skin crawl.

As the year went by, his comments became more and more inappropriate. I began to dread his class. He could turn anything we studied into something negative and degrading to women. It was humiliating. How could he treat us like this? Each time he made one of his comments, I wanted to say something, but I was too afraid of him. Besides, everyone called me "Miss Quiet and Shy." I didn't like speaking in front of other people and I would never talk back to a teacher.

Toward the end of the year, we started studying *The Canterbury Tales*, a Middle English collection of stories about a group of travelers. Mr. Barnes made a generic, stereotypical comment about the traveler in each tale we were reading. When we came to the tale about the

"Wife of Bath," I braced myself. Just as I suspected, he told us about how this woman was a typical wife. They only brought her along because they needed someone to cook and clean. I just couldn't take it anymore. What was wrong with us? Why did we all sit complacently, taking this abuse? The guys were laughing and acting like Mr. Barnes was a stand-up comedian. I looked at the girls and most of them just sat there with their arms crossed and their heads hanging down. It made me so angry. I felt like I was going to explode.

I don't know what came over me. Suddenly, I blurted out a "Hmm!" My teacher's head jerked up.

He glared around the room and asked, "Who said that?" No one said a word. It was so quiet that I heard the clock on the wall ticking for the first time ever.

I had a queasy feeling in the pit of my stomach, like I'd just gone upside down on a roller coaster. I could feel my face getting hotter as the blood rushed to my cheeks. My heart was pounding so loud and so fast that I thought it might jump right out of my chest. What was I thinking? I was "Miss Quiet and Shy," right? I was already in way over my head. Oh well, I thought, somebody has to stand up to this guy — here goes nothing. I opened my mouth and blurted out, "I said it." Everyone whipped around and stared at me with looks of horror. I wanted to crawl underneath my desk.

Mr. Barnes glared at me and said, "Do you have something you'd like to say?"

"Yes... I... do." I choked out. "I think your comments are stereotypical and rude. They are... um... inappropriate, sir." I stammered.

"Well," he said, "I'm sorry you feel that way. Thank you for your comments, Miss Westbrook."

I don't think I paid attention to anything else the entire class period. I couldn't believe what I had just done. Was that my voice I had heard? Did Mr. Barnes really just thank me for my comments? When the bell rang, I grabbed my stuff and ran down the hall to my locker.

By the end of the day, the entire school had heard what had happened. People I didn't even know were coming up to me and patting me on the back. All of the girls were so glad that someone had finally stood up to him, and so was I. I just couldn't believe that it had been me!

For the rest of the year, Mr. Barnes toned down his comments, at least in my class. He still told some awful jokes, but they were no longer degrading.

When I handed in my final exam, Mr. Barnes looked me in the eye and said, "You, Miss Westbrook, will go far in life. We need more leaders and fewer followers. Good luck next year." I was shocked—it seemed like he actually respected me for standing up to him. I smiled and felt proud. Who would have thought that "Miss Quiet and Shy" would have ended up being the boldest girl in class?

~Christy Westbrook

Changing the World — One Clip at a Time

*Never doubt that a small group of committed people can change
the world; indeed it is the only thing that ever has.*
~Margaret Mead

n 1998, principal Linda Hooper wanted to start a project that
would teach the students at Whitwell Middle School (Whitwell,
Tennessee) about tolerating and respecting different cultures. Mrs.
Hooper sent her eighth-grade history teacher and football coach,
David Smith, to a teacher-training course in nearby Chattanooga. He
came back and proposed that an after-school course on the Holocaust
be offered at the school. This in a school with hardly any ethnic and no
Jewish students.

Mr. Smith and eighth-grade English teacher Sandra Roberts held
the first session of the project in October of that year. The teachers
began by reading aloud from Anne Frank's *Diary of a Young Girl* and
Elie Wiesel's *Night*. They read aloud because most of the students
could not afford to buy books.

What gripped the eighth-graders most as the course progressed
was the sheer number of Jews put to death by the Third Reich. Six
million. They could hardly fathom such an immense figure.

One day, Roberts and Smith were explaining to the class that some compassionate people in 1940s Europe stood up for the Jews. After the Nazis invaded Norway, many courageous Norwegians expressed solidarity with their Jewish fellow citizens by pinning ordinary paper clips to their lapels, as Jews were forced to wear a Star of David on theirs.

Then someone had the idea to collect six million paper clips to represent the six million Jewish Holocaust victims. The idea caught on, and the students began bringing in paper clips from home, from aunts and uncles, and friends. They set up a Web page. A few weeks later, the first letter arrived — then others. Many contained paper clips. By the end of the school year, the group had assembled 100,000 clips. But it occurred to the teachers that collecting six million paper clips at that rate would take a lifetime.

The group's activities have long spilled over from the classroom. It's now called the Holocaust Project. Down the halls, students have created a concentration camp simulation with paper cutouts of themselves pasted on the wall. Chicken wire stretches across the wall to represent electrified fences. Wire mesh is hung with shoes to represent the millions of shoes the victims left behind when they were marched to death chambers. And every year now they reenact the "walk" to show their love and respect for those victims they never had a chance to meet. The "walk" also gives students at least an inkling of what people must have felt when Nazi guards marched them off to camps.

Meanwhile, the paper clip counting continues. Students gather for their Wednesday meeting, each wearing a paper clip on the lapel of their group's polo shirt emblazoned: "Changing the World, One Clip at a Time." All sorts of clips arrive: silver- and bronze-colored clips, colorful plastic-coated clips, small clips, large clips, round clips, triangular clips, and even clips fashioned from wood. The students file all the letters they receive in ring binders. With the collected paper clips, the students wanted to honor the victims with a memorial.

It was decided that the memorial would be more meaningful if the clips could be housed in an authentic German railroad car. With help from German citizens, the school obtained an authentic German railroad car from the 1940s, one that was actually used to transport victims to the camps. The car, transported from Berlin, Germany, to the tiny town of Whitwell, now sets in front of the middle school loaded with eleven million of these symbolic paper clips from all over the world. The principal, teachers and students took their vision and turned it into a reality. Having collected over twenty-nine million paper clips and over twenty thousand letters, the students and teachers at Whitwell Middle School have achieved a response that no one could have predicted.

For generations of Whitwell eighth graders, a paper clip will never again be just a paper clip. Instead, it will carry a message of perseverance, empathy, tolerance and understanding. One student put it like this: "Now, when I see someone, I think before I speak, I think before I act and I think before I judge."

Can one person, or one small group, truly do anything to help bring humanity together in understanding and peace? Just ask the students at Whitwell and all of those around the world who are helping them collect paper clips!

~Steve Goodier

You Get What You Give

If you find it in your heart to care for somebody else, you will
have succeeded.
~Maya Angelou

n 1953, moving into a newly built home in Levittown,
Pennsylvania, was the American Dream for a blue-collar worker
like my father. These affordable houses included modern auto-
matic clothes washers, radiant heating in the floor, carports and
complete landscaping. New schools cropped up, surrounded by parks,
pools and baseball fields. It was a dream come true for my family of
five, as well as hundreds of other families — providing they were white.
Levittown's builder refused to sell to blacks. As an eight-year-old, I was
unaware of this racial discrimination. I innocently played with neighborhood kids in the safe streets of Dogwood Hollow, one of the town's
subdivisions.

It was four years later when my eyes were opened to the harmful
and odious effects of prejudice. That summer, I turned twelve: the age
of accountability. I planted a flower garden. I went to a girls' camp with
my best friend, and we both changed our names. It was the summer
that I was awakened to life's lessons of hate and love, courage and
conviction, and the darker side of human nature.

Although Levittown's builder would not sell his homes to black families, there was nothing in the books that prevented a resale to blacks. That is exactly how the Myers family bought their house on Deepgreen Lane, just around the corner from my house. At first, neighbors thought that the black family had come to clean the house for the new residents. But when it became apparent that they were moving in, crowds began to gather around the house and in the street. The crowd turned into a mob that remained outside the house for weeks, terrorizing the Myerses with hurtful remarks, death threats and broken windows. Crosses were burned on roofs and lawns of any sympathizers. The Ku Klux Klan recruited angry homeowners who felt that their property values would decline.

As a naïve young girl, I was shocked and horrified by the events taking place in my neighborhood. I couldn't believe that people would hate other people because of their skin color. "Why?" I kept asking everyone. No one could give me an answer that made sense. The unfairness and hatefulness of it all pierced my heart deeply. I had to do something. I had to show this family that they were welcome in *my* neighborhood. I recruited my best girlfriend to help me.

The flower garden I had planted was now in full bloom, so I decided to pick some flowers and take them to the Myerses, my friend in tow. I was oblivious to any dangers or negative consequences of my decision to act. I didn't tell my parents of my plan either. I sensed that they wouldn't approve. Off went my friend and I, through the crowds and up to the front door of the Myerses' home.

Mrs. Daisy Myers answered the door. "Welcome to our neighborhood," I announced as I held out my bouquet of zinnias, snapdragons and marigolds. She smiled and invited us in.

The memory of her smile and her peaceful presence will forever inspire me. Here was a woman whose family was endangered, hated and victimized by members of my community and my ethnic group, yet she graciously invited my friend and me into her home. She trusted us enough to show her little baby girl to us, and she talked to us like equals. It was a time of transformation for me. I walked up to that door thinking that I was doing something good for that family, but it was *my* life that was changed. I saw courage, love, endurance and faith in the kindness that Daisy Myers offered me that day.

In 1999, forty-two years later, the city of Levittown invited Daisy Myers back so that a formal apology could be made to her. At the age of seventy-four, Mrs. Myers drove herself to Levittown from miles away, declining a chauffeur-driven ride in a government car. When I heard of the event, my heart nearly burst with joy. At last, I could be at peace with my hometown. I felt proud that they wanted to rectify the past injustices and create a new memory of acceptance and love. Daisy Myers lit the community Christmas tree in Levittown that year. Her memory still lights my heart.

~Terri Akin

A Lasting Lesson

As long as the world shall last there will be wrongs, and if no man objected and no man rebelled, those wrongs would last forever.
~Clarence Darrow

t was vacation time—two years before lung cancer would take Dad and twelve years before Mom would succumb to a different form of the same disease. But that was all yet to be. For now, we were all together—and all excited.

Mom, Dad, my two sisters and I were going on a trip. Vacations were rare in our family. We had love, caring, togetherness, and all the other intangibles that make a family name worth bearing. What we didn't have was money. We didn't have a car; meals in restaurants were an extremely rare treat. But at the age of six, I spent little time pondering such matters. My sisters, aged nine and eleven at the time, and I had food, good clothes to wear, and a safe and comfortable place to live. We also had the very best of parents.

It was a time of happy anticipation. My mother's parents had moved down to Florida and we were invited to visit. And while I was most excited about the train ride, I would leave that trip having learned a profound lesson from my mother that would stay with me forever.

It often took years before we grasped the meaning of Mom's lessons. Many times we didn't realize that a lesson had been taught—not until we experienced more of life, not until we had our own families, our own crises, our own sorrows. The irony of this whole manner of teaching and learning is that I don't think she ever realized what valuable training she was passing on to us.

She taught mostly by example, by living her life in a way that was unwavering in its commitment to the values she held to be true and important. We learned about honesty, respect for others, the importance of education; we learned how to face disaster with resolve and hope, when to be afraid, and when to be fearless. All this we learned by watching this simple, yet special, woman live her life.

The trip down to Florida was just as exciting as any six-year-old could hope for—gleaming railway cars, cities, farms, and open fields flashing past the window; sleeping in plush, reclining seats, our heads resting on fluffy, oversized pillows; listening to the sound of the conductor bellowing out the names of the various stops. These are all wonderful remembrances, but it was one incident that will always stand out. This "incident" is not something that made headlines, or caused any uproar of any kind. Indeed, it is unlikely that anyone beside my sisters and I recall what transpired. It is, however, something that eventually shaped many of my opinions regarding bias, hate, foolishness—and Mom.

It was a hot day in Florida, and we were reluctantly off on some mission with Mom. I don't remember where it was that we were going, but I do remember Dad had cleverly managed to avoid being dragged along. Not having a car, we headed for the nearest bus stop and waited for our ride to appear. When the bus pulled up, the driver yanked on a lever and the doors fluttered open. We pushed ahead of Mom, jumped up the couple of steps that led to where the driver sat, and immediately checked to see if our favorite seats were free. They were. While our mother dropped coins in the fare box, we made a dash for the back of the bus.

We reached the rear seat, which in those days was a bench-like design that spanned the width of the bus. This perch was desirable for two reasons: the rear window and the bounce. By facing backward and kneeling on the seat you could make faces at the people in the cars that followed. The bounce was the result of the primitive shock absorber system in use at the time. If the bus hit a good size bump in the road or a big enough pothole, the resulting jolt would cause the whole bus to bounce. This sensation was felt most strongly in the back. A really good hit could launch you a few inches above the seat, sometimes as much as a foot on those rare occasions when a poorly maintained bus met a sizeable imperfection in the road.

The back seat was empty that day and we ran to stake out our spots. Mom took a seat in the row in front of us. The driver pulled the door closed, but instead of speeding away from the stop, he got up and made his way down the aisle, much to the annoyance of my sisters and myself; we were anxious for the fun to begin. He stopped in front of our little group and, incredibly, informed us that we would have to move to the front of the bus. My mother responded that we would sit wherever her children wanted to sit; we were perfectly fine where we were, and not about to move.

Judging from Mom's northern accent, the driver apparently deduced that we were "foreigners." He explained that the back of the bus was where "colored folks" sat. White people sat in the front. My mother refused to move. The driver said he wouldn't move the bus until she did. She still refused. It wasn't until the driver threatened to bring in the police that she finally gave in.

To this day, I am convinced that if not for the presence of her children on that bus, she would have held her ground. Indeed, several years later, I would see her stand up to some New York City cops she felt were acting improperly, refusing to back down even after they threatened to arrest her.

Certainly, at the age of six, I had absolutely no idea of the roots of the coming civil rights struggles that would begin to right so many wrongs. For my part, I was just angry at these people in Florida who had somehow managed to usurp the best seats on the bus for their own use.

My reaction may seem ironic now, but it contains within it a very valuable lesson. I learned that by limiting the rights and freedoms of others, we are all impacted. Although such segregation can no longer be legislated, we still suffer the effects of the mindset that created it. Thanks, Mom, for this gift of understanding.

~Jim Dow

Finders Keepers

Goodness is about character — integrity, honesty, kindness,
generosity, moral courage, and the like. More than anything
else, it is about how we treat other people.
~Dennis Prager

When my daughters reached the third and fourth grades, I occasionally allowed them to walk to and from school alone, if the weather permitted. It was a short distance, so I knew they were safe and no trouble would befall them.

One warm spring day, a small friend followed them home after school. This friend was different from any other friend they had brought home. She had short stumpy legs and long floppy ears, with a fawn-colored coat and tiny freckles sprinkled across her muzzle. She was the cutest puppy I had ever seen.

When my husband got home that evening, he recognized the breed — a beagle puppy, not more than twelve weeks old, he guessed. She took to him right away and after dinner climbed into his lap to watch TV. By now the girls were both begging me to keep her.

She had no collar or identifying marks of any sort. I didn't know what to do. I thought about running an ad in the lost-and-found but I really didn't want to. It would break the kids' hearts if someone should show up. Besides, her owners should have watched her more closely, I rationalized.

By the end of the week she was part of our family. She was very intelligent and good with the girls. *This was a good idea*, I thought. It was time the girls took responsibility for another life so they would learn the nurturing skills they'd need if they decided to become mommies when they grew up.

The following week something told me to check the lost-and-found section in the local paper. One particular ad jumped out at me and my heart pounded with fear at what I read. Someone was pleading for the return of a lost beagle puppy in the vicinity of our grade school. They sounded desperate. My hand shook. I couldn't bring myself to pick up the phone.

Instead, I pretended I hadn't seen the ad. I quickly tucked the paper away in the closet and continued with my dusting. I never said a word about it to the kids or my husband.

By now we had named the puppy. She looked like a Molly, so that was what we called her. She followed the girls everywhere they went. When they went outside, she was one step behind them. When they did chores, she was there to lend a hand (or should I say, paw).

Homework proved a challenge with her around. More than once the teacher was given a homework page that the dog had chewed on. Each teacher was understanding and the girls were allowed to make it up. Life was definitely not the same at the Campbell household.

There was only one problem with this otherwise perfect picture: my conscience was bothering me. I knew in my heart I had to call that number and see if our Molly was the puppy they were desperately seeking.

It was the most difficult thing I've ever done. Finally, with sweaty palms, I lifted the receiver and dialed. Secretly I was praying no one would answer, but someone did. The voice on the other end was that of a young woman. After describing the dog to her in detail, she wanted to come right over.

Within minutes she was at my door. I had been sitting at the kitchen table, head cradled in my hands, asking God for a miracle. Molly sat at my feet the whole time, looking up at me with those big puppy-dog eyes — eyes the color of milk chocolate. She seemed to sense something was wrong.

A thousand thoughts crossed my mind before the woman rang the bell. I could pretend I wasn't home or tell her, "I'm sorry, you have the wrong address." But it was too late; the bell rang and Molly was barking. I opened the door, forcing myself to face my fear.

One look at Molly and the woman's face lit up like a Christmas tree. "Here, Lucy," she called. "Come to Mamma, girl." Molly (Lucy) instantly obeyed, wagging her tail in delight at the sound of the woman's voice. Obviously she belonged to the woman.

Tears stung at the back of my eyelids and threatened to spill over at any moment. I felt like my heart was being ripped from my chest. I wanted to grab Molly and run. Instead I smiled faintly and asked her to please come in.

The woman had already bent over and scooped Molly up into her arms. She awkwardly opened her purse and stretched out a twenty-dollar bill toward me.

"For your trouble," she offered.

"Oh, I couldn't." I shook my head in protest. "She's been such a joy to have around, I should be paying you." With that she laughed and hugged Molly tighter to her bosom as if she were a lost child and not a dog.

Molly licked her face and squirmed with delight. I knew it was time for them to go home. Opening the door to let the mout, I noticed a little girl sitting in the front seat of the van. When the child saw the puppy, a smile as bright as a firecracker on the Fourth of July exploded across her face.

My glance turned to a small wheelchair strapped to the back of the van. The woman saw me look at the chair and offered an explanation without my asking. Molly (Lucy) was given to the child to promote emotional healing after a car accident had left her crippled for life.

When the puppy disappeared from the yard, the little girl had gone into a deep depression, refusing to come out of the shell she was in. Molly (Lucy) was their only hope their daughter would recover emotionally and mentally.

"She formed a special bond with the puppy and Lucy gave her a reason to live," her mother explained.

Suddenly I felt very guilty and selfish. *God has blessed me with so much*, I thought. My heart went out to this family that had been through such a terrible time. As they pulled out of the drive, the smile on my face was genuine. I knew I had done the right thing—that puppy was exactly where she belonged.

~Leona Campbell

Chapter
2

Create Your
Best Future

Choosing to Be
Your Very Best

Playing Pretend

Go confidently in the direction of your dreams. Live the life
you've always imagined.
~Henry David Thoreau

In the middle of my sophomore year of college, I sat down to work at my desk. On one side, my economics textbooks remained unopened. On the other side, unstudied Chinese vocabulary flashcards were piled high. Months of skipping classes, partying and procrastinating had landed me there. I had to learn a semester's worth of knowledge in a week. I was miserable. Trapped and anxious, all I wanted was to burst out of my seat and pace back and forth. I wanted to be somewhere else. But, this was the life I had convinced myself I was going to live.

Somehow, I made it through that grueling week of finals.

While at home for winter break, a friend and I were out drinking at some unrespectable hour. I was in a cocky mood, riding high after surviving the semester by the skin of my teeth. So when another friend appeared in the bar's front window, with blood running down his face, I immediately charged outside to defend him. This is when I got blindsided by two assailants. The first punched me in the face. Then, as I fell to the ground, the second kicked me in the head.

When I wound up in the hospital later that night, a CT scan showed I didn't have a concussion. Instead, I had something much worse: a brain tumor.

Nothing in my life has come close to the fear I felt at that moment.

Death was my first thought. Would it be in six months or a year? How much pain would there be? How soon until I couldn't speak? When would I lose the ability to think?

The next day, my parents and I sat with a team of neurologists. They explained the tumor was located in the middle of my brain. It could not be removed through surgery. At considerable risk, I had a biopsy. It was the only way to determine if the tumor was cancerous. I had gone through life without a single symptom, which meant it could have been there all along, or it could have appeared a month before. When I woke up from anesthesia, my parents stood beside me. Their eyes were teary; their smiles were wide. The tumor was benign.

I returned to college and managed to get my studies on track. Those textbooks were open and read; those flashcards were memorized. But I still lacked passion for what I was learning and the business career that I expected to have. Every three months I would get a brain MRI to check the tumor's growth. It had appeared stable for more than a year. Then, on one beautiful morning, my mom called me. I could tell she'd been crying. The results of my latest scan had come back. The tumor was metabolically active.

Much like that night in the hospital, I felt crushed. My life had been taken from me a second time. By my twenty-first birthday, I had withdrawn from school and was undergoing radiation.

It was a strange feeling to have radiation on a brain tumor that had never given me a single symptom. Friends and family often told me how unfair it was: to be removed from growing up to face something so awful. I had endless stretches of time to think about that particular point of view. It was a surreal time spent on cold tables watching machines slowly circle my head; tired times that left me unable to get out of bed; energetic times once the neural steroids kicked in.

This time-out from life's normal direction gave me ample opportunity to think about grand ideas like happiness, purpose and passion. One morning, I found myself thinking about that long ago week I spent cramming for exams. Why was I so miserable? Why did I feel so lost? I knew there was something important underlying my desire to jump up and pace back and forth. I knew it reached back long before college, all the way back to one single moment of my childhood.

I was five years old, and had come across a book by the young-adult-fiction author, Lloyd Alexander. My father's name is Lloyd, mine is Alexander, and in my kindergarten mind, the coincidence translated as a calling. I was going to become an author. So, I started writing stories. I'd excitedly begin on the first page of my journal, continue to the second, and maybe even reach the third before it was left abandoned on my desk. Most often, the final sentence was unfinished, its last letter drawn down the page as if some monster had dragged me off.

Instead of sticking to the page, I would jump up from my desk and begin pacing back and forth. I'd start speaking my characters' dialogue, acting out their action, and before I knew it I was playing pretend. I played pretend constantly. It was like a drug; I couldn't function without my daily fix. And while playing pretend with friends is part of any childhood — whether as Power Rangers or princesses — I always preferred to play it alone.

Day after day I played out complete epics, building countless worlds with rules and citizens. Often my characters so enchanted me, their stories became so ingrained in my thoughts that after playing out their entire journeys, I'd start them over from the beginning. I'd replay entire narratives, exploring new details and alternate outcomes. So lost was I in these stories that by the time I rounded them all to a close I was an eighteen-year-old heading off to college.

My passion was to create stories. Unfortunately, it was stained with my embarrassment over playing pretend long past the age of five. So, I swore off it. When I sat down to study in my sophomore year, I wanted nothing more than to burst up and start playing pretend. But I wouldn't allow it. I would go into finance like my parents, and conform to my image of what I thought it meant to be an adult. But that too was just a fantasy.

While sick, I began playing pretend again. This time I benefited from the discipline of college. Pages of notes, timelines and sketches began to accumulate. I devoured books. I hadn't felt this passionate in a very long time. And it didn't take me long to realize why. It was clear where in my short life I had found the greatest joy. It was a place count-less measures of my energy were already sunk. Only when steeped in fantasy had I been truly happy. Yet it was a passion I had only allowed to exist in the margin.

For fear of rejection, failure and vulnerability, I had resisted what felt most natural. But being forced to face life's fragility at such a young age, I no longer cared. Sure it wasn't easy. When I returned to school, I crammed a four-year creative writing major into three semesters. I lived and breathed reading, writing and editing. I still have plenty of fears and doubts, but I know success doesn't come without risk.

I'm lucky for a lot of reasons. I'm especially grateful for my health — radiation sent my tumor into remission, where it will likely stay for a very long time. Above all, I cherish being given the chance to reevaluate my life. For me it took a brain tumor to realize that storytelling was more than just a childish whim. I've come to under-stand being successful is doing what makes you happy. Life is too short and uncertain to do anything else.

So I write, and simply hope what I create means to others what it has meant to me.

~Alexander Brokaw

It's a Great Day to Be Alive!

May you live life every day of your life.
~Jonathan Swift

stink at math. I really stink at it. Early in life, this lack of skill laid the groundwork for a strong dislike toward the subject and an ongoing effort to avoid it at all costs. So how is it that the most influential person in all of my educational career was my high school math teacher?

As a freshman in high school I was far from a math teacher's dream student. My mind was full of things that high school girls tend to focus on: boys, boys, and well… boys. I immersed myself in my social life, and my classes often took a back seat to other priorities.

I walked into Mr. A's classroom a chatty and bubbly fourteen-year-old girl. My primary focus was on picking a good seat, surrounded by my friends and with easy access to the door. From day one, I was very vocal about having a distain for math and I was even more vocal about my constant confusion. It was not uncommon for me to give up midway through an assignment, or zone out during a lesson because I didn't understand it. It wasn't that I didn't want to do well, but simply that I didn't think I was capable of doing well. "I can't," became my permanent state of mind in all things math related.

However, I was soon to learn that "I can't" was not an option in Mr. A's class.

On the first day of class, Mr. A greeted us with his arms extended as he proclaimed, "Welcome! Smile! It's a great day to be alive!" That phrase, which I would hear frequently over the course of the next four years, became an ever-present source of comfort and familiarity. From that moment forward, it was clear that Mr. A had a true passion not only for math, but for teaching. His positive and uplifting attitude never faltered. If Mr. A ever experienced the bad days of normal life, he never showed it. While some teachers forcefully told us not to cross them, they were "just having a bad day," Mr. A greeted us with that same enthusiasm each and every day.

This welcoming and uplifting personality mirrored Mr. A's teaching methods. Not only were his methods engaging, but his positive attitude was contagious. He encouraged each student, from the valedictorian to the self-proclaimed "I can't" student.

I found myself looking forward to math class, despite the fact that I still despised the subject itself. There was just something about being in Mr. A's presence that made me feel good, as if I had the potential to succeed. However, my story is not one of overnight success. I did not become a straight-A math student, and I continued to struggle with several concepts. In fact, it was in Mr. A's class that I received my first failing test grade, and I can still remember my eyes filling with tears as I stared at the 63 in bold red letters. I had failed. And more importantly, I had failed Mr. A.

This 63 became a defining moment in my math career. I could have given up and used the score as proof to Mr. A and to myself that I was not meant to do well in math. Similarly, Mr. A could have given up on me. But instead, he did the opposite. He became even more determined to help me with my math, and even more importantly, to help me see my potential.

As the year progressed, my determination to succeed grew. I spent an increasing amount of time on my homework, and I met with Mr. A weekly. My classmates began to do the same, and it became "cool" to have lunch with Mr. A. We didn't know it at the time, but he was transforming our attitudes. My hard work began to pay off and my grades slowly began to climb. There were road bumps, of course. Low grades and difficult concepts threatened to deter me, and sometimes succeeded in bringing me down. But a frown on my face almost always resulted in a bellowing, "Kate, smile! It's a great day to be alive!"

The year came to an end, and my classmates and I were surprised to find ourselves sad to move on from ninth grade math. We had found a home for ourselves in Mr. A's class, a comfortable learning environment which we feared would be impossible to replicate in a different teacher's classroom. And it was. Tenth grade proved to be a struggle: a new math teacher, new topics, and a sense of solitude. Mr. A's engaging lessons were replaced with hours of busy work, and my grades reflected this lack of personal attention. I longed to be back in Mr. A's class, and I was overjoyed to find myself there again the following year.

My junior and senior years were marked with many milestones: prom, the SATs, graduation. But perhaps the most important milestones were the accomplishments that took place back in Mr A's class. A's on the math section of my report card, a nearly perfect score on my math SAT, and a feeling of inner pride that I had never before experienced.

High school is undoubtedly a time of growth, both physically and emotionally, as well as academically and socially. I can honestly say that I experienced much of this growth sitting in my second row seat, just behind the door, in Mr. A's classroom. Today, when the work is piled up on my desk and I feel my mind beginning to think "I can't," I hear a deep voice in the back of my mind reminding me to take a deep breath and remember: it's a great day to be alive.

~Kate Lynn Mishara

The Two Saddest Words

Precaution is better than cure.
~Edward Coke

Two of the saddest words in the English language are "if only." I live my life with the goal of never having to say those words, because they convey regret, lost opportunities, mistakes, and disappointment. And sometimes the words "if only" go with terrible tragedies. Think about how many times you have heard about something awful happening, accompanied by "if only he had called her back to make sure she was okay..." or "if only I had investigated that noise..." or "if only they had made sure the gate to the pool clicked behind them..."

My father-in-law is famous in our family for saying, "Take the extra minute to do it right." He must be doing something right, since he's 91 years old and still making a lot of sense.

I always try to live by the "extra minute" rule. Sometimes it only takes seconds to make sure I write something down correctly, or check something on the Internet, or move an object out of the way before it trips someone. And of course when my children were young, and prone to all kinds of mishaps, I lived and breathed the extra minute rule. I always thought about what I could do to avoid an "if only" moment, whether it was something minor like moving a cup full of hot coffee away from the edge of a counter, or something that required a little more work such as taping padding onto the sharp corners of a glass coffee table.

I just read a news story about a student pilot who was thrown from an airplane when its canopy lifted off. The instructor, who was belted in, was fine. The student, whose seatbelt was not fastened, fell from the sky and his body was found on the ground somewhere in Tennessee. Imagine how many people are in mourning, and how terrified that man must have been as he fell from the plane and realized he was going to die. Imagine the chorus of "if only" coming from his family. If only he had been wearing his seatbelt… How simple would that have been?

I don't move my car one inch until I hear the seatbelt click on every passenger. I unplug the iron when I leave the laundry room for "just a minute." I'd hate to get distracted, not return to the laundry room, and start a fire with that forgotten iron. Imagine the "if only" I'd be saying then. After I realized that I could not be trusted with a teakettle — I left it boiling on the stove for an hour — I threw it out and bought an electric teakettle that shuts itself off. And I am paranoid about fireplace ashes. I wait till they are two weeks old, then shovel them into a bag on garbage collection day and put the bag 20 feet away from the house in the middle of the driveway.

When my teenage son was first driving, I worried that enforcing his curfew too strictly would cause him to speed and have an accident. A boy in the next town was killed when he drove too fast trying to make it home by midnight. So my son and I agreed on a plan — if he missed curfew he would just lose double those minutes the next night out. Ten minutes late meant 20 minutes shaved off the curfew the next time, consequences that were not so onerous that they would cause him to rush home.

When I was in a car accident a few years ago, resulting in spinal surgery and permanent nerve damage, I handled it well emotionally, because I wasn't the driver who was at fault. There was no "if only" thinking for me, and it's a lot easier to forgive someone else than it is to forgive yourself.

I don't only avoid those "if only" moments when it comes to safety. It's equally important to avoid "if only" in our personal relationships. We all know people who lost a loved one and bemoaned the fact that they had foregone an opportunity to say "I love you" or "I forgive you." When my father announced he was going to the eye doctor across from my office on Good Friday, I told him that it was a holiday for Chicken Soup for the Soul and I wouldn't be here. But then I thought about the fact that he's 84 years old and I realized that I shouldn't give up an opportunity to see him. I called him and told him I had decided to go to work on my day off after all. When my husband's beloved, elderly uncle pocket-dialed me several times yesterday with his new cell phone, I urged my husband to call him back, invoking the "if only" possibility. My husband called him and was glad that he did. Now if anything happens, my husband won't have to say, "If only I had called him back that day."

I know there will still be occasions when I have to say "if only" about something, but my life is definitely more serene because of my policy of doing everything possible to avoid that eventuality. And even though it takes an extra minute to do something right, or it occasionally takes an hour or two in my busy schedule to make a personal connection, I know that I'm doing the right thing. I'm buying myself peace of mind and that's the best kind of insurance for my emotional wellbeing.

~Amy Newmark

10,000 Hours of Perseverance

The road to success is dotted with many tempting parking places.

~Will Rogers

My dad always used to tell me that when I was two years old, I told everyone I met that I was going to be the next Michael Jordan. I told the clerk at the store, I told my aunt, and I told a stranger I met on the street. I'd never actually played basketball, but I'd seen Michael Jordan on the TV, and that was enough.

At first it was cute. My mom made me a bright orange basketball birthday cake and my uncle bought me my own small pair of Air Jordans. It was my dad alone, however, that took me seriously.

One day he sat my three-year-old body down at the table and looked me straight in the eye.

"You want to be the next Michael Jordan, huh?" he asked.

I nodded eagerly, squirming in my seat.

"And you're willing to do any amount of work in order to do this?"

I hesitated a moment, feeling the weight of his words, but then smiled brightly and nodded.

"All right," he sighed. Then he turned and produced a sleek, lined, business sheet of paper. He rubbed his brow and straightened his tie before handing the paper to me, warning, "This will be one serious, serious commitment."

He gave me a pen and gestured for me to sign my messy signature at the bottom of the page. Even without the ability to read what he'd written on the paper, I sensed the seriousness of the moment.

The next morning I had completely forgotten about the paper until, at the crack of dawn, my father shook me awake. I was shocked to see that for the first time in my three years of life, my father wasn't wearing a suit and tie. Instead he was dressed in a distasteful baggy T-shirt, shorts, and an old, ratty pair of gym shoes. I wrinkled my nose.

"What?" I asked.

"Get up," he ordered. "Basketball practice commences today."

I groaned, squirmed out from my warm alcove of stuffed animals, and followed my dad, still wearing my pink pajamas.

We headed out to the driveway and he revealed an old, beaten, orange basketball. He tossed it to me and I clumsily grabbed it with both hands, its bumps feeling foreign to me.

"First," he instructed in his firm, lawyer-practiced voice, "we will start with the art of dribbling."

I looked at him, unsure if he was serious, and threw the basketball with both hands back to him as he began to instruct me. I stood out in that driveway for three hours that morning, and never had I felt more exhausted in my three years of life. Every time my attention began to wander, my father would harshly drag me back to the present.

Although still unsteady on my own two feet, my father worked me until my pajamas were drenched in sweat and my wrists were aching from hitting the ball up and down. The neighbors out mowing their lawns had begun to stare at our strange scene — my father, a strict lawyer, standing in the driveway, domineering in ancient gym clothes, and me, a toddler perspiring in her pink pajamas.

Tired and voraciously hungry afterward, I went inside and devoured breakfast. My mother had brought out a feast of pancakes, sausages, muffins, and fruit, and simply pursed her lips and shook her head disbelievingly as I dragged myself in. Already, I was beginning to regret my decision to be the female version of Michael Jordan.

The next morning my dad dragged me out in the driveway at the crack of dawn, once again. This time I had come prepared. I was dressed in fresh shorts and a jersey, although, normally, I refused to wear anything but flouncy, flowery dresses.

Before I knew it, my dad was dragging me out for hours every morning. It was the same the next day, and the next day, and the next day. I began dreading the continuous lay ups, shooting, dribbling, and one-on-one. My only hope in my three-year-old brain was that soon, when winter came, I could take a break.

I couldn't have been more wrong.

Once the first flakes of snow started falling my dad started dragging me to the local gym to practice for four hours a day. I began complaining, sighing, and dreading each practice. My dad never gave up, though. Every time I screamed that I would never touch a basketball again he would take my signed piece of paper from his safe and wave it in my face, telling me that I couldn't take back my words now.

I wanted, in my dreams, to tear and burn that dreaded contract that bound me to four hours of practice seven days a week. I wanted to find his locked safe and burn it to the ground. Years passed and I began to accept basketball practice as just a fact of life. Even on days when I slept in, refusing to get up, guilt would soon overwhelm me, and I would head out to the driveway and find him waiting for me, knowing all along that I would come.

By the age of ten, after seven years of practicing (and approximately 7,350 hours) my dad predicted my skill was higher than any varsity player's in the state. He continued to coach me, day after day, from the sidelines of our driveway, pounding the knowledge into my brain about fakes, crossovers, and tactics. Our only days off in the year were work holidays and my birthday, which seemed way too far apart for my liking. But my dad kept a chart on the wall, measuring how much I practiced, and every 500 hours of practice time we would celebrate by heading to Dairy Queen.

My dad began telling me about his days as a star basketball player in college. He said that he had always dreamed of being the best basketball player in the world, but he had not had the perseverance to practice enough to become so. His theory was that in order to achieve the level of mastery associated with being a world-class expert, 10,000 hours of practice were required. Whether you were a writer, an ice skater, a guitarist, or a chess player. He said that one day, in basketball, I would become a true expert.

One fateful day, at the age of fourteen, I finally reached my goal. My 10,000 hours. The day was a Saturday, and from the morning I got up, I could feel something different as I met my dad out in the driveway before heading to school. A strange feeling of sorrow seemed to hang over me.

We practiced our usual four hours, and for once, I felt like I had learned everything there was to know about basketball. At the end of our practice session, my dad hugged me and said "Congratulations" before handing me that same old ratty basketball from eleven years back and saying, "It's yours now."

That evening we had more than forty of our friends and relatives over to a party, with a gigantic, basketball-shaped cake, and local newspaper journalists hugging the edge of the living room. On top of the cake sat five candles, with the numbers 1-0-0-0-0. I had never been so proud in my life. My dad made a speech about perseverance, and even his old coach from college came over to congratulate me. It was only when the cake's candles were lit that my dad finally handed me the forbidden contract I had signed on that fateful day at the age of three.

I felt tears well in my eyes as I traced the letters on that piece of paper, each word engraved in my heart. In my messy three-year-old handwriting I could still read my name signed in overly large backwards letters. "I hereby agree to practice basketball for as long as my father requires, until I have reached my goal of 10,000 hours." I read, for the last time.

"This is it," my father whispered, reaching for my hand. "10,000 hours of perseverance."

Those powerful words that had bound me for eleven years seemed so pointless now as together, we held the paper to the candle's flame and watched the paper slowly fold and crinkle into a brown paper mass. The crowd of family and friends cheered.

"So, are you going to quit now?" one of the journalists asked, speaking for the first time since the party had begun.

I looked around, staring at the many pictures of Michael Jordan, and of me playing basketball over the years. Then, without hesitation, I smiled and shook my head.

"Never," I whispered. "WNBA, here I come."

~Christine Catlin

I Wasn't Expected to Succeed

*Don't aim for success if you want it; just believe in yourself, do
what you love and believe in, and it will come naturally.*
~David Frost

t was the seventies. I was a poor kid from a large family, and a girl
to boot.

To make matters worse, I was a mediocre student. Math concepts eluded me, as did foreign language and science. I wasn't
musically inclined, either, though I did have a bit of creativity going
for me. Being creative, however, labeled me a cheat in ninth grade
when I got the right answers but the wrong equations in algebra class.
Because I couldn't breathe in gym class and lagged behind the rest of
the group, I was labeled "slow and lazy." No one ever suggested the
right label might have been "asthmatic." Being too shy to shower in
front of the rest of the class, I was written up time and time again as
disobedient.

They expected a truant student, so after a while, I complied. I was
a rebel, a ne'er do well. I wasn't up to standards. I certainly wasn't
expected to succeed.

My future plans included becoming a reporter and author, possibly an elementary teacher, but when I relayed that to my counselor,
I discovered we didn't see eye to eye. The word "college" wasn't even

mentioned during our "career directive" meeting, but words like "waitress" and "clerk" and "cleaning lady" were batted about the room like ping pong balls, all landing in my lap... and me without the proverbial paddle.

"I like to write," I said timidly. "I was thinking I'd like to be a reporter or an author... maybe write books for children."

His eyebrows rose and he nodded, considering....

And then... now that my portfolio had finally been opened... he had a brainstorm. I might consider becoming a secretary! After all, I had taken all of the secretarial classes, and I was a good writer. My spelling ability was above average. My shorthand was good; my office equipment skills were up to par.

"I don't really want... any... jobs like that," I replied.

He looked at me then, and smiled kindly. "I'd like to send you in a direction that would be more fitting with the skills you have," he said as he leaned back in his chair. "Of course... you'll want to get married and raise a family."

My heart fell. Regardless of what he was saying, what I heard was that once again I wasn't expected to succeed. Disappointment grew in the pit of my stomach. I thanked him and told him I would think about it. But as I walked back down the hall to my classroom, my cheeks burned with humiliation.

I didn't blame him. Based on the page in front of him, and what he had known of me as a student, he had tried to advise me to the best of his ability. What he didn't know was that the page in front of him wasn't me. None of my teachers knew the real me — they'd never taken the time to find out who I was. Or was it that I'd never believed in myself to begin with?

After graduation, I did exactly as my counselor suggested. As one of three secretaries in the Applied Mechanics and Engineering Science Department at the University of Michigan, I helped six professors help their students make their dreams become reality. Every day for two long years I watched other young adults make their way through college.

Within a few short years following high school, I had become a statistic.

At the age of twenty, I married my high school sweetheart and started my family. I didn't think about my career again until I had two toddlers underfoot and a burning need to discover what my mission on this planet was supposed to be. At the time, my husband was enrolled in evening classes to further his education, so college for me was out of the question.

Because of our family situation, I knew whatever I decided to do would have to be inexpensive and attainable from the comfort of my own home. By a stroke of sheer luck, I found what I was looking for in the back of a magazine. The Institute of Children's Literature was looking for people who wanted to write children's books. By cutting corners, I managed to save enough money to take the course by mail.

Since I was also the Girl Scout Leader for my daughters' troop, I double-dipped assignments and duties whenever possible. Class assignments revolved around troop activities and vice versa. After finishing each essay, I'd address one copy to the school and pop it in the mailbox, and slip a second copy beneath the door of the local newspaper. You can't imagine how pleased I was when the articles began showing up in the paper with my byline attached.

Of course, there was no pay, but I was ecstatic!

In March, 1986, the same month I finished my classes and delivered my third child, the publisher of the newspaper and I bumped into one another as I slipped yet another story beneath his door. He hired me on the spot and within two years I was named editor.

For seventeen years, I made a living as a journalist and photographer for *The Milan News* and several other local papers, including *The Ann Arbor News*. Since then, I have been published in more newspapers, magazines, and online newsletters and print anthologies than I can count. To date, my name also appears on the cover of eight books.

Finally — the hard way — my dreams have become my reality.

I realize now that the responsibility to succeed belonged to me, not my teachers or counselors. I was the one who hadn't expected me to succeed. I now also know it really doesn't matter what anyone else thinks about me or my abilities, it's what I think that matters. All anyone ever has to do in order to succeed is "expect" to succeed. These days I expect miracles every day of my life, and every day of my life I receive them.

~Helen Kay Polaski

The End of the Zombie Days

Education is not the filling of a pail, but the lighting of a fire.
~William Butler Yeats

was a zombie in high school, shuffling from class to class barely even awake. I played video games into the wee hours of the morning nearly every night. Luckily there was one teacher out there who slammed his hands on my desk and shouted at me one day, and in doing so startled me out of my stupor.

Ray Seabeck wore the same simple clothes every single day. He stood before me on the first day of class my senior year, as I was slumped in my desk in an eighteen-year-old haze. I was not expecting much from this man, from his gray, feathered hair and glasses. I yawned, not even bothering to cover my mouth, and he leapt — he literally leapt — from the front of the room to my desk in the second row, and slammed his hands on my desk when he landed.

"Do you like Shakespeare?" he screamed at me.

My mouth was stuck in mid-yawn, wide open.

"Well, do you?" he hollered.

"Yes!" I lied. I had no idea what Shakespeare was. But I was going to find out. What's more, this man would fan some smoldering cinder of interest in me, a cinder only he could sense.

I had a 1.7 grade point average in high school. I had stayed back in the fourth grade. Often I didn't even go to bed; I let myself become a slave to video games, sadly satisfied with accomplishments in the virtual world, while I barely noticed significant events of my real life speeding past, like mile markers on a New Hampshire highway.

We read *Hamlet*, and bit by bit I found that I enjoyed the psychological complexity. Why did Hamlet keep hesitating? Why?

I had done a good job rationalizing my poor grades throughout school. My excuse was this: I'm joining the Army, so what does it matter? I'd already enlisted in January of my senior year, so what did it matter? I was set to ship out in August after I graduated. But as my high school career wound down, my anxiety increased. Suddenly I'd begun liking Shakespeare, and then Hemingway, and then Fitzgerald, Wordsworth and Blake. What if—and it was an "if" of epic proportions—what if I could become an English teacher like Mr. Seabeck? What if I could read and write and talk about it, and get paid for it?

But on the other side I had the Army to look forward to. I'd always dreamt of being a soldier; I coveted the prestige that came with defending our nation.

I stayed after school one day to ask Mr. Seabeck what he thought about my conundrum. I told him of my choices, and my ambivalence. Of my desire to become a teacher, and a soldier. Want to know what he said?

"Hamlet!" he said, pointing at me. "You're Hamlet! Here you have two paths laid open for you—to be or not to be. To become a teacher or a soldier."

I said, "The thing is, I've already signed my Army contract. But I could still get out of it if I wanted to."

"Well that's curious," he said.

"What is?"

"That's the third time I've heard you say that—that you could still get out of your contract."

"But do you think I could even get into a college with a 1.7 GPA?"

"No college in the U.S. will turn you down, Ron, from enrolling in one class. Get an A in that, and maybe one or two more part-time, and you'd have a pretty good shot."

I left school that day with college in my eyes and ears. Just thinking of joining the thousands of students matriculating that fall made me feel electric.

And Mr. Seabeck was right. I did have to take a class part-time to get accepted at Plymouth State University, but get accepted I did. I graduated cum laude, and went on to earn my Master's degree in English Literature from the University of New Hampshire. And now, as I sit writing this twelve years later, I'm sitting at Mr. Seabeck's old desk. I took over his old position, teaching English at Laconia High School in New Hampshire. I can still see that wry grin of his, and I can still hear him screaming, "Do you like Shakespeare?" I might never have known that I, in fact, love Shakespeare, if not for the spark he lit in me that caused me to examine my life, my habits, and my desires. I will forever bear his stamp, and the evidence is in my high school yearbook. My senior quote reads as follows:

"Tis now the very witching time of night,
When churchyards yawn and hell itself breathes out
Contagion to this world. Now I could drink hot blood,
And do such bitter business as the day
Would quake to look on."

— *Hamlet, Act III, Scene II*

~Ron Kaiser, Jr

Trials and Tribulations

To win without risk is to triumph without glory.
~Pierre Corneille

I was thirteen when my Binghamton, New York, Boy Scout troop planned a camping trip. I wasn't afraid of being out in the woods at night, but the thought of being with a group of people terrified me. I stammered severely, and kids sometimes made fun of me.

However, I summoned up the courage to go on this outing for I knew that there would be at least one person I could spend time with: my best friend. A friend who had never been put off by my disability, whose father owned a meat market a block away from where my father operated an Army/Navy store. A friend with a "fantastic" imagination. Sitting apart from the other campers, in the dark of the woods, alert to the spooky night sounds, my friend would tell stories of life on other planets, of beings he imagined would be found there, of time traveling to other worlds, of ghosts, of the meaning of dreams, of reincarnation, of the ability to read minds. I sat spellbound as he elaborated a string of "what if" stories. He wanted to be a writer, and I was certain he would be.

My friend's name was Rod Serling. He became the fantastic writer he dreamed of being and more. As creator of the television show *The Twilight Zone*, his influence on science fiction has been "astronomical."

I was so certain that Rod would attain his dream that I was almost too embarrassed to tell him mine. I wanted to be a defense attorney like Clarence Darrow and Sam Leibowitz. I'd read everything I could about them, including transcripts from their trials. I'd spent hundreds of hours alone at the library, imagining myself a golden-tongued attorney pleading sensational cases before juries.

But I knew I could never be like Clarence Darrow and Sam Leibowitz because of my speech impediment. "You'll make it," Rod would say, never once discouraging me. "Don't worry. The stammering will go away, and you'll be a great lawyer one day." When I felt discouraged, Rod would cheer me up with a tale about an attorney defending a three-eyed creature from another planet. I'd laugh and feel better, his confidence in me encouraging my own confidence in myself.

Eventually, I did attain my dream of becoming a lawyer. Still, it was preposterous to think a stammerer like myself could perform in a courtroom. I conceded as much and planned to return home, to help my father run his Army/Navy store, and then perhaps to branch into legal research where I could silently earn a living.

Thoroughly depressed, I sank into my chair at the 1951 University of Miami Law School commencement. When I looked up, I couldn't believe my eyes: There at the podium stood the keynote speaker, Sam Leibowitz! Leibowitz was the famous New York attorney who had saved the lives of nine Alabama black men falsely accused of raping two white women in the famous "Scottsboro Boys" case. That afternoon Leibowitz, his voice filled with conviction, told us that defense attorneys were the key to keeping America free, that the protective ideals of the U.S. Constitution and the Bill of Rights were constantly under attack, that "authorities" were chipping away our rights to a fair trial, to the presumption of innocence, against unreasonable search and seizure, and to proof beyond a reasonable doubt. He warned us that the old guardians were dying out and that without a new generation to take up the fight, America would succumb to a reemergence of robber barons and torture chamber confessions, and that the average man and woman would be stripped of dignity and liberty, and would then be legally and economically enslaved.

Leibowitz challenged us to take the torch he was passing, to become defense attorneys, and to protect America. I felt as if he were speaking directly to me.

Because of Leibowitz's speech, I remained in Miami to become a defense attorney, stammering or not. Soon I got my first case: A black man named Henry Larkin, who had shot and killed a man in the hallway of his apartment building, was charged with murder. Larkin said the man he shot had come after him with a knife.

Since there were no public defenders in those days, groups of young attorneys would mill around the courthouse volunteering for cases and hoping to be appointed. I was doing just that when someone told me about Henry Larkin. He nearly cried when I offered to represent him.

The day before the trial (my first!), I read in the *Miami Herald* that Leibowitz, then a New York judge, was back in town for another speech. I searched him out, and soon I stood at his hotel door, briefcase in hand. Stammering an apology for my intrusion, I asked for his help.

"I was in the audience at your ca-ca-commencement address here; I became a defense attorney because of you. Now I'm facing m-m-my first case tomorrow."

Leibowitz smiled and invited me in. I told him about the case. He raised his eyebrows every time I tripped over a word, but never said a thing about my speech impediment and then proceeded to outline my entire defense.

The next day I stood before twelve people in a court of law, with the life of Henry Larkin in my hands, or more precisely, in my misfiring mouth. Then something strange came over me: not fear, but confidence.

My own troubles vanished, replaced by the far greater problems of Henry Larkin. He was a good man who had never broken the law in his life. It was up to me to convince a jury that he had acted in self-defense. I talked for four hours that day, remembering everything Sam Leibowitz told me as I pled for Henry Larkin's life. The jury took three minutes to decide he was "not guilty."

One thing missing from the next day's newspaper report is that

I had not stammered once during my entire argument. I tried to call Sam Leibowitz, but he had left town. Needing to share my multi-faceted victory with someone, I called Rod and told him about the miracle of my untangled tongue. He exuded elation, and then grew serious. "Ellis, it's a sign! You've found your place in time. You were destined to speak for the innocent and oppressed. Never forget that!" Rod was quick to see some unexplained, universal phenomenon in practically everything. In his eyes, what happened was the result of what can only happen in *The Twilight Zone*.

For whatever reason, Rod's words have stayed with me throughout my life. I've been in thousands of trials and have always tried to do my best to defend the "poor and defenseless." Some people, including my wife, feel I've overdone it. I have spent a great deal of time on "pro bono" cases.

I've also had my share of wealthy clients, including celebrities, rich businessmen, doctors, and a billionaire Arab oil sheik. Payments come in many forms, such as a handshake, a hug, a baby's smile, a holiday card, a home-cooked meal, a friendly face in court, even a picketer carrying a sign outside of jail. Henry Larkin, my first client, came by every Friday for the rest of his life and handed me an envelope with a five-dollar bill in it. He never missed a week.

~Ellis Rubin as told to Dary Matera

Just One Drink

Drinking and driving: there are stupider things, but it's a very short list.
~Author Unknown

There's a small cross by the side of Highway 128, near the town of Boonville. If this cross could talk, it would tell you this sad story:

Seven years ago my brother, Michael, was at a friend's ranch. They decided to go out for dinner. Joe arrived and volunteered to drive—after just one drink.

Lightheartedly, the four friends traveled the winding road. They didn't know where it would end—nobody did. Suddenly, they swerved into the opposite lane, colliding with an oncoming car.

Back home we were watching *E.T.* on video in front of a warm fire. Then we went to bed. At 2:00 A.M. a police officer woke my mom with the devastating news. Michael had been killed.

In the morning, I found my mother and sister crying. I stood there bewildered. "What's wrong?" I asked, rubbing my sleepy eyes.

Mom took a deep breath. "Come here..."

Thus began a grueling journey through grief, where all roads lead to nowhere. It still hurts to remember that day.

The only thing that helps is telling my story, hoping you will remember it if you are tempted to get into a car with someone who has had a drink—even just one drink.

Joe chose the road to nowhere. He was convicted of manslaughter and served time. However, the real punishment is living with the consequences of his actions. He left us with an ache in our hearts that will never go away, a nightmare that will haunt him — and us — for the rest of our lives. And a small cross by the side of Highway 128.

~Chris Laddish

Dedicated with love to the memory of Michael Laddish

Head-Butting the Wall

*Every action we take, everything we do, is either a victory or
defeat in the struggle to become what we want to be.*
~Anne Byrhhe

I grew up in a small town in New Jersey where I felt bored and
trapped. My family life was all about, "Mom works, Dad works
and kids are expected to go to school." My parents didn't have the
money to buy me stuff I got interested in, and we didn't have any
time to spend together except during meals. That didn't cost anything
or take up any extra time.

I was angry and frustrated most of the time — it seemed that no
matter what I did or said, I felt like I was head-butting the wall and
getting nowhere. No one could get through — not my parents, my
teachers or my guidance counselor. No one could help me.

Then I started high school, and a lot of the people I knew began
using drugs and alcohol. Because I wasn't interested in that, I found
myself on the outside of my peer group. I was totally alone and I hated
the world.

I started roaming the streets looking for trouble. I fought older,
tougher guys around town and gained a reputation for being crazy.
I'd take any dare. If someone said to me, "Smash your head on this
rock for five bucks!" I would.

I was well on my way to prison or the morgue when I stumbled on punk rock music. The whole idea of a punk lifestyle sounded cool. So, I spiked my hair and took on a whole new identity until, one day, some *real* punkers came up to me in the hall at school.

"Hey, man, are you punk?"

"Yeah, yeah, man, I'm punk," I fumbled.

"Oh, yeah? What bands do you like?"

I didn't know any bands — none.

"Who do you listen to?" I didn't know one band from the other. Then my eyes landed on their band-logo T-shirts.

"Dead Kennedys, Black Flag, The Misfits…" I thought I had them fooled. But I was pretty much busted.

"Stop looking at our shirts. You don't really know any punk bands, do you?"

Totally busted. *Where do I go with this?* I thought to myself. Before I could come up with a strategy, one of them dared me to come home with them to his house. We went down into his basement and they shaved my spikes off. Then they said I was really punk. The next thing I knew, I was meeting up with them after school and hanging out.

Some of my new friends would occasionally get a hold of a skateboarding magazine, and they'd show me pictures of some decks. When I saw the boards, I connected. I became obsessed. I wanted to get my hands on a board and more of those magazines. One kid, the younger brother of one of my friends, had a stash. I cruised over to his house and knocked on the door.

"Hey, man, can I take a look at some of your skateboard magazines?" I asked.

This guy was hardcore. He wasn't about to let me *touch* his prized possessions, but he let me stand on his back porch and look at them through his screen door as he turned the pages, one by one. That's when I saw an article about street skating and a photo of a guy jumping off a car.

"I can do that! I can totally do that," I tried to convince him. He looked at me, doubting every word, but he got his board out and challenged me right then and there. I took the dare, grabbed the board and got up on his grandpa's car. Slam! I hit the ground. I got back up. I went through the same thing over and over — biting dust every time. Then finally… I landed it!

He screamed, "You did it! You're a skateboarder!"

I was hooked, rushing on adrenaline. I wanted to experience it again and again.

I began to follow a group of guys in my neighborhood that had boards. I'd beg them to let me skate. They treated me like dirt, but because they had boards, I took it.

I *had* to figure out how I could get my own board. I finally conned my mom into giving me money for a board by promising her that it would be my one and only Christmas present. I ordered a board and when it arrived, I was totally stoked. Then my mom made me hand it over. Her words, "Sorry. You can't have it until Christmas, Mike," were torture.

Weeks later, Christmas came and *finally* I got my board. I skated every spare second I could. I went from skating a few minutes a day to hours a day. I'd skate to and from school, after school, after dinner and after homework. When I started trying to skate the half pipe, I'd get nothing but grief about my style. I was doing everything I could just to gain the speed needed to get up the other side of the ramp. I'd flap my arms to get momentum. "Look at the chicken-man," guys would taunt. I didn't care — whatever it took, I'd try it. I lived and breathed skateboarding. It was my sanctuary and my salvation; it was my "thing."

I easily navigated the traps and pitfalls of high school and adolescence by just getting on my board and riding. But it wasn't just the physical act of skateboarding that made an immediate and lasting impact on me; it was the entire subculture of doing your own thing. Instead of following the crowd, I had discovered my individuality. My small town that once felt full of dead-end streets suddenly opened up. I found a wide-open country of possibilities. At fourteen, that's some vital stuff.

I truly believe everyone needs to find something to help them discover their identity and give them a sense of purpose, meaning and direction. For me... it just happened to be skateboarding. Skateboarding saved my life. It gave me the ability to express myself, connect to a passion and offer something unique back to the world. Now, as a professional, I travel the world, skateboarding and sharing my life story.

I'm still head-butting the wall, the difference is that now I'm fighting to keep the sport of skateboarding open to everyone and anyone — regardless of how good they are, what they look like or where they live. I want everyone to know that if they just believe in themselves and have a passion for the sport, anything is possible.

~Mike Vallely

Editor's note: To find out more, log on to www.mikevallely.com.

Hidden in Plain Sight

The real acid test of courage is to be just your honest self when
everybody is trying to be like somebody else.
~Andrew Jensen

t was a Thursday, and school was almost out. Our teacher was out of the classroom. Our homework sat on our desks. I fiddled with my pen while I listened to Joel and Bryan talk about a certain group of girls that we all knew.

"I like them," Bryan said, "but none of them would ever try drugs or even drink."

So what? Nobody does that stuff, I thought, but I didn't say it.

Joel just nodded.

"Actually," Bryan continued, "Lisa wants to try them, so she's talking to me about it. Everyone thinks I'm the biggest druggie in the school." He paused. "Well, basically I am."

My pen fell out of my hand and bounced on the floor. I stared at him, waiting for him to laugh, to smile — do anything — just to show that he was kidding. No one our age did drugs. No one did drugs except for those huddled people on the sidewalks who were so lost in their minds that they didn't even know who or where they were anymore. Bryan's mouth stayed in a straight line, though. No smile tugged at the corners.

"We're meeting at the park tonight," Bryan continued. "I'm not gonna charge her anything this first time. I just want her to like it. I'm bringing some friends, too. Joel, Lance, you wanna come?"

"Sure," Joel said. My whole body locked up. What could I say? What should I say?

Then, the door flung open and our teacher reentered the room. We all turned to our homework and began scribbling.

I turned and looked at Joel. *No*, I thought, *this isn't happening*. I always knew that Joel wasn't the perfect child, but who was? He certainly wasn't like Bryan, who ditched school, stole and even did drugs. But Joel had agreed to go to the park. I had known his family since I was born. He was always smiling, cracking jokes, and we hung out together almost every day. Yet he expected me to go to the park with him.

Don't worry about it, I said to myself. *My parents won't let me go to the park that late at night anyway.*

That night after I had finished dinner, I sat on the couch watching TV. The doorbell rang. When I opened the door, Joel was standing there. "What's up, Lance?" he asked.

"Not much," I said.

"So, are you coming to the park tonight?" he asked.

"I don't know," I said. "I have to ask my parents."

"No, you don't," he said, making a face as though he had just eaten something rotten. "Ask if I can spend the night and we'll just sneak out."

I frowned. "Why don't you just spend the night, and we don't sneak out? We'll have more fun here, anyway."

He groaned. "Well, I should have known that you wouldn't want to do anything slightly risky. I guess I'll find someone else." He turned and began walking away.

"No, no," I grabbed his arm. "I'll go."

He smiled.

It was ten-thirty. Lying in bed, I stared at the ceiling. In my mind, I kept thinking of ways to phrase the question, *Aren't you surprised that Bryan does drugs?* Or, *Do you think many kids are doing them?* Or even, *Do you do drugs, Joel?* I couldn't be sure now that I even knew my lifelong friend anymore. *Am I the only one who didn't know about*

Bryan's drug habit? Was I the only one who thinks that it matters? I turned and stared at Joel. *Is there a side of him that I didn't even know about?* His sleeping bag ruffled as he crawled out.

"Let's go," he whispered. I opened the window, grimacing at the sound.

It was ten-fifty. We walked until we were about one hundred yards from the park. A heavy silence laced the air. I glanced at Joel. He was staring toward the dark playground.

"We don't have to go, Joel," I said.

"What's wrong with you?" he turned and faced me. "You worry about everything. We're not little kids anymore, Lance. It's time to realize that not everything adults tell us is true."

He turned and walked forward. I followed.

When we arrived at the playground, slides and swings were the only things there. I glanced at my watch. Ten fifty-seven. "Maybe they aren't coming after all," I said.

Joel groaned and kicked the sand into the air.

I stuffed my hands into my pockets and gazed out at the lights in town. I looked back at Joel. We had come to this very park so many years before. We had spent endless hours on the swings. He always boosted himself so high into the air. I wanted to be like him, to be able to swing that high, but I couldn't do it. He was the risk taker. I looked at him again. *I guess it's only fitting that he'll take the big risk tonight*, I thought. *It's just his nature.*

A laugh erupted through the silence. Joel and I turned.

"It came from the creek," Joel said. We ran through the forest toward the water. We stopped when we got to the dense trees. I squinted to try to find footprints that led somewhere. Where was the brown, wooden picnic table that I had eaten lunch on so many times? Indented lines in the dirt caused by the legs of the table showed that it had been dragged deeper into the trees. I looked at Joel and saw that his eyes were focused on the tracks as well. "Come on," he whispered.

We followed the tracks until we reached a clearing surrounded by trees.

A white, powdery substance covered a mirror that lay on the picnic table. Jim, the kid I did a book report with in third grade, lay on the ground next to the picnic table. He trembled as if he were having a seizure. Beads of sweat lined his face. He squeezed a straw that he held in his hand. His eyes stared up into the sky. They looked as if a layer of Saran Wrap covered them. My eyes darted around. The people I grew up with were passing a pipe around in a circle. Robert, the first kid who talked to me in preschool, was taking shots of alcohol.

Bryan approached me. He squinted at me with his red eyes. A smell that made me want to gag surrounded him. "Come with me, Lance," he said. "We're taking some pipe hits."

I looked around me. *This is reality, isn't it?* I thought. *Everyone was doing it, and I never even knew about it. This is what I've been missing out on.*

I followed Bryan. The kids in the circle turned and looked at me. I stared back. These were the kids I had played with since preschool.

Something tapped my shoulder. I turned and saw Joel.

"Where are you going?" he asked. I pointed at the circle. "Let's go," he whispered. I shook my head.

"You were right, Joel. Everybody we've ever known is here. This is just the way it is."

"No," he said. I turned and walked away. He grabbed the collar of my shirt and pulled.

"We're going," he said. The respect that I had always felt for him forced me to follow. When we got out of the trees to where the picnic bench used to be, we began talking again. "I didn't know it would be like that," Joel said.

"Everyone's doing it, Joel," I said. My voice cracked. "We're the only ones not doing it."

"Not everyone's doing it, Lance. I'm not. You're not. We both have our lives ahead of us."

I nodded as we walked away.

The streetlights glared down on us as we walked on those same sidewalks that we had passed over for so many years. I looked over at Joel. He stared down at the sidewalk, his hands in his pockets. I kept wondering why he had been the one who didn't try the drugs. After all, he was always the risk taker. He was always the one who pushed himself to his limits just like that time on the swing.

We reached my house. "I think I'm going to go home and sleep," he said. I nodded.

I pulled myself into my room through the window and collapsed onto my bed. *What had kept Joel from doing what I had almost done?* I wondered as I curled up in bed.

Finally, I made sense of it all. Joel took risks, and he had taken the biggest risk of all. He *hadn't* done what everybody else was doing. He had a sense of originality that drew all those who met him to admire him. He had what he wanted in life, and drugs would only set him back.

I looked over at a picture of Joel and me on my dresser. In the picture we were both kids, swinging on the swings, laughing our heads off. That's when I knew that we could get higher than any of those kids who were stumbling through the trees behind us, just by being ourselves.

~Lance Johnson

Editor's note: For the straight scoop on drugs, log on to: www.kidshealth.org (key word search: "drugs").

Chapter 3

Create Your Best Future

Looking Past Stereotypes

Duerme con los Angeles

Walking with a friend in the dark is better than walking alone
in the light.
~Helen Keller

All summer, I waited apprehensively for the letter. Through the hot days in June and sticky days in July, I ran out to the mailbox and returned empty-handed and disappointed. After what felt like years, the crisp white envelope sealed with a blue Hofstra University crest finally arrived. No, this wasn't the letter declaring my acceptance or rejection to the University—that had come ages ago. This letter would reveal the name, address, and telephone number of the girl I'd be stuck with for the first year of my true adult life, and while I was anxious to find out who this stranger would be, I was not thrilled about having to share closer-than-close living quarters with a stranger.

In late July, the letter came. Ana Galdamez was her name, and she hailed from Flushing, Queens. I wasted no time, eager to learn whatever I could about her. I picked up the phone and dialed her number. After three rings, an answering machine clicked on, and a woman's voice streamed through the receiver.

"*Hola, no nos encontramos en este momento, porfavor dejenos un mensaje y le devolveremos la llamada lo mas pronto possible....*"

Spanish? The girl's answering machine recording was in Spanish? Of all of the horrors I feared (smelly feet, obnoxious habits, ugly bedding...), I never considered the possibility of being paired up with someone who might not even speak English. I slammed the phone down before the beep, my heart racing and my stomach churning. My knowledge of the Spanish language extended only as far as the Taco Bell commercials I had seen on TV. This was going to be worse than I thought.

In the next few weeks, I shopped, primped, and prepared for what I hoped would be the most exciting four years of my life. I stuffed my car with frilly pink bedding, sheer white curtains, sequined pillows, and all sorts of pretty trinkets. The impending stress of choosing a major, taking tests, and buying books wasn't really a concern; I was more excited to get to school as early as possible to claim the better bed, newer dresser, and bigger closet in my new room before my mystery roommate arrived.

On move-in morning, my family and I arrived before the suggested check-in time of 8:00 A.M., and I was surprised to see a line already forming outside my new dorm building. Despite all my efforts, a girl was already in my room—okay, our room—with some of her belongings unpacked, chatting cheerfully in Spanish with her own mother. She didn't seem to have a lot of things with her. I assumed they were still in the car.

Ana spoke before I could. "You must be Cassie! I'm so excited to meet you. I'm sorry we didn't get to talk this summer. I was away for most of it! Oh my gosh, you brought so much stuff! This is my mother. I saved the good furniture and the bigger closet for you; I don't really need the space!"

So she spoke English after all. Embarrassed about my assumption, I processed her words. She said she had saved the better set of furniture for me, and she wasn't kidding—I glanced around and noticed the furniture on my empty side of the room was made of polished wood, with a brand new plastic-wrapped mattress resting on top of my bed. Her furniture looked old and shabby, her mattress stained and torn and her closet significantly smaller than mine. A twinge of guilt passed through me.

I took a closer look at her now, feeling more at ease. She was pretty in a wholesome way, dressed in solid-colored clothes with no makeup or nail polish. I noticed a large, heavy-duty camouflage backpack next to her green bed.

"What's with the army bag?" I inquired.

"Oh, right. That. Well, I'm sort of in ROTC," she explained. "I wake up at four in the morning a few days a week. It's not a big deal."

Four in the morning? My stomach flipped. "Like, army training?" I knew my tone was offensive, but she didn't seem to notice. She smiled and nodded.

That evening, our parents left us to our own devices in our new half-earth-toned, half-frilled room. It took a great amount of effort for me not to grab my mother's ankles and beg her to take me back home with her. Sure, the girl seemed nice enough, but I still wasn't ready for this.

Surprisingly, we got right to talking. She was a hopeless romantic, her family was her life, and she had heaps upon heaps of exciting plans for herself and her future. As she talked, her eyes were bright, and each sentence she spoke rang with contentment and optimism. I had less to say, but was surprised to find myself wanting to learn more about her, even after we turned off the lights to go to sleep. I rested in my new bed, feeling guilty thinking of the time I wasted with my pretentious thoughts about her before we even met. I knew I had a lot to learn.

"*Duerme con los angeles,*" Ana whispered, sounding like she was already half-asleep.

"Huh?" I mumbled.

"*Duerme con los angeles.* It means 'sleep with the angels,'" Ana explained, and her soothing voice wove itself into my dreams as I slept.

That year, without knowing it, Ana taught me invaluable lessons about patience and caring for others. Her own career and life goals rubbed off on me as I carefully chose a major and studied hard. She taught me to slow down, enjoy the coming years, and appreciate what I learned in my classes. Most importantly, she taught me not to give in to quick judgments as I always had before I met her.

We lived together — by choice — for the next two years. We grew and adjusted to our new home together, every day of college life bringing new challenges to each of us. No matter what changed, however, our nights ended the same way — with a whispered "*duerme con los angeles,*" followed by a peaceful night's sleep.

~Cassie Goldberg

The Stranger Within

After the verb "to love," "to help" is the most beautiful verb in the world.

~Bertha von Suttner

It was one of those sweltering, hot days in the middle of July when all you can do is dream of the cold winter days that you hated only months earlier. One of those sultry days when you either yearn for a swim in a pool or crave a cool drink. In my case, all my friends who had pools I could invite myself into were away on vacation, and the public pools were out of the question unless I could learn to enjoy suffocating myself in chlorine with hundreds of other delirious people. Instead, I decided to go to the neighborhood café where they sold my favorite dessert, frozen yogurt. Since my parents hadn't given me a car for my sixteenth birthday, the only option I had was to walk.

Dragging a friend along, we headed for the ice-cream shop, almost passing out from the burning heat of the angry sun on the way. As we trudged along, my friend continuously grumbled about the heat and why she had so foolishly decided to come with me on this hair-brained quest for frozen yogurt. I just shrugged, perspiration dotting my forehead, mumbling.

"We're almost there. Just think of cool air conditioning and the sweet taste of frozen yogurt on your tongue. It'll be worth the walk," I assured her.

I had to admit to myself that the café was quite a distance from our house. I was beginning to get extremely thirsty, and my head was reeling from the smoggy air.

When we were about a block away from the café, I noticed her for the first time. She was old, somewhere in her mid-seventies I guessed. She had this awful arch in her burly shoulders as if she couldn't hold the heavy weight of her large chest. Her curly hair was frizzy from the heat and dyed a horrible greenish-yellow, which was clashing dreadfully with her neon pink shirt. She was struggling, pushing a squeaking grocery cart full of what appeared to be beauty-salon items.

Besides all her extraordinarily gaudy clothing, her most dominant feature was the deep frown she wore. At first, I thought it was from the harrowing heat, but with each step toward us her scowl increased, creating a more disturbing picture of a very unhappy soul. It seemed as though she hated the very air she breathed, reminding me of the cantankerous lady who used to live on our street, the one my friends and I called The Witch.

I glanced at my friend to see if she had noticed her. I could tell she had, for she was wearing the usual disgusted face she wore when she disliked something and somehow felt superior to it. My friend was the type of person who was very conscious of what others might think of her. She wanted to remain flawless to the world so, when she was presented with someone who was different in any way, she became arrogant and condescending.

As we drew closer to the lady pushing the grocery cart, my friend directed us as far away as she could, until we were nearly walking on the road. I began to observe the many others that were passing by. They, too, were avoiding her at all cost as if she were a leper or a criminal of some kind.

The lady stared blankly ahead, her wobbling knees hitting the sides of the cart. Somehow, I felt ashamed at my reaction, but that didn't stop me from hurrying by. Just as we made it past her, I heard this horrible sound from behind me and quickly turned around to see what it was.

The lady's cart had been knocked over and her soap, perfume and shampoos were scattered across the pavement. Shocked, I looked at the lady's hunched back trembling as she slowly bent with great care to begin collecting her items.

I gulped. Many things were running through my head. I looked at my friend inquiringly. "What should we do?" I asked quietly.

"What should we do? We shouldn't do anything!" my friend said, rolling her eyes heavenward.

"Yeah, I know, but it looks like she needs help," I responded softly as the lady began feebly assembling a couple of perfume bottles into her lap.

"Well, I'm sure she's okay. Someone else will help her. Besides, we didn't knock her cart over…" my friend said with cold logic and then started to walk ahead. I stood there for a minute thinking. Something was tugging at the strings of my heart and, all of a sudden, I felt great compassion for this pitiful lady. At that very moment, I knew what I had to do.

"Are you coming?" my friend called over her shoulder impatiently.

"No, I'm going to help her," I said with determination as I began to head back toward the lady.

"What? Amy…" my friend groaned through clenched teeth, giving me that look that said, *Don't test me, and don't expect me to follow you.*

I didn't pay attention to my friend as I cautiously knelt down beside the lady who was now furiously attempting to set her cart upright once more. I could feel the inquiring, skeptical eyes of the passersby. I knew they were thinking I was crazy for helping her or, worse, that I had clumsily knocked over her cart and therefore was assisting her out of duty.

"Here, let me help you," I said gently, as I began to position the cart upright.

The lady slowly glanced up, her large eyes filled with such fear, sadness and pain that I was frightened by her stare. I gulped and then, hesitantly, began putting the items back into her cart.

"Go away," she grumbled, throwing a tube of cream into her cart. "I don't need your help."

Shocked, I backed away from her seething stare and looked up at my friend who was haughtily standing by, glaring with her arms folded smugly against her chest. I sighed.

"No, I want to help you," I continued, putting three more shampoo bottles into the cart. The lady peered at me as though I was crazy. Maybe I was, but I knew that I was supposed to help her. She didn't stop me this time so I helped her put away the rest of her items. I was stunned by how many people walked by and hopped over certain disarrayed items in their paths, not even offering a sympathetic word or glance. What astounded me even more was when a cute guy whom I had liked for as long as I could remember was one of the uncaring, selfish people who strolled by. I was embarrassed by his reaction when he first saw me in a humiliating situation and then disgusted by his self-centered attitude.

When the last item was put back into the cart, I slowly rose to my feet, flinching as the lady awkwardly stood as well. I supposed she would walk by without looking at me, but then I realized I was guilty of misjudging her character.

I waited as she straightened her bent head, sniffled and slowly peered up at me. Her large dejected eyes were filled with a wonder I couldn't express in words. As an innocent tear dribbled down her ashen cheek, I was sure I could see a hint of a smile.

"Thank you," she whispered in a hushed tone. My throat tightened and tears threatened to fall down my cheeks.

"You're welcome," I murmured, offering a smile.

And you know what? She smiled then and a beautiful peacefulness washed over her once-stern countenance. I grinned widely as she cordially nodded her head and continued down the street, slowly creeping out of my life as quickly as she had appeared. Yet I knew that her smile and gratefulness would always be imprinted upon my life and heart.

When I finally had my frozen yogurt and my friend was still complaining about the embarrassment I had caused her, I felt gratitude well up within me. At that very moment, I didn't care anymore what other people thought. I was going to do the right thing, even if it meant losing or embarrassing my friends. I smiled to myself because even though I had helped that lady in such a small way, she had helped me more by showing me how I could be different in the world and how good that could feel.

~Amy Hilborn

John

Optimism is the faith that leads to achievement.
~Helen Keller

Gathering my things as I headed out of the office, I said, "I'm off to pick up my brother from the light rail."

My coworker shot me a sideways glance. "That sucks," she said, then paused. "I thought you said your brother was older than you. He doesn't drive?"

"Nope."

"And you have to pick him up every day?"

"Well, yes, and no. Yes, every day. No, but I don't *have* to. I *get* to."

John, two years older than me, has Down syndrome. Reactions to that vary. Like Great-Uncle Fred who, when John was born, voiced his opinion that John should be institutionalized, as that was the only thing to be done with "kids like that." I didn't even know I had a Great-Uncle Fred until my late teens when Mom mentioned him. Our family hasn't spoken to him since that episode.

In contrast, people who meet John before meeting me always say, "You're John's sister! He talks about you all the time. You are so lucky to have him around! You know, John always calls you 'my beautiful sister, Meghan.' Isn't that the sweetest thing ever?"

Those who know me well will occasionally get up the nerve to ask me the tough question: Was it hard growing up with John in the house?

The short answer is no.

The longer answer is, "Well, there were some differences...." John required a lot of Mom and Dad's attention when we were young, but I never felt neglected. My parents faced some challenges—finding the best programs for John, helping him learn motor skills that come naturally to most children, learning how to communicate with him. But for me, all those things were normal, because John had been there my entire life and that was all I had ever known.

Growing up, I had friends who would tell me about horrible fights and strained relationships with their siblings. In particular, my friend Kathryn's brother screamed that he hated her. That was the first time I realized how different my relationship with John was from the "normal" brother/sister dynamic. When I got home from Kathryn's house that evening, John met me at the door with a smile, a jubilant "Meghan!" and a gigantic hug.

But more than just loving my brother like crazy, John has taught me about dedication. He has an almost unnerving ability to state a goal and achieve it, no matter how unlikely it seems.

When John was in seventh grade, while he and my parents prepared for John's IEP meeting, he said, "I don't want to take all special ed classes anymore." With Mom and Dad's help, John lobbied the teachers and principal. By his senior year in high school, he took mostly normal classes with an aide and only took a small number of special ed classes.

In his freshman year of high school, he saw the homecoming parade and declared he wanted to be Homecoming King. Mom and I glanced at each other, thinking we had to find a way to let him down easy. "John, I don't know if that's going to happen," Mom said. "We'll just have to see."

Three years later, my friend Tess nominated John for Homecoming King. John came home with a card from the student council wishing him good luck. He was beside himself. "I'm going to be Homecoming King!"

Every few days for the next two weeks, the student council had runoffs to narrow the field of contenders. Each time, John brought home another card that read, "You're still in the running!"

Eventually, John was in the top four. At the rally, the nominees were announced one by one.

"Danny Hochstetler!"

Polite applause followed Danny's name, as it did for Todd White and Stephen Wright.

"And John Maste —"

We couldn't hear the last part because the gym erupted into screams, cheers and applause. For a second, I worried — loud noises scared John — but he charged through the doors with his signature smile and his eyes alight. The cheers redoubled as he stepped up to the platform next to the other contenders. The other boys put their arms around John's shoulders, and everyone smiled as the cameras flashed.

John had won.

But John wasn't finished. Next, he said, "I want to go to college!"

John attended the transition program at Sacramento City School District and was wildly successful. He graduated in December 2008. He was the only person slated for graduation that winter, but the program made sure to hold a ceremony just for him. We ran out of chairs half an hour before the ceremony began. My brother's graduation was a standing-room-only event by the time he walked to the makeshift stage.

But that's not all. After Arnold Schwarzenegger was elected to the governorship, John said, "I want to meet the governor... No, I want to work for the governor."

His contacts at the transition program set up John with an internship in the governor's mailroom at the Capitol. John became friends with the governor and Maria Shriver, and he met all sorts of visiting dignitaries. My favorite picture of him at work shows John standing between Governor Schwarzenegger and the president of Mexico.

John asked the governor if his internship could be a real, paid job. A conversation was had, papers were signed, and on his twenty-second birthday John took his oath of office. He has worked as an employee in the gubernatorial mailroom ever since.

Part of John's success comes from his dedication. He sets a goal and goes for it without restraint. He'll tell all his friends about it, gather support, and have at it. I have never seen him fail.

Though I am biased, John is wonderful. Since John is so fantastic, people are excited for him, willing to help him on his way, and go the extra mile.

So, no, it wasn't hard to have John around. In fact, it was inspiring to watch him grow up into the incredible man he has become. And every day, I sling my bag over my shoulder, grab my keys and head for the train, because I get to pick up my brother.

~Meg Masterson

Homeboy Goes to Harvard

Intolerance is the first sign of an inadequate education. An ill-educated person behaves with arrogant impatience, whereas truly profound education breeds humility.
~Aleksandr Solzhenitsyn

As I walked into the building, I heard whispering among them. Hidden behind dark glasses with a red bandanna wrapped around my head, I approached the front of the room. I wore a long, black coat, a blue shirt buttoned to the collar, baggy trousers and black patent leather shoes. I strutted across the stage and bellowed out the words, "How dare you! How dare you look at me as if I am a good-for-nothing lowlife doomed to be dead!" I looked around again. Their eyes quickly shifted away as my eyes made contact. It was as if I had a disease.

They were educators who had come to hear a speaker talk about gang prevention and intervention, about the increase of violence in schools. They expected to meet Mr. Richard Santana, a Harvard graduate. Their eyes continued to shift.

"They call me Mr. Chocolate... and I'm here to talk to you about life."

I've always known my life was different. My mother died when I was three months old, and my father left before then. I, along with my two older sisters, was moved from foster home to foster home in Fresno, California. My parents were caught in the juvenile justice system and the welfare system. I am a product of the system. I hated it.

I was introduced to gangs, drugs and violence at an early age. My uncle, a tall, strong man covered with tattoos, came into my life after serving a sentence in the state penitentiary. He was part of the largest institutionalized gang in the state of California. My uncle played an instrumental role in teaching me the rules of the barrio — the school of survival. This, along with drugs and alcohol, gave me strength to deal with the shortcomings of my life.

I grew up fast, and I developed an inner strength that made the homeboys I ran with gravitate toward me, making me the leader of the gang. My homeboys' trust in my leadership gave me courage and a deep sense of comfort. I held them close. I was prepared to die for them.

I was proud of all this, yet I often wondered, *Why can't others outside my gang see the strengths that my homeboys see in me?* Lack of acceptance by adults around me fed my resentment. So I grew intolerant of anyone who denigrated or disrespected me.

Funny thing is that even while I was rooted in the street life — the drugs, the violence, as well as the love and empowerment of being a gangster leader — part of me was elsewhere. I lucidly saw everything my life was about, as though I were looking at my own life and the lives of those around me from a watchtower high upon a hill. This wasn't a single and sudden moment of lucidity; rather I always had this perspective.

From this watchtower, I saw my homeboys' lives growing shorter each day. Whisper, a talented soccer player who was recruited for the U.S. junior team to compete internationally, gave up his dream when he got his girlfriend pregnant. Menso's ability to take pictures of life with his mind and create beautiful artwork through his hands was lost to his love affair with a syringe. I could name more. Despite how affirmed and familiar I felt with the street life, I knew I wanted another way to live.

One day while looking for a job, I dropped by the Chicano Youth Center (CYC), which offered after-school jobs regardless of my affiliation as a gang member. Through CYC, I went to Washington, D.C. for a student-leadership conference and gave a presentation on issues related to gang violence. This marked a turning point in my life — a point when I realized that I could make a positive contribution to society. As a result of this trip to D.C., I was recruited through the Educational Opportunity Program to attend California State University at Fresno.

In college, I learned about my heritage and the sacrifices made by my race. The protest for access to the university and the struggle for equality had a tremendous impact on my perception of life. I grew to appreciate my culture. Yet I was still heavily involved with the violent realities of the streets. I felt split between being a college student and a street thug.

While in my first year in college, I was approached by the campus police and frisked. When I asked why I was being searched, they informed me that they had received a phone call claiming that someone fitting my description had threatened to shoot a professor for not getting an A in the class. When the officers found nothing, I smarted off, "Well, you better get busy 'cause there's this dude looking just like me about to shoot a professor." Naturally, they didn't appreciate my humor.

If they would have checked my student status, they would have found that I was getting straight As. I knew at that moment that I would always be treated differently, dehumanized because of the way I looked. For this reason, I made a commitment to dedicate my work toward breaking down barriers that prevent other homeboys and homegirls just like myself from entering college.

I dress as a gang member, enter a room with an audience and speak to them on a variety of educational issues; I then take off a layer of clothing to reveal a shirt and tie. I make many people uncomfortable; I have caused many eyes to shift, many bodies to squirm. But by presenting my life story, I have been able to teach others ways in which they can put aside those biases and prejudices that push youth down.

~Richard Santana

The Bus Stop

*Memories of our lives, of our works and our deeds will continue
in others.*
~Rosa Parks

This particular day began as usual. I got up, got dressed and
headed for work.

I walked the usual four long blocks to the bus stop.

As I arrived, the same old faces were in the old same
places. I kept to myself and attempted to avoid all eye contact. I was
determined not to engage any of them in conversation. In the past,
nothing any one of them had said was truly of any consequence. So I
stood in back of the bus bench and leaned against the wall.

I didn't have to look for the bus because the others each took turns
leaning over to look for it.

Late again, I thought to myself.

So there I was at the bus stop with all those losers who didn't have
lives or cars. I justified my place among this particular crowd: *I would
have had a car and a better job, if my dad hadn't run out on us, making it
impossible for me to go to college. If I had gone to college, then I wouldn't be
at this bus stop.*

I looked around and noticed the white couple in their early six-
ties, who dressed alike every day. They sat extremely close together.
They were probably afraid of us. They spoke constantly in some foreign
language.

I looked over at the man I referred to as the "Dirty Old Man." He always made dirty remarks. No one paid attention to him. Besides, he still wore leisure suits. I'm sure he was Mr. Personality back in the day. He and the older couple who appeared to be joined at the hip always sat in the exact same seats.

Daily I could count on a variety of strangely dressed, loud, ignorant-acting teenage boys at the bus stop. These teenagers made a point to speak loudly enough for everyone within a block to hear every word of their conversation. I don't know why someone didn't tell them to shut up.

Then there was the "Book Worm," a girl with thick glasses. Daily she wore an oversized jacket that probably belonged to her brother. She never spoke to anyone, and she never looked up from her book and that was fine with me.

There was the "Music Man," a man in his early thirties. He wore the largest sunglasses on the planet and some kind of uniform. His earphones appeared to be attached to his head. He would blast the music so loud that you could hear it five feet away.

Lastly, there was an older woman about seventy-five. She wore a purple scarf over her head every day rain or shine. She and I leaned against the wall. She stared at me, but we never spoke. I was sure that she was a domestic worker.

Now on this particular day, I wondered why the bus people couldn't be as well groomed as I was. I wondered if they were Christians like me. I wondered if there was a reason we were always there together.

My thoughts were interrupted by the terrifying screech of skidding tires; the sound appeared to come from out of nowhere. My eyes frantically searched back and forth attempting to determine the source. Suddenly, there was a loud, horrific crash. The impact felt like a bomb, it shook everyone. Right in front of our eyes two cars collided, and one began to spin in a circle, totally out of control. The screeching became louder and louder. Everyone began to scream as the car came out of the spin and headed directly toward the bus bench and all of us.

Within a flash and without a thought for their welfare, the teenage boys, who just moments before I had called ignorant, grabbed the old man and the couple sitting on the bench and pulled them to safety. The Music Man, instead of running to get out of the way of the speeding car himself, risked his life by running over and pulling the girl reading the book out of the path of the oncoming car.

As the car jumped the curb, barely missing the teenage boys, it plowed through the cement bus bench and debris flew into the air. All I could see was a cloud of smoke heading right toward me. I closed my eyes and said, "Lord, please save me." I felt someone tugging on my right arm; I felt my feet fly off the ground. The back of my head was smashed into the wall, and I lost consciousness for a few moments.

When I finally opened my eyes, all I could see was the hood of a car right in my face, and I could feel the bumper pressing against me. The car was so close that I could see the face of the unconscious driver behind the steering wheel.

One of the teenage boys was holding my arm. He was pinned against the wall by the bumper of the car. He had risked his life to pull me from the fatal path of the car.

Immediately, I looked to my left and I saw a hole in the wall. Then I remembered the old lady who was standing next to me. I looked for her and saw that she had been hit by the car and smashed through the wall. I reached over to touch her. She looked at me and reached for my hand.

She asked, "Are you okay, honey?" as sweetly as if she were my grandmother instead of a familiar stranger at the bus stop. I said, "Yes," somewhat disbelievingly as I was certainly in shock and had not yet performed an overall assessment of my well-being.

She smiled and said, "Thank God." This was the first time we had ever spoken, in all our days at the bus stop.

Then, in a soft voice just above a whisper, she said to me, "I have watched you for months, and it made me so proud to see you looking so sharp and going to your important job. I'm so happy that you are safe."

I told her that help was on the way, but it was too late. She tenderly squeezed my hand, drew her last breath, and I felt her hand slowly slip away from mine. She closed her eyes as her head lowered. She looked so peaceful; I knew she was gone.

A pain shot through my heart. I couldn't breathe. We couldn't have been more than a foot away from each other. I was spared while she was taken. I kept asking myself why I hadn't spoken to her while I had the chance. She was proud of me even though I never even bothered to say hello or wish her a good morning. *What kind of person am I? What kind of Christian am I? I didn't even know her name.*

All the bus people, who just moments before I had called unintelligent and losers in my mind, had all clearly displayed genuine character and heroics. Without giving any thought to their own safety, they all responded, put their lives on the line and helped each other to safety. They literally saved the day.

Since then, I have learned to respect and love people, no matter what their station is in life — or what I may *think* their station is.

I continue to walk the four long blocks to the bus daily.

Only the walk doesn't seem as long because I know when I get there my friends at the bus stop will be waiting for me.

~DeAnna Blaylock

Taxi!

A moment's insight is sometimes worth a life's experience.
~Oliver Wendell Holmes, Sr.

I eagerly positioned my cab at the end of the taxi lineup outside the fancy marina resort hotel. It was a good location, and I was sure to get a passenger who would tip well. While I was waiting my turn to be first in line, I wondered if the other drivers in this lineup were as thankful as I was to be in this land of freedom and opportunity. I doubted that any of them had planned to be taxi drivers. I certainly had not.

My thoughts wandered over the long journey I had made to be here. I had grown up in Somalia, in eastern Africa, and dreamed of becoming a businessman. After graduating from the university, I had started an import/export business where my ability to speak Italian, Arabic and some English was useful. Soon my business was flourishing. Unfortunately, Somalia erupted in a civil revolution, and I found myself in danger. To stay in Somalia would have meant certain death. There was no choice but to abandon my business and flee with my young family to America, seeking political asylum. We arrived with very little means. I quickly took a job driving a taxi, something I could do immediately, in spite of my limited English. We were doing all right now, with the second job I got at AT&T, and finally I was able to tell my wife to relax and stay home with our three children. I was filled with a sense of well-being.

"Taxi! Taxi!" The voice of the hotel doorman jarred me out of my reverie. I put my cab in gear and pulled up. The doorman opened the back door of my cab and held it as a fair-haired, young business-man got in.

"Good day, sir." I smiled as the man settled himself in the back seat. "Where would you like to go?"

The man looked up and stared at me. "Where are you from?" he bluntly asked.

"I'm from Somalia, sir."

The man continued to stare at me. "Are you Muslim?" he asked suspiciously.

"Yes, sir," I answered politely. "I am Muslim."

The man abruptly opened the car door, got out of the cab and called to the doorman. I was startled by his behavior, but I was interested in this man now. I wanted to talk to him, to understand him and his fear. I pulled my cab out of the drive-through line.

The doorman looked at the young man and asked, "What's happened, sir?"

"I don't want this guy," he said pointing at me. "Please call me another taxi!"

The doorman just stood there, not knowing what to do. At this point, I jumped out of my cab and approached the now visibly agitated man, saying, "Sir? May I talk to you?"

I gestured to the cabs waiting in line. "Look. All these cabbies are Muslim, sir. None of them will hurt you, but please ride with me. I will give you a free ride wherever you want to go! Ask the doorman; I am a dependable driver. You will be safe."

The man looked at me with distrust, then at the doorman for reassurance. The doorman nodded his approval. He shrugged and warily got back in my cab. "Oceanside," he directed, somewhat defiantly, but with a questioning look on his face.

"That's okay, sir. I said I would take you for free, and I will." I smiled, even though I knew the drive to Oceanside was a hundred-dollar fare and would take nearly two hours of my time. "Please be comfortable, sir. Would you like a cigarette?"

The man accepted the cigarette and appeared to relax a little. We drove in silence for a few minutes. Then I asked, "Why didn't you want to ride with a Muslim, sir?"

As I expected, the man began to talk about the September 11 terrorists' attacks and the thousands of innocents who had been killed. He concluded this litany with an emphatic declaration: "That's what Muslims do!"

Even though I had expected the response, the words still hurt. Ever since September 11, I had felt shame that men claiming to be Muslims had committed such terrible acts. I wanted this man to understand that those men were not behaving like Muslims, that they were crazy.

"Sir? You have ten fingers on your hands. Right? Each finger is different from the others. Right? People are like that. Whoever was involved in September 11 was against Muslims, against Christians, against Jews. No religion in the world says that violence is the right way." There was silence in the cab as I negotiated the traffic on Interstate 5. Then I asked, "What about the bombing in Oklahoma, sir? Was that a Muslim?"

"No." "Where was he from, sir?" "America." I persisted with my questions. "What religion, sir?" "Christian," my passenger reluctantly responded. "Did the Christians agree with what he did, sir?" "No!"

"It is the same with Muslims and these sick, crazy guys that did this terrible thing on September 11!" I felt triumphant. "Please, please, please don't think every Muslim would do what those crazy men did on September 11. You know that Christians do not do what that crazy man did in Oklahoma. Let's go forward with that reality."

There was a moment of silence.

"Yes. You're right, you're right," came the soft and thoughtful reply from the back seat.

"Okay! Okay!" I eagerly responded. "I'm Muslim. You're Christian. We're brothers. If you were about to die right now, right here, I would not let you die. I would help you. And you would do the same for me, right? So we are brothers! It doesn't matter what religions we are; we are Americans. We can help each other that way when we forget about the religion. We are Americans — that's it!"

"Right! Right!" We arrived, and the man attempted to pay the fare. "No, no, sir! I told you that this would be a free ride, remember? Here is my card. I am Nur Ali. Please call me when you need a ride. You can pay me back that way!"

About three hours later, I got a call from the man to pick him up and bring him back to his hotel. The fare was $98, and the man gave me $128. He was staying at the hotel for three days. For all three days, he faithfully called me to take him wherever he needed to go.

The last day of his stay, I took the man to the airport. As he got out of the cab and paid me his fare and a tip, he said, "Good-bye, Nur. I am sorry. Please forgive me."

"Of course, of course," I told him. I couldn't stop smiling, which I'm sure left no doubt in his mind that my forgiveness was sincere. "We are brothers. We are Americans. We must forgive each other."

I was still smiling as I returned to the resort hotel and maneuvered into the taxi lineup. I was glad to be in America. I was free. I was at peace.

"Taxi! Taxi!" It was my turn. I looked expectantly at my next passenger.

~Nur Ali as told to Barbara Smythe

Thirty Cents Worth

Things do not pass for what they are, but for what they seem.
Most things are judged by their jackets.
~Baltasar Gracián

Whispering voices and laughter fill the hallways of my school as I walk with my friend toward our next class. I resist the impulse to become yet another person using these few moments to judge others in order to make myself feel better. I repeat to myself, *Thirty cents*, as I continue to walk in silence, something I rarely do. My friend digs her elbow into my side and grumbles, "That's just gross. Why would anyone want blue hair? That's so nasty!" I think before my tongue springs into action. Ordinarily, I would just give the expected giggle and nod — but for some reason, I hesitate.

My thoughts turn back to the previous Sunday afternoon. After flying through the house grabbing and tossing things into my soccer bag, I discovered that I was out of Blister-Block Band-Aids, an essential for the next day's game. After some persuasion, I coaxed my mom into taking me to Walgreen's. She dropped me off and assured me she'd be right back. I rushed inside and snatched the goods.

There was a line at the register, as usual, and I waited my turn. I slowed down for a minute and examined the man in front of me. I was appalled.

He was old and reeked of gasoline and cigarettes. His hair was unkempt and reached below his shoulders. He wore a red vest matted in dust and jeans faded beyond recognition. His blue eyes were glassy and tired, and his dark mahogany face was etched with deep wrinkles carved by hard times.

He reached the counter and greeted the saleswoman with a nod. She averted her eyes as he pointed to the cigarettes behind the counter. She grabbed the carton he was pointing to and quickly rang him up. He grabbed the plastic bag and slowly ambled away.

I gave her four one-dollar bills and the Band-Aids as she nodded in agreement with my disgust. "Sorry," she said. "You're thirty cents short."

"Oh, no… I don't have thirty cents! My mom isn't here… She'll be right back. Can I run out to the car real quick?" As I was pleading my case, the cashier was visibly annoyed by the delay I was causing. I could feel the blood rush to my face as the people behind me in line started looking at each other with the same judgmental eyes I had just shared with the cashier. Just as I was about to run out of the store without my Band-Aids, I got a strong whiff of cigarettes and gasoline.

A dirty hand with yellow fingernails placed four nickels and a dime on the counter. I was awestruck and at a loss for words. I quickly offered to pay him back.

"That's okay. It's only thirty cents," he said with a warm smile and a wink. The man I had just judged as a foul creature had done something amazingly kind.

Now when I start to judge somebody based on their looks, I stop and repeat "thirty cents" to myself as a reminder to look beyond appearances. When I do that, I see beauty in everyone I meet.

~Trish E. Calvarese

Troubled

Christmas is not as much about opening our presents as opening
our hearts.
~Janice Maeditere

A song sung by Faith Hill in the blockbuster movie *The Grinch* asks: "Where are you, Christmas? Why can't I find you?" Well, sometimes the Christmas spirit is like a misplaced sock—you find it when you aren't looking and where you'd least expect it to show up.

I found it at a quarter past one in the morning.

On my way home from work, I stopped at the neighborhood doughnut shop. After parking in its ghost town of a parking lot, I was headed toward the door when I spotted trouble.

What lit a warning light on my intuition radar was a group of teenagers—three boys and a girl. Understand, I wasn't alarmed by their tattoos (the girl included) or their earrings (boys included—eyebrows as well as each of their ears). Rather, it was the extremely late hour and the fact they loitered on the sidewalk in a semicircle around an elderly man sitting in a chair. Wearing a tattered flannel shirt and barefoot, the man looked positively cold and probably homeless.

And in trouble with a capital T.

Against my better judgment, I went inside the store and ordered three doughnuts—while keeping a worried eye on the group outside. Nothing seemed to be happening.

Until I headed toward my car.

Something was indeed "going down." As ominously as a pirate ordering a prisoner to the plank, the teens told the old man to stand up and walk.

Oh, no, I thought. Capital tee-are-oh-you-bee-el-ee.

But wait. I had misjudged the situation. And I had misjudged the teens.

"How do those feel?" one of the boys asked. "Do they fit?"

The cold man took a few steps—maybe a dozen. He stopped, looked at his feet, turned around and walked back. "Yeah, they'z about my size," he answered, flashing a smile that, despite needing a dentist's attention, was friendly and warm on this cold night.

The teens, all four, grinned back.

"Keep them. They're yours," one of the boys replied. "I want you to have them."

I looked down. The teen was barefoot. The kid had just given the cold-and-probably-homeless man his expensive skateboarding sneakers—and, apparently his socks, as well.

The other two boys sat on their skateboards by the curb, retying their shoelaces. Apparently, they, too, had let the man try on their sneakers to find which pair fit the best. The girl, meanwhile, gave the cold man her oversized sweatshirt.

With my heart warmed by the unfolding drama, I went back into the shop.

"Could I trouble you for another dozen doughnuts?" I asked, then told the clerk what I had witnessed.

Christmas spirit, it seemed, was more contagious than flu or chicken pox. Indeed, the cold night got even warmer when the woman not only wouldn't let me pay for the doughnuts, but added a large coffee, too.

"These are from the lady inside. Have a nice night," I said as I delivered the warm doughnuts and piping-hot cup. The old man smiled appreciatively.

"You have a nice night, too," the teens said.

I already had.

~Woody Woodburn

Nameless Faces

*Human beings, by changing the inner attitudes of their minds,
can change the outer aspects of their lives.*

~William James

I was nineteen years old the first time I saw my own true character. I wish I could say I was proud of what I saw, but that would be a lie. At least I can say that my true character changed that day. My overall outlook on people managed to take a 180-degree turn in less than ten minutes. Who would have thought that the first person to change the way I viewed humanity would be a complete stranger?

For about a year, my voyage to and from work each day included a subway ride followed by a ten-minute walk through the heart of downtown Toronto. As with most large cities, the homeless population of Toronto often congregated on downtown corners, asking pedestrians for their spare change. Like most busy citizens, I learned to ignore the nameless faces who begged me for money each day. When it came to homeless beggars, my limited life experience had led me to one assumption — you are on the streets because you choose to be, probably due to drugs or alcohol.

I remember noting how particularly cold the weather had been that season. It was mid-December, and the temperature was a chilly –20 degrees Celsius. I walked with my head down, desperately wishing that my office was closer to the subway stop. I passed the usual mobs of homeless beggars, ignored all of them, and continued walking. As I crossed the intersection of Queen and Yonge streets, I saw him sitting against a building, wrapped in several layers of thin cloth, holding a white cup in front of him. I heard his shaky, pathetic voice target me as I sped past him.

"Spare some change?" he asked. "I would really appreciate it."

I didn't even bother looking up at his nameless face. I briefly pictured him walking into the closest liquor store and stocking up on whiskey with whatever money he managed to conjure up that day. Or, maybe he needed another hit of cocaine. Clearly, if he had ever been married, his wife would have literally kicked him to the curb when he couldn't get his habit under control. See, like most teenagers, it took me only moments to pass judgment on his life.

"I have no money on me," I said quickly.

Looking back now, I feel as though fate had set out that day to teach me a lesson. And it succeeded. Just a few feet past him, I managed to find the only ice patch on the sidewalk. As I slipped, I tried to position myself so the impact would occur on my hip and thigh, but unfortunately my aim was about as good as my judgment of character, and I managed to land square on my right knee. The pain seared through me as I lay on the ground for several moments wondering if I had fractured my kneecap. As I tried to come to grips with the notion of actually getting up, I heard a familiar, gruff voice only inches above me.

"Are you all right?" he asked.

I knew immediately that this was the man I had just rushed past. Even in pain, I still took a quick moment to sniff for the faintest smell of alcohol on his breath. There was none. Before my eyes began to well up with tears, I saw the smooth, sympathetic look in his eyes. He wasn't drunk or high.

I held his hand as I struggled to get to my feet. He held my arm as I hobbled to the nearby bus stop and quickly sat on the bench. The pain in my leg told me that I had definitely done more than simply bruised my knee. I needed an X-ray.

"My name is Mike," he said, as I tried to find a comfortable position on the bench. "You really shouldn't try walking on that leg. That was quite a fall you took, and you really need to get it checked by a doctor," he said with deep concern.

"This bus goes past the hospital," I said quickly, pointing to the bus sign above me.

Mike paused, and a look of sudden realization crossed his face. He reached into his pocket and pulled out his small white cup. He dumped the meager amount of change into the palm of his hand and counted it. He held only money out toward me, and after a few confusing moments I looked up at him in sheer bewilderment.

"I know you don't have any change on you," he said, "but I can always give you this. I think there's just enough here for you to take the bus."

I was overwhelmed with guilt as I remembered the lie I had told him only a few short minutes earlier. I turned away from his offering hand and reached for my purse. I pulled out my wallet and dumped my own change into the palm of my hand. I felt Mike's eyes on me as I counted through the money that I had told him didn't even exist. I had at least ten dollars worth of change in my hand. I counted out enough money for me to take the bus to the hospital and then turned to Mike to offer him the rest. He held out his cup as I placed the handful of change in it. I wished I had some bills to give him, but I hadn't been to the bank yet that day.

"Thank you," he said quietly. It was by far the most sincere "thank-you" I had ever heard in my life. Just behind him, I heard the bus approaching. He held out his hand to help me stand up.

"Thank *you*," I said as the bus slowed down in front of me. "You take care of yourself," I said sheepishly. Both of us knew that five minutes earlier I couldn't have cared less what happened to him.

"I will," he said. "And you take care of that leg."

"I will."

I hobbed onto the bus and took a seat by the window. I watched Mike as he clung to his cup of change, cherishing it as if it were the first gift he had ever received. Despite his gratitude, I didn't feel absolved for my actions. A half-cup of change seemed too small a gift for the man who gave a name to every nameless face I've ever seen.

~Alexandera Simone

Switching Roles

With honesty and a little digging, we have the opportunity to
identify our gifts and harness them in the service of our best
self — our own unique noble purpose.
~Tom Hayes

have a beautiful older sister, Sarina, who just so happens to have Down syndrome. From my earliest years, I was made to believe that I was to take care of her, as she would never be able to care for herself. I remember promising my mother that I would.

When I went off to college at seventeen, Sarina stayed home with my parents. I lived in Nevada, and she lived in Massachusetts. When I turned twenty-one, Sarina wanted to move to Nevada with me, as my parents were not giving her as much independence as she wished, and she was steadily regressing. I thought about this, wondering if I could take care of my sister and finish off college. *Wouldn't she be a lot of work? Could I actually get her all the things she would need and still maintain a life of my own?* We decided to try. In all honesty, I was not prepared for all the challenges that faced us. I worked nights, went to school during the day, and slept when I could. In between, I was teaching Sarina the ins and outs of taking care of herself. I took her along to everything — parties, clubs, casinos, vacations — all over the West Coast.

On Halloween 1992, we were going to a nightclub in our costumes. She was Catwoman and I was a gypsy. A car ran a red light, hitting us head-on. Sarina went through the windshield, and I was a mess — broken knees and hands, and a fractured skull. Sarina sustained no injuries but a scratch on the nose and neck.

When we were discharged from the hospital, I could barely walk and was in constant pain. Sarina had to cook, assist me in the shower, help me get dressed, and do my hair — basically everything I had done for her previously. She was amazing! She had retained all that I had taught her and was able to apply it to real-life situations, not only for herself, but also for another. We had switched roles — I was now being taken care of by my sister.

After five years, I decided to move back to the New England area. Sarina and I climbed Calico Basin in Las Vegas on Christmas day, and when we got to the top I told her that I wanted to go back. She very clearly said to me with a smile, "You go, my sister. I stay here."

I asked her who would take care of her, and she said, "I take care of myself." I had little doubt she could, but I just couldn't leave her alone in Las Vegas, so she gave in and moved back to New England with me. After we got settled, she got her own apartment with twenty hours of assistance and took college classes.

I will never forget how I wondered if I could take care of Sarina. Now I wonder if I could have accomplished all I did if I didn't have her in my life. She has shaped my career, my personality, my parenting skills, and my life. I love you, my sister.

~Gina Favazza-Rowland

The Hardest Lesson

*No human race is superior; no religious faith is inferior. All
collective judgments are wrong. Only racists make them.*

~Elie Wiesel

When I was five years old, my mother and father
moved to the South Bronx, New York, leaving me
in the care of my grandmother in Santurce, Puerto
Rico. Although we were poor and food was scarce,
I lived an idyllic life with my grandmother and my *tíos* and *tías* and
cousins, surrounded by the loving faces of my extended family, emerald
green oceans, trips to the countryside, to *El Yunque*, little kids' games
and bedtime stories. I missed my mother and father, especially my
mother, but I never wanted to leave the island. I was happy and loved,
and I felt safe there.

When I turned eight, my mother wrote to my grandmother and
asked her to send me to New York. She and my father were managing
to scrape out a living, had a small apartment in a stable neighborhood
and were making progress. It was time for me to join them, and so I
went, sadly leaving behind the only world I knew.

When I got to the South Bronx, my mother enrolled me in the public elementary school, and although I didn't speak a word of English,
I found myself stuffed into overcrowded classes of English-speaking
children and teachers. Luckily, there were some other Puerto Rican
kids, although they were very different from me, most of them having

been born in the United States and speaking much more English than Spanish. But they were able to communicate with me, and the little conversations that we shared at recess really kept me going. I was scared and I felt alone, like nobody else in the world had ever gone through what I was going through. My parents weren't any help since they didn't speak much English. In fact, they were pressuring me to learn the language so that I could help them handle daily transactions that had to be carried out in a language they didn't speak. It was a tough time, and I remember it very well.

A month after I started school, things started to get better. I was beginning to understand some English, I had made a few friends, and I was feeling a little more at home in my new surroundings. But that was about to change. One day, as we were getting our daily math lesson, I felt the kid behind me nudging me on the back. When I turned slightly to see what he wanted, he stuck out his hand and showed me a small piece of paper that was sloppily folded into a little square. I understood that he wanted me to take the paper from him, so I did, and I put it on my desk. I didn't realize it at the time, but the teacher had observed the passing of the "note," and she was quickly standing over me at my desk.

I remember feeling scared and small as my tall, blonde teacher reached down and grabbed the folded paper out of my hand. Mrs. Jones's face turned red and her squinted eyes seemed to get smaller and smaller as she glared at me. Although I couldn't really understand the fast string of staccato words that came out of her mouth, I did hear her call me a "Dirty Puerto Rican." I didn't understand the word "dirty," but whatever it was, it felt like an accusation. And I had no idea what I had done to earn my teacher's wrath.

The next thing I knew, Mrs. Jones yanked me up in front of the class and announced that I was being sent home. Soon my mother appeared, and I watched as she came in through the hall door and started making her way toward me. I was so relieved to see her that I ran as fast as I could and buried myself in her waist, holding on to her desperately. But my sense of security was quickly shattered as she pushed me from her, unfastening my grip on her waist and staring down at me with fiery eyes. My mother's face was redder and angrier than the teacher's; she was furious and didn't ask me any questions. I could see her eyes filling with tears although she was trying hard to blink them back.

"*Por qué lo hiciste?*" she screamed at me, demanding to know why I had done what I had "done." I knew it had something to do with the paper that the teacher had snatched off my desk, but I didn't know how to begin to answer her. And then, without another word, she slapped me in the face, hard.

I felt so betrayed by her and so humiliated in front of my class-mates. I ran out of the room and hid under the water fountain down the hall. My mother came out and found me, wiped my tears, hugged me and took me home.

When we got there, she asked me why I had been so foolish as to pass around a note with filthy words on it. This was the first clue I had about what had happened and why I had gotten into trouble! It didn't help me feel any better about things. I hadn't even opened the note, and even if I had, I wouldn't have understood any of the cuss words that the boy behind me had written on the paper. I didn't even know bad words in Spanish, let alone in English!

When I explained to my mother exactly what had happened, she was filled with sadness and remorse; she explained that a lot of people in New York didn't like Puerto Ricans, and that I would have to be careful about that. She said that in order to avoid these "problems," I would have to behave better than the Anglo kids. I would have to look cleaner, neater and more decent than them, always speak properly and only when spoken to, and never bring suspicion on myself or my fam-ily. How I missed my life on the island right then.

Looking back on this incident as a grown woman, I understand what my mother was trying to do for me. Although she definitely made the wrong choice that day, I've come to understand that "choices" don't come easily when people are living under stress. I was also able to understand that my mother did what she did, ironically, to try to pro-tect me. She wanted Mrs. Jones and the class to know that I came from a "good" Puerto Rican family, and that I would be disciplined harshly by her if I crossed any lines. My mother meant well; she just didn't have the resources to make a better choice.

Racism is evil. It isn't something that anyone should have to put up with. It is one of the ultimate injustices of life. But still, I am grateful that my mother set me straight at a very early age so that I could better deal with the life that she and my father had chosen for me. I learned so much from that one experience and from others that followed, and I have become much better equipped than my parents to struggle for myself and my family. As a Latina, as an American and a Nuyorican, I always remember that my greatest resource is believing in myself, believing in us, in our inherent dignity, and in our right to live and thrive in this country.

It's a life worth struggling for.

~Caroline C. Sánchez

Chapter 4

Create Your Best Future

Developing Self-Esteem

A Lifetime
of Stuttering

*Awakening is the process of overcoming your false self and
discovering your True Self. It begins when you decide to grab
the tiger by the tail and ends with the tiger tenderly licking the
sweat off your brow and face.*
~Steve Baxter

For the first decade or so of my life, my older brother and I
were the only two kids I knew who suffered from the speech
disorder known as stuttering. Miraculously, around the age of
twelve, my brother's stuttering stopped. I was very happy for
him and equally excited for my future. I was thinking "two more years."
Thirty years later, my stutter is still going strong and I wouldn't want it
any other way.

If I had a nickel for every time I was made fun of, I could have
potentially retired at twelve. It's not easy being a kid, and it's especially
difficult when you're different.

The biggest fear for most Americans is public speaking, so imagine being a stuttering child having to read aloud a paragraph from
Charlotte's Web as the entire class looks, listens, and laughs. It's not
easy. Imagine sitting at your desk with your palms sweating, pulse racing, and heart pounding as if you're about to testify against the Mafia,
when, in fact, you're simply sitting there waiting to read a paragraph

from *Where the Red Fern Grows*.

That all changed for me in the eighth grade when I decided to ease my anxiety by volunteering to read each and every time. My hand was always the first to go up and stayed up for most of the class. I chose to be in complete control of what and when to read. If kids laughed, they laughed. I'd usually have a witty one-liner to shoot back at them, which would ultimately shut them up. From that point on, I never again looked at my stuttering as a significant challenge.

Fast forward to 2012 and I'm a comic, a speaker, and a soldier with three tours of duty in Iraq. I currently hold the rank of Captain in the Alabama National Guard.

When I started out in comedy, my goal was simply to make the audience laugh. After each show or online video, I'd get feedback on how my comedy helped educate them with respect to their family and friends who also suffered from this speech disorder. I was blown away. Until seeing my routine, they'd never considered the challenges a person who stutters faces on a daily basis. Imagine the fear of talking on a telephone. Imagine the fear of ordering food at a restaurant. Imagine the fear of not being able to say your child's name.

I also get random messages from young men and women who aspire to serve in the military but feel they are not qualified due to their speech disorder. Being able to inspire them to follow their dreams might be the highlight of what I do. Stuttering is no joke but having the ability to inspire and create awareness of stuttering through humor has truly been a gift from God.

Stuttering is still one of the great unknowns. I've been stuttering for forty years and still can't explain it. I can probably do a better job of explaining the Pythagorean theorem. I do know, however, that four out of five people who stutter are male and that only around one percent of the world's population will ever know what it's like to get "stuck" on the simplest of sounds. I, just like any person who stutters, have my good days and bad days and everything in between. Additionally, we don't always get hung up on the same sounds, words, or sentences. And finally, the number one pet peeve for most of us is having people finish our words or sentences. We have something to say, so let us say it.

I've had the great fortune of attending the last two National Stuttering Association (NSA) annual conventions. The convention is not a pity party. It's a fun and inspiring celebration filled with education, awareness, acceptance, and empowerment.

Because of my upbringing and military service, I've always been an adapt-and-overcome kind of guy, but attending the NSA convention has even opened my eyes to the difficulty many of my fellow stutterers face each and every day. I've even met people who stutter when they sing.

The NSA convention is a four-day conference. In 2011, we had the writer for the Academy Award winning film *The King's Speech* as the keynote speaker. I may be the only person who stutters who has not seen the film. Another great film featuring a person who stutters is *Star Wars*. James Earl Jones, the voice of Darth Vader, endured severe stuttering during his childhood but has gone on to have one of the greatest voices of our time. He truly beat the odds. Of course he did have one slight advantage; he was a Jedi.

There are days when I, too, wish I was a Jedi, but that has nothing to do with my speech.

Whether it's a big nose, ugly toes, or a run in your pantyhose, we all have perceived flaws that each of us should embrace, because if we don't embrace them ourselves, how can we possibly expect it from others?

~Jody Fuller

I Own It

*A successful person is one who can lay a firm foundation with
the bricks that others throw at him or her.*
~David Brinkley

My mother used to say "I would give you all of my hair if I could." She used to try on my wigs, turning her face from left to right, and back again. Angling her chin, fluffing the synthetic bangs with three fingers. I would watch her from behind her vanity table, silently taking everything in. Alone there, in her room, I never felt ashamed, or different because of my alopecia. Would I ever be like her, so confident, brave and strong, brimming with sureness and beauty? But this was my alopecia, my hair loss, not hers. When she took my wig off, her golden curls bounced around her face, and perhaps she never gave it another thought. My cold hands absentmindedly rubbed my bald head.

I will never forget the day I lost my hair. Not because it affected me so, but because my mother acted as if the world had ended, collecting waist-length locks into plastic bags and storing them in the china cabinet in the dining room "just in case anything could ever be done."

At four years old, I had no sense of worry about losing my hair. On the contrary it was painful for my mother and sister to vice grip me between their knees, hushing me as they brushed out my tomboy snarls. I would cry and wriggle and beg for them to just cut it off.

Then overnight, against my cool cotton pillowcase, out it came, lying all around me in clumps as if a ghostly hairdresser had come in the night and razored most of it off.

Even amidst all of the doctor's appointments, the cortisone treatments and the pull tests, still I did not feel any differently. Pictures of me in horrid 80s clothing, dashing across the cameras frame, bald head wild and free, I never even stopped to consider that I was different.

Because alopecia had touched my life so early, none of the children in my elementary school minded. Girls with silky, thick pigtails used to line up in the bathroom for a peak under my hats. They would ask month after month if there'd been any change, any growth. I was everyone's personal peep show, but it was also harmless, and I was accepted. Things were okay.

There was nothing more beautiful, and I never had a closer sense of self, than when I was young, before I was made aware of my physical differences. Alopecia felt good. It was light, and airy and it was just me.

Junior high was the year when everything changed. School went from being a place where I was loved and accepted, to a place where I was bullied and tormented. I went to a junior high that had an open enrollment program. That meant kids would be bussed from Detroit to the suburbs surrounding Detroit. That meant there were new children who didn't know about my alopecia. It was an abrupt change, one that no one had prepared me for. When I accidentally singed the bangs of my new wig in seventh grade, there was nothing my father could do; he could not afford to buy me a new one.

It became apparent that I wore a wig, and now, instead of my differences making me popular and loved, they made me a target to children who were unaware and angry. One girl in particular bullied me for what felt like the longest year of my life. She and her friends would play football with my wigs. They would walk up behind me and with the slightest of hand movements pull my hair from my head, earning me the nickname of "snatches." Teachers and lunch ladies, friends and janitors would watch in horror, but no one said a thing. It made me feel as though I was not worth anything, since no one, not even the adults, would stand up for me. And I was too ashamed to stand up for myself.

Somehow I made it through to high school but then we moved. I would have start a new school and face telling everyone about my alopecia, a condition that was now something I tried my best to hide. I reinvented myself. I told people I was sick and was dying. Cancer was much more glamorous than simply having no hair. When other students would question me, I would panic and spend that class period in the bathroom, hiding, from them, from myself, breathing hard, internalizing my anxiety, and hoping to just disappear. The next day, and the day after that, I would stay home sick. I just couldn't bear the possibility of going through what I went through before. Yet still, I made it through, just as I had before.

Something happens the older and older you get. Women with alopecia bloom. Maybe it's the experiences we endure, tucked under our belts like weapons, like armor. I can't tell you the specific day or time my alopecia no longer shamed me, but empowered me. With each person I told about my hair (or lack thereof), it became easier and easier to do so. Slowly, I started to have fun buying wigs, enjoyed being different from all of the other girls. I had knowledge, and I had gone through things no one else I knew had ever experienced. The stronger I became about my alopecia, the less people cared, and the more they supported me.

Even if adults behaved the way those junior high kids did, I would still be proud to be who I am — a strikingly beautiful twenty-eight-year-old writer with alopecia totalis.

Now I spend a lot of time in front of the bathroom mirror, wig off, lights burning bright, admiring the things about myself that are enhanced by my alopecia. I have amazingly high cheekbones. Because my hair does not grow, I have the softest skin of anyone I have ever met. I can change my hairstyle, color, and length in an instant, and then change it back if it suits me. I will never have a bad hair day. I have experienced swimming bald, and nothing will ever compare to that. When I go to sleep at night, my pillow comes up soft and cool to meet my warm head. I am beautiful and desirable, and I stand out, with or without my wig on.

I gained that confidence I watched my mother have for me. Except it is mine. It is stronger than hers, more wild and sincere than hers. It is mine. Because I earned it. I understood that being proud of having alopecia was a dream my mother had for me, but I ran with it and made it my own.

~Kate White

Follow Your Dream

Don't live down to expectations. Go out there and do
something remarkable.
~Wendy Wasserstein

have a friend named Monty Roberts who owns a horse ranch
in California. He has let me use his house to put on fundraising
events to raise money for youth at risk programs.

The last time I was there he introduced me by saying, "I
want to tell you why I let Jack use my house. It all goes back to a
story about a young man who was the son of an itinerant horse trainer
who would go from stable to stable, race track to race track, farm to
farm and ranch to ranch, training horses. As a result, the boy's high
school career was continually interrupted. When he was a senior, he
was asked to write a paper about what he wanted to be and do when
he grew up.

"That night he wrote a seven-page paper describing his goal of
someday owning a horse ranch. He wrote about his dream in great
detail and he even drew a diagram of a 200-acre ranch, showing the
location of all the buildings, the stables and the track. Then he drew a
detailed floor plan for a 4,000-square-foot house that would sit on the
200-acre dream ranch.

"He put a great deal of his heart into the project and the next day
he handed it in to his teacher. Two days later he received his paper
back. On the front page was a large red F with a note that read, 'See

me after class.'

"The boy with the dream went to see the teacher after class and asked, 'Why did I receive an F?'

"The teacher said, 'This is an unrealistic dream for a young boy like you. You have no money. You come from an itinerant family. You have no resources. Owning a horse ranch requires a lot of money. You have to buy the land. You have to pay for the original breeding stock and later you'll have to pay large stud fees. There's no way you could ever do it.' Then the teacher added, 'If you will rewrite this paper with a more realistic goal, I will reconsider your grade.'

"The boy went home and thought about it long and hard. He asked his father what he should do. His father said, 'Look, son, you have to make up your own mind on this. However, I think it is a very important decision for you.'

"Finally, after sitting with it for a week, the boy turned in the same paper, making no changes at all. He stated, 'You can keep the F and I'll keep my dream.'"

Monty then turned to the assembled group and said, "I tell you this story because you are sitting in my 4,000-square-foot house in the middle of my 200-acre horse ranch. I still have that school paper framed over the fireplace." He added, "The best part of the story is that two summers ago that same schoolteacher brought thirty kids to camp out on my ranch for a week. When the teacher was leaving, he said, 'Look, Monty, I can tell you this now. When I was your teacher, I was something of a dream stealer. During those years I stole a lot of kids' dreams. Fortunately you had enough gumption not to give up on yours.'"

Don't let anyone steal your dreams. Follow your heart, no matter what.

~Jack Canfield

Inner Sustenance

*Believing in yourself is one of the greatest things that you could
ever do for yourself. But the greatest is loving
yourself unconditionally.*
~Edmond Mbiaka

All I ever wanted was to be popular. Have the coolest friends. Be in a hot rock band and date the best-looking men — simple wishes for a young girl. Some of my dreams even came true. I started a rock band. And the cutest guy at Melbourne High School even asked me out.

I answered yes of course, but within a week, he complained, "Your hips are too big. You need to lose weight to look thin like the other girls in your band."

Immediately, I tried several different diets to lose weight. For one, I ate grapefruit and vegetables only. That didn't work; I felt faint and had to eat. The second week I tried skipping breakfast and dinner. When I did that, I became so hungry by the time dinner came, I splurged and eventually started gaining weight. Ten pounds I added in a month trying to please my boyfriend. Instead of praising my efforts, he cut me down even more. "You look like a whale," he said, making me feel not as pretty as my other friends who wanted to date him. I felt self-conscious and didn't want to lose him as a boyfriend, so I desperately searched for another way to lose the pounds that were keeping him at bay.

I didn't even think that he was the problem: just me, it was just me. Whatever I ate made me fatter. Whatever I wore, I looked hideous. I was now 110 pounds, a complete blimp!

One evening after a date, I got so angry by his "whale" remarks that I ate an enormous piece of cake. The guilt made me want to try something I had seen other girls in my school doing at lunch break: throw up. I went to my bathroom and without even thinking of the consequences, stuck my finger down my throat and threw up in the toilet.

All I ever wanted was to be as pretty as a model. I wanted my boyfriend to look at me the same way as he did those bikini-poster girls.

It was so easy. That cake I just enjoyed didn't cost me any unwanted calories.

Once a day soon turned into three forced vomits. Becoming malnourished, I was constantly hungry, so I ate more, threw up more. It wasn't until I strangely gained another fifteen pounds and tried to quit a month later that I realized I couldn't stop. I fought to, for several weeks. As soon as I got up from the table, my stomach began convulsing. Now my own stomach somehow believed that's what it was supposed to do. I had to run from the table. I was throwing up without even sticking my finger down my throat or even wanting to!

I wasn't in control anymore. I was caught in a whirlwind. I thought bulimia would help me lose pounds but after the months of doing it, not only hadn't it controlled my weight, but the purging had opened up the pits of hell.

I needed help. My boyfriend's comments and my weight were the least of my problems now and I knew it. At age fifteen I didn't know what to do. Desperate for a solution, I broke down into tears and confided in the only person I could trust: my mom. Unsure of how she would react and wondering if she'd stop loving me if she knew, I mustered up the courage to write the truth on a note and leave it on her dresser:

"Mom, I'm sick. I tried forcing myself to throw up to lose weight, now I am vomiting every day. I can't stop. I'm afraid I'm going to die."

I locked myself in my room the entire night. My mother knocked on my door several times. I could hear her crying. The next morning she pounded harder and told me she had made a doctor's appointment for me. "Get out here before we're late!" she said.

I opened the door. Instead of a hard and loud scolding, I received a hug. Being in her understanding arms, I had the confidence to go to the doctor with her.

The first meeting with the doctor, I'll never forget. He told me that by using bulimia to lose weight I was actually retaining water, losing hair, ruining the enamel on my teeth and was now developing a very serious stomach condition called gastritis. He informed me I was malnourished and in danger of losing my life. He strongly recommended that I check myself into a hospital for treatment.

Knowing that I would be apart from my friends and my mother, I didn't want to agree. Going to the hospital seemed to be a way of walking away from everything I've ever known. I was terrified about leaving home. I'd never been away from my house, my school or my friends before. I was wondering if anyone would even stay my friend or if they all would think I was a freak. I thought about telling the doctor I wouldn't even consider it, but my conscience reminded me, *If I don't go I'll be spending the rest of my days, however many more I have left, throwing my life away, literally down the toilet.* I told the doctor I would go.

The first day and night were the hardest. Nurses gave me a study schedule for both educational and counseling activities. I would attend six different classes each day: math, English, science, group counseling, PE and a personal session with my doctor. All the people were complete strangers. Most of the patients my age weren't there for eating disorders but for severe mental illnesses or violent behaviors. In my first class, math, I sat down and said hello to the girl sitting next to me. She turned her head and ignored me. I shifted in my chair and waved to the girl on my left and asked what her problem was. She didn't answer and mumbled something about needing medicine. I quickly learned that the other patients were hard to relate to or on heavy medication. They didn't seem to have any desire to make friends. That night, I cried myself to sleep, feeling more alone than I ever had.

The next morning, I was told that my blood work reported that I was not only dehydrated but also starving. The doctor said he wouldn't release me until I was strong inside and out. Months passed like this and I continued attending classes with screaming, irrational kids. I felt so isolated. The doctors tried several types of medicines; none of them seemed to be working to keep my food down. They started feeding me intravenously. A needle was stuck in the top of my hand and stayed there, taped, twenty-four hours a day. It was so gross, having a big needle sticking out in my hand. Every morning they would attach a liquid-filled bag that dripped nutrients into my bloodstream. Each night they gave me pills that made me nauseous and want to throw up. I was becoming more and more discouraged. *Will I ever be normal again?* I wondered. Still, I wouldn't give up. I knew what I had to do and I tried yet another medication.

When that didn't seem to do anything, a nurse came into my room, took that morning's medication out of my hand and suggested that I stand in front of the mirror one hour after each meal and repeat to myself these words, "Yes, I am perfect because God made me."

I thought she was nuts! If modern medicine couldn't work, how could saying a few words do the trick? Still, I knew I had to try it. It couldn't hurt and if it got me off the feeding tube, it was worth it no matter how crazy it sounded. Beside, if it didn't work, I could tell the nurse that it wasn't the cure and that at least I tried.

The next meal, I said the words for several minutes. Religiously. I said them for an entire week extending the time every day. After a while, I realized I began saying them as if I meant them and I had been keeping my food down. My bulimia was becoming under control because my mind stopped focusing on throwing up, and started focusing on saying those words! Within a week I stopped needing to be fed through tubes, my stomach had stopped rejecting food and my compulsion to vomit ceased. My mind had been tricked into more positive thinking!

With the support of my counselors and nurses, I continued searching for ways to bolster my self-esteem, so that I would never again be so vulnerable to the judgments of others. I began to read self-esteem books and the Bible to further my self-image. By then, my boyfriend had dumped me. Most of my friends had stopped coming to see me. Even on the day I celebrated my newfound ability to keep my food down, I called my brother to tell him the good news and he said, "You're making all this up for attention, aren't you?"

I can't tell you how much that hurt. Still, I wouldn't let the outside world's cruelty diminish my victory or my newly found self-esteem of loving myself no matter what my weight was. Finally, I realized with this new strength, I was well.

I began feeding myself and choosing to be full— literally, spiritually, emotionally and physically. My self-esteem strengthened as I ate, repeated those words, and learned to love myself. By gulping down food, I became the vessel God had created me to be. I was special regardless of what others thought. And, I saw that old boyfriend for what he really was: shallow, close-minded, inconsiderate, and not even worthy of my love in the first place.

It had taken months in the hospital with nurses and counseling to learn a lesson I'll never forget. Being popular is just an illusion. If you love yourself you are in the "in" crowd. You are an individual gift from God to the world. It's comforting to know joy comes from being who I am instead of trying to become somebody else's perfect model.

My first day back to school, my ex-boyfriend actually came up to me and asked me out again. "Wow, you look great. You're so thin! You want to go to the football game on Friday?"

"No," I answered, without regret. "I'd rather date someone who loves my heart."

Me! Accepting me suddenly became a daily celebration of life. I love me! Those three words sound so simple, but living them, believing them makes living so tantalizingly delicious!

~Michelle Wallace Campanelli

Second Lead Syndrome

We find comfort among those who agree with us — growth among those who don't.
~Frank A. Clark

have sold my first young adult novel; it's being published any day now with a major publishing house and with any luck, I'm going to spend the rest of my life writing books for teens. I'm a key player in a really amazing non-profit that I think is going to change the world one day. I've traveled the world. I've earned my undergraduate and master degrees. I got that job, rocked that interview, earned my own money and even, briefly, went to school with the Prince of Wales.

I've achieved personal and professional success, and there is so much more I'm looking forward to.

And I wouldn't have done any of it if someone had actually believed in me.

Maybe that's a little overdramatic to say, but I didn't get it. I never got it. And not in the sense of understanding — it wasn't that I didn't comprehend "it." What I mean is that, in a constellation of gold stars, I was the dying light of a red dwarf planet — dim, flickering, and completely overshadowed by the glowing lovelies around me. Whatever "it" happened to be — success, praise, extra credit — I wasn't going to get it.

That was high school for me. That was life for me. I went to an all-girls Catholic school and, despite having uniforms for equality, I somehow managed to look sloppier and less put-together than other girls. In junior year, when we all applied for the exclusive AP History course that you could take as a junior (as opposed to the more widely offered, less exclusive APs we could all take in senior year) I had the PSAT scores to qualify for the class—but since we had something like eighteen merit scholars in my grade, the class was filled by girls who had higher PSAT scores. Rather than start another class for the "extras" who qualified, we just got bumped.

I was just on the cusp of qualifying for several different honors societies in high school (which looked fabulous on college transcripts) but didn't quite make it.

When I went out for the school play... oh, well, who am I kidding? I was lucky just to be cast in the school play. I can't sing, dance or act. It was a miracle I didn't take the theater down in flames as a dancing, singing, acting turtle that was purposefully cut out of most other versions of *Alice in Wonderland*.

For my senior bioethics project, we had to design a personal manifesto—our own Code of Ethics. I agonized over the thing; I dearly loved it. I wrote these short stories about my friends and about what my ethics really meant to me, about how I saw the world working and what I could do to make it better. I wrote about how being a strong, empowered girl was important to me. I made it beautiful; I was one of those artsy kids so I knew my way around a glue stick and some quotes. And when I handed it in like a prized pony, it was returned to me with a three page note on pink notepaper in red ink (yes, I still have it, and the Code of Ethics) that accused me of demonstrating an utter lack of belief in God, and grading me accordingly.

Never mind that I do have a ludicrously strong faith in God. Never mind, even, that the project assignment hadn't even mentioned that. When it came down to it, I just wasn't the favorite. I wasn't the darling of high school.

For a long time, I had the biggest chip on my shoulder about this. I thought it was the teachers' faults: how could they not see my potential? Then I blamed my fellow students: What does she have that I don't? Can't they see she doesn't deserve any of this?

I was a grumpy teenager. I was always coming up short; I would never be the first in line, I would never be the star, I would never be appreciated. I was smart and I was driven and I wanted for one moment to be the best. I had English teachers who encouraged me and supported me and said my writing was good, and yes, I did have people who believed in me. My mom seems to be a big fan of mine, but I suspect nepotism at work.

I was never the star.

I'll tell you what; being the star is thoroughly overrated. In some of the work I've been doing lately, I've had the honor of getting back together with some of the girls from my high school, and we all sing the same song — we were never the favorites. We were never the stars. One of them is a singer and songwriter. One is a successful business lady. One founded and runs the non-profit I work with. One works for the archdiocese and rocks her Catholic for all it's worth (though we kind of disagree that she wasn't anyone's favorite). In short, they are some of the coolest people I know.

We all came out of high school with righteous anger and resentment because things weren't handed to us. We came out with the "Well I'll show them!" promise tattooed on our foreheads. We all doggedly worked harder and longer than our illustrious high school counterparts because we had something to prove.

For me, every day I was chased by the idea that someone thought I wasn't good enough — because I disagreed. I knew I wanted to be a writer from a really young age, but I kept getting told that it wasn't smart, I wouldn't make it, I couldn't succeed. I wasn't the valedictorian, I wasn't good enough for AP History, and I was a god-awful turtle. But I knew, better than anyone else, what I was capable of.

When someone tells you that you can't, the worst thing you can do is believe them. There will always be people in life and in high school that don't seem to earn the things they receive; there will be people who doubt you and don't see the passion and fire you have within and relegate you to the role of second lead.

But do you know what the most amazing thing about personal success is? Proving every single one of them wrong. Because it just so happens that in the process, when you trust your own heart, you demonstrate to the world the infinite power of believing in yourself.

~AC Gaughen

The Enemy Within

What a man thinks of himself, that it is which determines, or rather indicates, his fate.
~Henry David Thoreau

I suffer from a self-diagnosed disease. It's called self-hatred, and it's a writhing serpent that has infested my brain since my teenage years, continually attacking me, releasing its venom and paralyzing me. I conspired with this entity to create a stream of propaganda against myself in a twisted pattern of reverse psychology. No one could reject me because I had deemed myself unworthy of love.

I must first present some backstory on the origins of my self-hatred. Shortly after entering high school at age fifteen, my family physician referred me to an endocrinologist. I had complained to my parents that the other kids were sprouting while I had remained the same height as the year before.

The endocrinologist ordered a battery of tests, including a skull X-ray to determine my biological age. The scan showed a gray spot that was later diagnosed as a craniopharyngioma, a benign brain tumor near the pituitary gland. This type of tumor can cause headaches, hormonal imbalances and vision problems if left untreated.

Surgeons at Upstate University Hospital in Syracuse, New York removed the tumor in 1984. The surgery was successful, but it left me with panhypopituitarism, a deficiency of all of the hormones the pituitary gland produces. Puberty was delayed. While my friends continued to grow and mature as we headed for college, I remained physically unchanged.

I looked like a fourteen-year-old boy when I began my freshman year at St. John Fisher College in Rochester, New York; some of my classmates mistook me for an academic prodigy. I had to explain to them I was of normal intelligence — only scoring 970 on the SAT — but appeared young for my age due to an illness.

No female at the school took me seriously as a potential boyfriend, as I was considered cute in the way a teddy bear is cute — soft and safe — the antithesis of sexy.

My self-hatred festered during this period.

Without testosterone and growth hormone, my body was a soft shapeless mass and I loathed my round baby face with peach fuzz on the upper lip. My feminine features and a high-pitched voice meant people would sometimes confuse me for a girl.

While waiting to order a drink at a college bar near campus one night, I drew the attention of two mustached men, dressed in jeans and Carhartt jackets, who were sitting at the bar, nursing draft beers. One of the men looked at me and then turned to his friend and asked, "Is this a guy or a chick?" I caught the second man gazing at me, and he whispered to his friend, "I'm not sure." I left the bar right away. I walked back to campus in the cold night air with hot tears stinging my face.

I retreated into a world of shame, unable to control the revulsion I felt when a mirror or photograph reflected my image back at me. And I could do nothing to shed my child-like exterior.

But the endocrinologist prescribed growth hormone and testosterone shots. In time, my body grew and my face matured, if only slightly.

I graduated from college, earned my master's degree and began working in the journalism field. My self-hatred simmered, but I was able to keep it under control.

A series of health crises then altered my perspective. One of the most memorable happened while I was living in Phoenix in 2004. Over the course of a Sunday afternoon I began vomiting and my legs became heavy and weak. I still intended to go to work that night at my job as a copy editor. But as I got ready to take a shower, I fell in the bathtub and struggled to climb back out. I called in sick and my roommate drove me to the hospital.

Blood tests revealed dangerously low sodium levels. Doctors in Scottsdale determined my blood had become diluted because the dosage of desmopressin I had been taking to replace vasopressin, a hormone that controls urine production, was too high while the dosage of cortisone was too low.

I spent a week at the hospital with IV fluids pumping through my veins. My sodium levels rose and I left the hospital on a bright sunny afternoon with clear blue skies overhead. Woody, a volunteer with white hair, a white mustache and muscular forearms, wheeled me outside to the curb; the sun felt warm and the desert smelled clean, with hints of sage and wildflowers wafting in the air.

As I waited for my roommate to bring the car around, I talked with Woody, and his positive attitude and the joy he expressed in helping people made an impression on me. I felt thankful for being restored to full health. I was alive. I could walk and I didn't have a serious disease that required surgery or further treatment.

And I made the decision then to stop hating myself, to turn off the negative thoughts I had allowed to flow into my brain. The futility of my self-defeating philosophy became clear to me. I asked myself, what good had all this self-hatred brought me? How had it served me?

It had controlled my existence but produced nothing of value, while robbing me of energy and time, time I lost and could never recover.

My parents' deaths from lung cancer — my father in 2007 and my mother in 2011 — solidified my thinking. Seeing them wither as the cancer spread made me realize that our bodies are only finite machines. They hold no power besides the functions they are able to carry out.

I have tried to put aside my obsessions with the self. I've come to the conclusion I can't rearrange the molecules of my being and construct a new face, a new body or a new voice. This is who I am, and I need to stop rejecting myself or wishing for a better version.

In 2011 my craniopharyngioma returned, only this time with greater intensity. The tumor pressed against my optic nerve, causing headaches, a drooping right eye and double vision. Surgeons at Upstate performed a transsphenoidal (through the nose) decompression of the tumor and my vision was restored. I could see again and gratitude swelled inside me.

And although I would never claim victory over my self-hatred, gratitude cancels it out; the two cannot share the same space. You can't hate yourself if you feel lucky to be alive, if you celebrate the gift of life, breath, body and mind.

The bad thoughts about myself are still stored inside, archived for future use, and they can be accessed anytime.

In order to dispel negativity I often repeat a silly slogan in my head. It's a variation of Popeye's mantra of "I yam what I yam and that's all what I yam."

An adapted version I started using in 2004 goes, "I am who I am and I can't hate this man." I have since revised it to: "I am who I am and I must love this man."

I don't always succeed at taking this advice, but I also don't condemn myself when I fail.

~Francis DiClemente

Finding a Vision

*People are like stained-glass windows. They sparkle and shine
when the sun is out, but when the darkness sets in, their true
beauty is revealed only if there is a light from within.*
~Elisabeth Kübler-Ross

Six years ago, I went blind. Due to a severe herpes simplex virus in my eyes, I lost one of my most precious possessions: my eyesight. Tiny cold sores covered the surface of my eyes, scarring my cornea. I wasn't allowed to stand in direct sunlight or even in a brightly lit room. The light would penetrate my eyelids and cause too much pain. At the age of seventeen, I was unprepared to find myself in a dark world. Who would I be without my ability to see?

All I wanted throughout the entire summer was to be able to see people. What new cute bathing suit styles was everyone wearing? Who had cut their hair or dyed it purple? I would have a conversation with someone and realize that I had no idea what facial expressions he was making. I no longer had the ability to make eye contact, a privilege I had taken for granted before. I longed to talk with my eyes. I just wasn't whole without my vision.

My parents became my sole support system. Hoping for a miracle, they took me to an eye specialist every day. No one was sure if I would ever completely recover, and if so, how long the healing process would take. Meanwhile, Mom and Dad adjusted their own lives in order to keep my spirits up. They would take me to baseball games and out to dinner — anything to get me out of the house. However, going places was difficult. I had to wear eye patches and dark sunglasses to ease the pain of bright light. As a seventeen-year-old, this wasn't exactly the fashion statement I was trying to make.

My parents had to take care of me everywhere. At restaurants they ordered my food, arranged it on the table, and then explained where everything was on my plate so I could finally eat it. My fifteen-year-old brother took this opportunity to rearrange the food on my plate. My mom was amazing. Each day she would brush my hair and lay out a decent looking outfit so I could walk out of the house with a little bit of pride. She was determined to keep my self-esteem as high as possible. I relied on my mom to make me feel pretty. At an age when I should have been gaining my independence, I found myself becoming increasingly dependent on my parents.

I wasn't able to drive or visit my friends. Movies were completely out of the question. Life seemed to just go on without me, as if I was never there. Fortunately, I had a wonderful friend who knew how to make me feel special. Donny and I had dated a couple of times before I lost my vision, but at that time we were just friends. He would come to my house to sit and talk with me. If the TV were on, he'd watch and I'd listen. One time, Donny took me to a baseball barbecue and introduced me to all of his friends. I had never been so happy in my entire life. He didn't care that I couldn't see his friends. He held my hand proudly and led me around. I may not have been able to see all the people I met that day, but their voices are clear in mind. I can still separate whose laughter belonged to whom. When I close my eyes now and try to remember that day, I mostly see darkness. But I can still smell the sausage and brisket cooking on the grill. I can hear the happiness around me and Donny's voice saying, "This is my girlfriend, Talina."

I slowly began to make progress toward the end of the summer. Little by little, I was able to open my eyes. My vision was still blurred but this achievement called for a celebration. My parents were still concerned and Donny continued to stay by my side. Then I began to worry, *Will I have to start my senior year wearing my thick glasses that everyone still refers to as Coke bottles?* I didn't want to think about it. August crept up on me, though, and I started school with limited vision and thick glasses. As I walked through the halls, I struggled to look confident. I had a harder time cheering at pep rallies and football games. My lack of clear vision and concern with my physical appearance took the fun out of everything that I used to love. My level of self-confidence had diminished to an unrecognizable point.

At a time in my life when I expected my only concern to be to have fun, I was learning a powerful lesson. I could no longer rely on appearance to make me feel better about myself. I had to go deeper. With the support of my family and friends, I realized that feeling good about who I am on the inside is far more important. Believing that I can overcome the obstacles that I face is crucial. My identity wasn't my thick glasses. My identity was my inner strength. This inner strength allowed me to love life even when I was unable to see it. Losing my eyesight could not take away my ability to hear the voices of the people who love me. It could not steal away the fresh smell of morning or the lingering aroma of my mom's cooking. Most important, my loss could never take from me the feel of my boy-friend's hand around my own.

Six years later, I continue to need steroid eye drops to keep the virus from reoccurring. The scar tissue is slowly improving. Recently, I began to wear both contacts, which is a huge accomplishment. A day doesn't go by that I am not thankful for my progress and the lesson I learned. I am incredibly thankful for my special friend who visited me, introduced me as his girlfriend and is now my husband.

I am currently preparing for my first year of teaching. I think about which of my personal qualities I might be able to share with my students. I know how difficult it is to grow up and I want my students to believe that I understand them. If I can't teach them any-thing else, I hope I can get across the lesson that changed my teenage experience: True beauty is not about what you *see* on the outside but what you feel, sense and love from within.

~Talina Sessler-Barker

Defining Myself

Without a struggle, there can be no progress.
~Fredrick Douglass

My dad died when I was four. My brother was two and my sister only one. Soon after, our family grew to five children, as I found myself with a half-sister and then a half-brother. We lived in the poorest part of the city; the projects were only a block away.

My mother, a widow in her twenties with five kids, couldn't handle it. She became an alcoholic and a drug user. Her expensive drug habit caused her to use all the money she could get her hands on for drugs. Although we were on welfare, she didn't use the money for the food we needed. Instead, she used the money to help support her drug habit. Her routine became a normal occurrence: she sent each one of us kids to the store with a food stamp. We'd buy something for a quarter or less, then give the change to her. We soon began to rely on the food given out by homeless shelters in order to eat. We would receive a bag and walk through a line as donated food, such as TV dinners or canned green beans, was dropped in our bags.

Not only were we deprived of a proper diet, but our poverty prevented us from experiencing the normal joys that kids look forward to, such as Christmas. Although we swallowed our pride when we had no choice but to seek food donations, it was hardest during the holidays. Each winter, our thin, hand-me-down clothing and holed shoes forced us to accept free clothes and a voucher for new shoes at the local church, which we then exchanged as Christmas gifts. Knowing that our clothes came from this organization made it impossible to believe in Santa, tainting our holiday spirit.

Soon, my mom began disappearing for days at a time. In a way, it was better when she wasn't around because we didn't have to live in fear of her mental and physical abuse, like the beatings and heartless name-callings. One night, after my mom threw a lamp at me, nailing me on the side of the head, and a plastic vase at my sister, hitting her in the eye, I made the toughest decision that I ever had to make. I called Child Protective Services, while my sisters cried beside me, begging me not to. Although my mom had been reported before for abuse and neglect, we had always been prepared, cleaning the house beforehand and lying about our situation. Since I was a good student and none of us were troublemakers, we were convincing. We made everyone believe that we had a great life. But while we could lie to everyone else, we could no longer lie to ourselves.

We were put into foster care. My sister and I were placed with an elderly couple in the country, my brother stayed in the city with another family, and my half-sister and half-brother went to live with their dads. We were permitted to visit with my mom once a week, that is if she showed up. When she did come to see us, which averaged about once every two months, she promised us that she was getting an apartment so that we could live together once again.

It's been four years now since I made that call. No one has heard from my mom in over two and a half years. We don't even know if she's dead or alive. Although my brother walked down the wrong path for a while having stolen a car, he was released from detention center early for good behavior and vows to turn his life around. My sister has been adopted by a family who lives in a nice neighborhood. She's on a swim team and finally getting good grades. My half-sister still lives with her father. Her dad remarried a wonderful woman who treats her like her own daughter. Unfortunately, we lost contact with our little half-brother, and we haven't had any luck finding him. He'll be turning six soon.

And me? I'd like to say that I'm doing pretty well. I just turned sixteen, and I have finally found stability in my life, which has helped me excel and succeed in many areas. I've been on the honor roll for five years, and I'm involved in way too many school activities. I'm even in a volunteer group that promotes the fight against drugs and alcohol. I'm a good advocate of the anti-drug campaign because I know from firsthand experience what happens when drugs run your life: they ruin not only your own life, but the lives of those around you. I tell my story and amaze people with my positive attitude, despite all that I've been through. My adoptive mom says, "You've definitely made some sweet lemonade out of all the sour lemons you've been handed."

What I went through, all my hardships and pain, they're part of who I am. I'll always feel like I'm different, and I'll always have to fight the feelings that I wasn't good enough, not even for my own mom. But I'm not going to let those feelings define me. I will only let them make me stronger. And I know that I'm going to be somebody. Actually, I already am.

~Morgan Mullens-Landis

Label This!

The best person I will ever be, is myself.
~Torild S. Bruun

You don't have to listen
To the rumors and hype
Or let others brand you
With a stereotype
You don't need the clothes,
Or the shoes, or the car
Just believe in yourself, and be who you are

You can try hard in school
Without being a geek,
'Cause there's way more to life
Than the popular clique
Joining the band doesn't make you uncool
It's those who say otherwise who are the fools
Join a team, or a club, or try out for the play
Don't wait any longer, go for it today

You don't have to be great, just get out there and start
And whatever you do, let it come from the heart
Be it music, or writing, or drama, or sports,
Don't let anyone else make you think you fall short

Oh, the things you can do,
If you be who you are,
Just be true to yourself, and you will go far

Oh, the people you'll meet
Of all different kinds
Just forget about labels
And open your mind
Oh, the things you will learn

And the worlds you will see
If you say to yourself:
"I'm glad to be me!!"

~Emily Adams

She Didn't Give Up on Me

She never once gave up. My mom is my hero.
~Kimberly Anne Brand

lay on the floor, furiously kicking my legs and screaming until my throat felt raw—all because my foster mother had asked me to put my toys away.

"I hate you," I shrieked. I was six years old and didn't understand why I felt so angry all the time.

I'd been living in foster care since I was two. My real mom couldn't give my five sisters and me the care we needed. Since we didn't have a dad or anyone else to care for us, we were put in different foster homes. I felt lonely and confused. I didn't know how to tell people that I hurt inside. Throwing a tantrum was the only way I knew to express my feelings.

Because I acted up, eventually my current foster mom sent me back to the adoption agency, just as the mom before had. I thought I was the most unlovable girl in the world.

Then I met Kate McCann. I was seven by that time and living with my third foster family when she came to visit. When my foster mother told me that Kate was single and wanted to adopt a child, I didn't think she'd choose me. I couldn't imagine anyone would want me to live with them forever.

That day, Kate took me to a pumpkin farm. We had fun, but I didn't think I'd see her again.

A few days later, a social worker came to the house to say that Kate wanted to adopt me. Then she asked me if I'd mind living with one parent instead of two.

"All I want is someone who loves me," I said.

Kate visited the next day. She explained that it would take a year for the adoption to be finalized, but I could move in with her soon. I was excited but afraid, too. Kate and I were total strangers. I wondered if she'd change her mind once she got to know me.

Kate sensed my fear. "I know you've been hurt," she said, hugging me. "I know you're scared. But I promise I'll never send you away. We're a family now."

To my surprise, her eyes were filled with tears.

Suddenly I realized that she was as lonely as I was!

"Okay… Mom," I said.

The following week I met my new grandparents, aunt, uncle and cousins. It felt funny — but good — to be with strangers who hugged me as though they already loved me.

When I moved in with Mom, I had my own room for the first time. It had wallpaper and a matching bedspread, an antique dresser and a big closet. I had only a few clothes I'd brought with me in a brown paper bag. "Don't worry," Mom said. "I'll buy you lots of pretty new things."

I went to sleep that night feeling safe. I prayed I wouldn't have to leave.

Mom did lots of nice things for me. She took me to church. She let me have pets and gave me horseback riding and piano lessons. Every day, she told me she loved me. But love wasn't enough to heal the hurt inside me. I kept waiting for her to change her mind. I thought, "If I act bad enough, she'll leave me like the others."

So I tried to hurt her before she could hurt me. I picked fights over little things and threw tantrums when I didn't get my way. I slammed doors. If Mom tried to stop me, I'd hit her. But she never lost patience. She'd hug me and say she loved me anyway. When I got mad, she made me jump on a trampoline.

Because I was failing in school when I came to live with her, Mom was very strict about my homework. One day when I was watching TV, she came in and turned it off. "You can watch it after you finish your homework," she said. I blew up. I picked up my books and threw them across the room. "I hate you and I don't want to live here anymore!" I screamed.

I waited for her to tell me to start packing. When she didn't, I asked, "Aren't you going to send me back?"

"I don't like the way you're behaving," she said, "but I'll never send you back. We're a family, and families don't give up on each other."

Then it hit me. This mom was different; she wasn't going to get rid of me. She really did love me. And I realized I loved her, too. I cried and hugged her.

In 1985, when Mom formally adopted me, our whole family celebrated at a restaurant. It felt good belonging to someone. But I was still scared. Could a mom really love me forever? My tantrums didn't disappear immediately, but as months passed, they happened less often.

Today I'm 16. I have a 3.4 grade point average, a horse named Dagger's Point, four cats, a dog, six doves and a bullfrog that lives in our backyard pond. And I have a dream: I want to be a veterinarian.

Mom and I like to do things together, like shopping and horseback riding. We smile when people say how much we look alike. They don't believe she's not my real mom.

I'm happier now than I ever imagined I could be. When I'm older, I'd like to get married and have kids, but if that doesn't work out, I'll adopt like Mom did. I'll pick a scared and lonely kid and then never, ever give up on her. I'm so glad Mom didn't give up on me.

~Sharon Whitley

Editor's note: A version of this originally appeared in *Woman's World*.

Rediscovery

Believing in our hearts that who we are is enough is the key to a
more satisfying and balanced life.
~Ellen Sue Stern

S
even. The age of ballet lessons and Barbie dolls, of learning to add and subtract simple numbers; the time when the family dog is your closest companion. Seven. The age of innocence.

I was a typical-looking child. I had long, straight brown hair that fell past my shoulders. My almond-shaped hazel eyes were always full of adventure and curiosity. And I had a smile that could brighten a bleak winter day.

I was a happy child with a loving family, and many friends, who loved to perform skits on home videos. I was a leader in school, not a follower. My best trait was my personality. I had imagination. But what made me special was not seen from the outside: I had a special love for life.

At age twelve, my life had a huge breakdown. It was then that I developed obsessive compulsive disorder (OCD). OCD is a disorder that is the result of a chemical imbalance in the brain. People with OCD don't think the same way as people with chemically balanced brains. People with OCD do rituals. I started to wash my hands ten times an hour to avoid germs, and I constantly checked my kitchen oven to make sure that it was off. This way of life for me continued for four agonizing years, and by then, my OCD had led to depression. I was no longer the happy little girl I had been.

In the tenth grade I finally confessed to my mother that I was suffering from depression along with my OCD. I couldn't take the emotional pain anymore. I needed help if I wanted to continue living.

My mom took me to a doctor the same week. I started taking medicine that would hopefully cure my OCD and depression. Over the course of a few months, the medicine did help the OCD. I stopped doing rituals. I no longer took four showers a day to avoid germs. But one thing didn't change; I still was overwhelmed with depression. I still was constantly sad and I started to believe that my life no longer mattered.

One autumn evening two years ago, I hit rock bottom. I thought that my life no longer had meaning, because I no longer brought joy to other people like I did when I was little. I decided suicide was the only solution to my depression problem, so I wrote a suicide note to all my friends and family. In the note I expressed that I was sorry for deciding to leave them, but that I thought it was for the best. As I was folding the note, my eyes fell on a photograph. It was a picture of an adorable little girl with natural blond highlights in her brown hair from spending so much time in the sun. She was wearing her red soccer uniform and held a biking helmet in her small hands. She had a carefree smile on her face that showed she was full of life.

It took me a few minutes to realize who the girl in the photo was. The photo had been taken one weekend at my uncle's house when I was seven years old. I almost couldn't believe that smiling child was me! I felt a chill go down my spine. It was like my younger self had sent me a message. Right then and there I knew I couldn't kill myself. Once I had been a strong little girl, and I had to become strong like that again.

I tore up my suicide note and vowed that I would not rely only on my medicine to help my depression. I would have to fight the depression with my mind, too. I could make myself happy again.

It has been two years since I "rediscovered" myself. I am OCD- and depression-free. I still take medicine to keep my disorder at bay, but the real reason I am healed is because I took action and refused to let depression ruin my life. I learned a lifelong lesson: Never give up. Life is good. Everyone has challenges in life, but everyone can survive. I am living proof of that. Also, it is important to keep smiling, because in the end, everything will work out.

Of course my life can still be a struggle, but I pull through with a smile on my face. I know I can't give up on life. I am here for a reason. Sometimes, I think it was strange that I had to look to who I was as a little girl in order to regain faith in myself at age eighteen. But I think everyone can look back on their early years and see that it was then that they knew how to live in peace and happiness.

I have plans for myself now. Once I graduate from high school this spring, I plan on going to college to major in journalism. I want to be a writer someday. And I am prepared for whatever challenges life may bring. I have a role model to look up to for strength, and who is guiding me through life. My hero is a seven-year-old girl, smiling back at me from a photo on my desk.

~Raegan Bake

Editor's note: For more information regarding obsessive-compulsive disorder, log on to www.ocdresource.com.

Chapter 5

Create Your Best Future

Volunteering and Giving

One at a Time

*We ourselves feel that what we are doing is just a drop in the
ocean. But the ocean would be less because of that missing drop.*
~Mother Teresa

A friend of ours was walking down a deserted Mexican beach at sunset. As he walked along, he began to see another man in the distance. As he grew nearer, he noticed that the man kept leaning down, picking something up and throwing it out into the water. Time and again he kept hurling things out into the ocean.

As our friend approached even closer, he noticed that the man was picking up starfish that had been washed up on the beach and, one at a time, he was throwing them back into the water.

Our friend was puzzled. He approached the man and said, "Good evening, friend. I was wondering what you are doing."

"I'm throwing these starfish back into the ocean. You see, it's low tide right now and all of these starfish have been washed up onto the shore. If I don't throw them back into the sea, they'll die up here from lack of oxygen."

"I understand," my friend replied, "but there must be thousands of starfish on this beach. You can't possibly get to all of them. There are simply too many. And don't you realize this is probably happening on hundreds of beaches all up and down this coast? Can't you see that you can't possibly make a difference?"

The man smiled, bent down, and picked up yet another starfish, and as he threw it back into the sea, he replied, "Made a difference to that one!"

~Jack Canfield and Mark Victor Hansen

The Shopping Trip

Every action in our lives touches on some chord that will vibrate
in eternity.
~Edwin Hubbell Chapin

ane, hurry and get your coat. We're going to the store." I ran to do as my father instructed. A shopping trip with Dad was a rare treat. He traveled a great deal of the time, and I cherished the unexpected opportunity to be alone with him.

Once in the car, I asked, "Where are we going?"

Dad only smiled. "You'll see."

To my surprise, we didn't take the usual turn to the area's one department store. (This was in the pre-mall era.) Instead, we turned down an alley where small row houses lined the road. Dad parked the car, got out, and walked to the front door of the first house on the street. Within a few minutes, he returned with Connor, a boy from our church.

I tried to hide my disappointment. I had wanted my father to myself. Now it looked as though I would have to share him with someone else.

"Hi, Connor," I mumbled, barely able to keep the resentment from my voice.

"Hi," he mumbled back. He looked as uncomfortable as I felt.

Dad drove to the store. Once inside, he steered us to the boys' clothing section. My indignation bubbled over. Not only did I have to share my dad, I had to endure looking at boring clothes for boys.

"Connor is going to receive his confirmation tomorrow," Dad said. "He'll need a suit to wear for the occasion."

Connor looked with wonder at the row of clothes.

Dad must have noticed my stiff posture for he drew me aside.

"We have an opportunity to help someone in need," he said in a quiet voice.

Finally, I understood and was ashamed at my lack of compassion. Connor came from a family of modest means where his single mother worked to provide for her four children. I guessed that Sunday clothes had no place in the budget.

With Dad's help, Connor chose a dark suit. I watched as Dad gently encouraged Connor to add a white shirt, tie, dress shoes, and socks. Connor's eyes grew wide as the purchases mounted.

"Th... thank you," he stuttered when we returned him home.

Dad smiled broadly. "You're welcome. And remember, this is our secret. Only your mother knows."

"Yes, sir."

"Thanks for coming with me," Dad said once Connor had gathered up his bags and run to the front door. "What if we stop and get a chocolate milkshake?"

I nodded, but without my customary eagerness for my favorite treat. I had a lot to think about. Other things began to make sense. I recalled holiday dinners where the table was filled with widows and others who were likely to be alone.

"Why," I had asked Dad at one time, "do we always have to invite those ladies to dinner? They never invite us to their houses."

Dad's answer has remained with me. "It's easy to invite those who can return the favor. Taking care of those who can't do something for us in return is the hallmark of love."

I didn't realize it at the time, but in those few words my father had given me the greatest definition of charity I would ever hear.

~Jane Choate

A Mom's Blessing

One must be poor to know the luxury of giving!
~George Eliot

n the late 1960s, I was a single mom of four children five years apart in age. My husband was an alcoholic and upon leaving home, told me "I'll see you living in a slum. The kids won't know the difference, but I know it will bother you." I understand he wasn't in his right mind at the time, but I never forgot those words. Determined never to fulfill his parting wish, I was lucky enough to find a part-time job in a law firm that allowed me to work until the kids came home from school. Needless to say, I lived paycheck to paycheck, struggling to raise the kids in a nice neighborhood. They wore hand-me-downs, but always had a roof over their heads and nourishing food to eat. I could only afford the basics, so I made it a point to be sure that they always had fruit, ice cream and home-baked cakes — there was no money for potato chips, soda or fast food (lucky us!).

I always taught them to respect each other's personal things. That meant they didn't take each other's things, and my pocketbook was also one of my "things" that was off-limits.

Bill was able to have a paper route when he was twelve years old, which he and his eleven-year-old brother Michael shared. They delivered papers seven days a week, worked out the responsibilities and finances (learning to record collections and share profits) together. It was their only way of getting "spending money." Often when there was a snowstorm, the neighbors would call to see if one of the "boys" could shovel their walk. If, for some reason, the boys were not available, my daughter Debbie would beg me to send her in their place. The first time, our neighbor was so excited, I heard her say with glee, "Honey, this time we're getting a girl!" Stephen, the youngest, was responsible for taking his grandfather for a walk around the block each day after school. Pop had a stroke and the doctor wanted him to get up and out. Stephen took this responsibility very seriously and would always give Pop whatever he made in kindergarten that day, and then insist they go for their walk.

I could not afford to give them an allowance or even buy school lunches. I packed lunch for the four of them every day — snacks from the outlet store usually came in packages of twelve, which meant divided by four, those snacks were good for three days of packed lunches. I often went to work with just a dime for a phone call, should it become necessary. I really didn't care — we were in a good school district, unusually healthy and happy.

I thought I was successful in not worrying the kids about money, although apparently they knew it was an issue. Due to the circumstances, I always knew exactly what I had in my purse — to the penny. I had to be careful not to overspend at the grocery store because in those days, cash was the only method of payment — there was no credit card or overdraft protection.

Then came a day when I looked into my purse, knowing I was broke but hoping for a miracle, and finding one. I went from penniless to having four dollars. I couldn't imagine how I could have forgotten those four dollars. When it happened a second time, I was truly at a loss, until the day I came upon the kids whispering around my pocketbook (where they were not supposed to go). I surreptitiously watched and discovered four sneaky little angels putting their hard-earned money into my wallet. The next day when I made a point of exclaiming about the money, no one said a word. I almost admired their ability to keep the secret as I much as I did their unselfish love.

I often regret not being able to give them more, but it was a blessing in disguise — it somehow made them into confident, responsible and caring adults. I am grateful for the lesson to us all. God balances hardship with blessings. We need only the capacity to recognize them when they arrive.

~Maureen T. Cotter

Lost and Lonely

I wondered why somebody didn't do something. Then I realized,
I am somebody.
~Lily Tomlin

The first day I transferred to a new college was heartbreaking. Why did I leave my friends? Why did I choose a school that was farther from my family? I didn't know anyone on campus and I didn't know how to find the buildings for my classes. The world had just celebrated another New Year's holiday and I was sitting alone in a dorm room, surrounded by painted white brick walls and with an unknown roommate. What had I done?

I wandered around campus, consulting my flimsy paper class schedule and the buildings that I passed. I bumped into shoulders and backpacks. Bikes whizzed by me, clipping my heels as my eyes welled up with tears. I was late to chemistry class twice. I felt very lost and alone.

As a runner on the school's cross country and track teams, I looked forward to practice each afternoon. It was a chance to be part of a group, to escape the loneliness. It was a chance to be me. The pounding of my footsteps on the city sidewalks gave me a chance to discover myself. I began to think that feeling lost and alone might sometimes be a good thing. If we never felt lost then why would we search for the deeper meaning of life?

When an injury kept me from practice, I found myself with

numbing amounts of free time. I had nothing to do but sit in my small dorm room. I began to swim laps in the campus pool, but I still felt trapped. I needed something more.

Having grown up with pets in our family home that I had rescued, I missed having a pet around. When I found the address for the local animal shelter in the phone book, I invited a running teammate to visit the shelter with me.

"Can you believe this place?" Amy asked in awe on our first day. The dark building looked like something from a horror movie, surrounded by a barbed wire fence. A small sign covered in dust hung sideways on the latch of the tall gate.

"It says they're open right now." I shrugged, thinking we must have the wrong place. The building had only one small window and not a shred of green grass.

A few minutes later a man emerged from the dark building wearing a red flannel shirt and blue jean overalls. "What do ya need?"

"We were hoping to volunteer, to spend time with the animals... ." I stuttered, wanting to run back to the car and drive away quickly.

"Come on in," he muttered as he shuffled towards the door, cigarette pressed tightly between his lips.

Our first day of volunteering led us to the cat room. The cat room was a small 4x10 area with wire crates stacked one on top of the other, filling the entire room from floor to ceiling. Most of the food and water bowls were empty, some filled with dust, which told me the cats must have been hungry. Many of the cats were ill, and all were starved for attention. They were clearly lonely and they were scared. I could relate and they instantly won my heart. Cats of every age, size and color lined the walls. Their paws reached forward through the rusty steel bars of the cages, begging for help, pleading for attention. They meowed with force, letting us know that they needed help. Amy and I stayed at the shelter until they closed that day.

We went back to the animal shelter every Sunday. We walked the dogs, we provided food and water to every cage, we let cats out of their cages one by one to stretch their legs and feel the sunshine that poured through the tiny window in the next room. We brought pet treats and we made toys. The following year we organized a volunteer day where more than fifty track team members came to walk the dogs and spend time with the lonely pets. Before I knew it, I wasn't lonely anymore; I wasn't sitting quietly in a silent dorm room. I was in the city, I was giving back to lives that were in need and I was living life. I was learning not only about a great need of our society, but a great need in myself — the need to give back to those who can use a helping hand.

The animal shelter was changing my life as much as we were changing the lives we intended to help. Adoptions were increasing, the quality of care had risen by leaps and bounds, the shelter euthanasia rate was dropping and more people were signing up to volunteer. I was ecstatic! I was in awe that one person could really make a difference. I began to learn that we each have the power within us to make miracles happen. It takes three elements: effort, persistence and a positive attitude. With those three qualities, I learned that anyone could make a difference.

A few short years later, Amy Beatty and I co-founded Advocates 4 Animals, Inc., a non-profit animal welfare organization helping to save the lives of death row shelter pets in need. I had turned my loneliness and fear into positive action and change. I had learned to live outside the confines of the comfortable walls that I once called home. And most of all, I had learned to use what I had already possessed to create something that so desperately needed to exist. Through my desire to discover the world, I created a no-kill animal rescue, rehabilitation and adoption group that continues to help thousands of homeless animals annually. Feeling lost and lonely sure led to some amazing miracles for thousands of lost and lonely pets.

~Stacey Ritz

Listening to My Heart

Wherever you go, go with all your heart.
~Confucius

The fall of my senior year of college I was an emotional wreck. When I looked ahead to my bright, shining future all I saw was a cubicle with my name on it. This was not the future I wanted, but to me it seemed as though the major forces in my life (mostly my family, friends and the college career center) were forcing me in that direction. Without ever stopping to ponder what I actually wanted to do with my life after graduation, I had begun applying for positions at Fortune 500 companies because that's what I "should be" doing. In the busy hustle of college life I had forgotten that I had a choice, and the inner turmoil that resulted was crushing me.

Luckily, I was given the opportunity to travel to a conference focused on finding "the life worth living." The conference centered on living with purpose and spiritual direction. I was placed in a group of fifteen total strangers, but that was where I found my direction.

During one session we were asked to read an article called the *"Cup of Trembling,"* and then to individually reflect on what fears were holding us back from following our dreams. When it was my turn to share I heard things coming out of my mouth that I didn't even know I had been thinking. I shared my fear of the nine-to-five desk job and the lack of direction that I felt looking past graduation. I shared my fear of living in poverty, and the fear of leaving the nest and beginning my own life.

This group of random people listened to me pour out the contents of my soul and then they probed me for more information. They genuinely wanted to help me straighten myself out so that my future matched what my heart was saying. They asked me to put aside all of the barriers and excuses I made for myself, and to reflect on what I would most like to do.

I explained that I wanted to serve others, to go somewhere and be in a program like the Peace Corps, where I could dedicate my life to something that would make a difference in other people's lives. Speaking the words out loud made me realize that if this was my goal I had the power to make it my reality.

I felt renewed and ambitious. I returned home with a new perspective and a fresh energy. The sadness and anxiety was replaced with a sense of purpose. I researched the Peace Corps, and started discussing my decision, but I didn't tell my parents until I was reasonably sure that it was the direction I wanted to take. I was a little apprehensive about their reactions. I envisioned the conversation taking a variety of directions. I felt they would see my decision as irresponsible. I feared they would think that now was the time in my life to grow up and to start earning money to pay back my student loans or that I was somehow trying to back away from my responsibilities as a young adult. How on earth could I go so far away and expect that they would take care of things for me while I was gone? I was worried they would take my decision personally. I remembered back to high school when it was time to choose a college. My mother felt that four hours was too far away. How would she feel about her only child moving across the world?

I told my father first. I was nervous and afraid, but I knew that my father would embrace my ambitions more easily than my mother. After I told him, I felt the immediate flood of release: it was as though telling him made it real and now it had been decided that this is what would happen just by speaking the words. He responded by helping me find out more and explore my options. Overall, he seemed supportive and a little excited.

My mom was less enthused by my new ambition. She made it clear that although this wasn't the direction she had hoped I would take, she didn't think it was a bad decision and she still loves me. That was enough for me, so I endured the lengthy application process. I wasn't sure how it would all turn out; I prayed about it and asked God to place me where I would be most useful. During my interview I didn't express any preferences for location, but I did mention that I would like to learn French or Spanish. My recruiter's eyes lit up as she explained that she would like to find me a business assignment in French-speaking West Africa.

And here I am one week away from leaving the familiar comfort of everything I have known for the past twenty-one years. One week away from turning my life upside down. One week away from moving to Africa to serve as a Peace Corps volunteer for two years in Mali, a country I had previously never even heard of.

Sometimes life takes you places you never expected to go. The call to follow one's own heart is not always a voice of reason. This is what I must remind myself every time I ask the real questions weighing on my mind: What on earth am I thinking? How am I ever going to survive? Am I tough enough to face the challenges ahead? Will I actually do any good? Wow, am I prepared for this?

As my parents will surely attest, no, I am not prepared for this. I have lived a pampered life so far, and this will most certainly be one of the hardest times of my life. However, I feel deep in my soul that God would not call me to service if it weren't something we could get through together.

~Danielle M. Dryke

A Place to Call Home

*Unselfish and noble actions are the most radiant pages in the
biography of souls.*
~David Thomas

didn't quite know what to expect the first time I drove down to
St. Vincent's. I had volunteered on a whim when I decided to stay
behind in Baltimore for the summer following my freshman year
of college. Right before freshman year, my family moved from
Pennsylvania to Maryland. Going "home" over the summer wasn't
exactly an option for me — staying at school to work made more sense.
When Marya, my boss at the campus community service center, asked
me if I'd be interested in driving a van of students bringing sandwiches
and drinks into downtown Baltimore every Tuesday evening, I thought,
"Why not?" I figured it'd be a good way to help pass the time until
school started up again.

Loyola College's Care-A-Van program normally runs from
September to May, when the regular academic year is in session.
Student and adult volunteers travel down Baltimore's winding
Interstate 83 until they reach this open lot situated right next to St.
Vincent's Church. Some people call the place Tent City on account of
the makeshift houses erected using some rope, tarp, and two trees.
Father Jack calls it People Park. Regardless, if you've never had an
encounter with a homeless person before, the lot next to St. Vincent's
would be the place to start.

Traditionally, volunteers arrive bearing ham and cheese sandwiches and containers filled to the brim with iced tea and water. In the winter they bring hot chocolate. During the summer, we brought lemonade — lemonade, sandwiches, as well as some good company and conversation.

It was desolate. The grass that once blanketed the lot had died off, replaced by a morbid, dusty brownness. Cars zoomed by the place, kicking up dust in their panic to get to the safety of the highway. Sometimes people stopped at the red light glanced out their windows at the people there; staring emptily, apathetically, they often returned immediately to the comfort of their cars' front windowpanes. "This is it," I thought. This was pathetic, sad: an empty, ominous, dirt lot, decorated with a few dying trees here and there and boxed in on three sides by asphalt. St. Vincent's stood on the fourth side, mocking the conditions there. For any religious homeless folk, the irony of having God so near and yet so far must have been unbearable.

And then there were the people. They lived in blue-tarp tents held up by some sticks and white rope; the Boy Scouts would've been proud. Others slept on benches, their clothes folded up in piles underneath, covered by today's newspaper, which doubled as a blanket in the night. One man rested on an old, musty mattress, dressed only in boxers and an undershirt. No pants; no socks; no shoes. Father Jack would later tell me that the guy had AIDS, as well as a drug problem. No dignity either, I suppose. I was numb.

"Would you like water, iced tea, or lemonade, sir?" What the hell was I doing here? Me, a nineteen-year-old preparatory school graduate. I had both my parents, a car, a nice life; I was the quintessential Prince of Suburbia, and now I was hanging in downtown Baltimore.

I tried starting conversations with some people. How do you talk to a person who's homeless? I was nervous — I thought they all resented me. I hated being "well off." I shouldn't have, but I couldn't help it. What could I possibly do for anyone here?

This one guy — his name was Eartle, which was easy enough to remember, since it sounded like "Myrtle Beach" — was lounging against a tree that still had some life in it, using its leaves to provide shelter from a sweltering June sun. Summers in Baltimore are hot, even at 6:30 at night. I went over and introduced myself, feeling guilty because I couldn't stop my darting eyes from absorbing the scene around me: Eartle on a makeshift cot, surrounded by a couple of trash bags holding his personal belongings and an overturned cardboard box he was using as a table.

We talked; he called me Prince Andrew to remind him of what my name was. "Yep, that's me," I thought. "Prince Andrew of Suburbia." I told him I used to live near Philadelphia. He had some friends up that way. He asked what I did at school.

"I'm an editor of *The Greyhound.*"

"Yeah? They came down here and interviewed me once."

Next Tuesday night I was back. Eartle was still there, under that same tree. I brought him a couple of sandwiches and hunched down next to him. He invited me to have a seat on his cot. He asked me how my week had been. "Rough," I replied. "Busy at work, and I'm taking a summer class."

"Just keep pluggin' away," he said. We sat in silence for a couple seconds. Then it happened.

"How'd you end up here?"

I shouldn't have done it. It was rude and misguided; this guy sleeps on a cot at night, and I had the audacity to ask him how it happened.

Eartle laughed. "Choices, Andrew — it's all about choices."

And then he went on and on about his life. He had served during the Vietnam War. According to him, a bullet had been lodged in his brain for some time; it was out now. He played baseball during the war on a traveling team. They went around the States recruiting soldiers. I just sat and listened.

He had been to a lot of hospitals. A lot. They all had cute nurses, though. Eartle was an expert in cute nurses. He had a million different jokes, and they were all funny. We laughed it up, Eartle and I. I learned he was Native American, and he told me stories about festivals he'd been to in Baltimore's Patterson Park. Eartle was starting to feel like a second uncle to me. Oftentimes I'd forget that I had to get up and leave at 7.

Tuesday night became the best night of the week. When work ended at 5, I was busy helping to get stuff ready for my weekly trip to People Park. I raced down I-83. After my job for the night was finished, I sauntered over to my seat on Eartle's cot. We talked baseball. We talked about journalism and newspapers. Actually, Eartle did most of the talking, always pausing every ten minutes or so to see if I minded. I never did. I just sat there and listened, and baked in Baltimore's summer sun.

I laughed to myself later on. In Baltimore, I was about two hours from my life in Pennsylvania. In a way, then, I too was homeless. But Tuesday nights were different. With Eartle, I had one good hour every week where I could just forget the world and get wrapped up in conversation about anything. I forgot that Eartle was homeless. Instead, I remembered that I had a buddy, a friend — a semblance of home.

~Andrew Zaleski

Emily, the Soccer Star

The love we give away is the only love we keep.
~Elbert G. Hubbard

"BZZZZZZZZZ." The sound of my alarm clock was enough to make me jump. I turned over with a groan and stumbled out of bed. From the second my feet touched the carpet, I could tell today was going to be another scorcher. I pulled on my hospital pants and white T-shirt. Although I tried to eat, the butterflies in my stomach won the battle, and I settled for apple juice. Today, I would begin my summer job. I was volunteering at the hospital. When I had decided to work there I had been excited, but now I was very anxious about what I would be doing.

At the hospital I learned that most of my job would be to take patients to their rooms and to do other odd jobs. On Fridays, however, I would spend time in Pediatrics, visiting with a child. The first few days passed quickly. By Friday, I had forgotten about my date on the Pediatrics floor. So when I was instructed to go meet Emily, a leukemia patient, I tried to plaster a calm smile across my face, but inside I wanted to cry. Even with her lack of hair and an IV in her arm, she mustered the strength to smile and speak with me.

I soon learned that Emily was eight. She loved going to the beach and playing with dolls, and she had an older brother named Ryan. She was on the town soccer team and proudly informed me that she had scored more goals than anyone else on her team. With our incessant chatting, that first Friday very quickly came to an end.

When I told her I would be back in a week, she begged and pleaded for me to visit on Monday. I couldn't resist her toothless grin, and so I "pinkie-swore" to be back after the weekend. It wasn't long before I was spending lunch breaks with Emily and leaving the hospital long after my shift had ended to spend time with her in the game room.

On days she felt strong enough, we played soccer, even though it was not allowed. It was hilarious to see the nurses turning their heads away, pretending not to notice when Emily's infamous and most prized possession — her black and white soccer ball — would fly through the air. On rare occasions, her illness would get the best of her, and we couldn't play. On those days, I would read her favorite children's books to her or we would play Barbies on her hospital bed. On one occasion, we even cut off Barbie's hair so she could be Emily's twin.

I discovered many things that I admired about Emily. I was most impressed with her will to live. Not once did I see her shed a tear over the pain she must have been hiding behind those clear blue eyes. In addition, her constant optimism, along with her contagious laughter, made her unlike any eight-year-old I had ever met. She was wise beyond her years, and her incredible physical and emotional strength made her an inspiration.

Toward the middle of the summer, her "yuck days" (as she called them) began to outnumber her good ones. I can remember one particular day when I arrived at Emily's room to find her in an unusual state: she was quiet and in a deep sleep. After talking to her mother, I learned that Emily had been given her life "sentence" — she only had a couple of weeks left.

I went home that night with a pit in my stomach and a lump in my throat. I retreated to my room without dinner and cried for hours. I felt so helpless and would have given anything to take her pain away, but all I could do was hold her hand as she vomited from the medication being forced into her tiny body. Even more, I hated this disease that had wreaked havoc inside her and cut her life far too short. It was then that I decided to make the best of these weeks with Emily.

Even during her last few days, Emily brought joy into the lives of those around her. She laughed and giggled with everyone who visited, and she marveled at all the cards and stuffed animals she received.

One evening after dinner, we played soccer — a special occasion because it was something she hadn't had the strength to do in quite a while. Ending the night with her favorite book, *Cinderella*, I once again "pinkie-swore" I would be back the next day for another round of soccer. She gave me the biggest hug that her frail body could muster.

The next day, I sprinted down the corridor to see my favorite patient but instead was greeted by her mother. Through her tears she told me that Emily had passed away earlier in the morning. Her mother told me how wonderful I had made Emily's last few months, but that didn't help ease my aching heart. Just as I was about to leave, her mother handed me an envelope with my name written in red crayon. I knew immediately it was Emily's handwriting because of the backward S scribbled across the front. Opening the envelope in the car, I found a drawing of us playing soccer. On the top was written "To my favorite soccer player." The tears that I so desperately tried to keep inside sprang from my eyes. At that moment, I realized I had been truly blessed by the presence of this amazing eight-year-old.

Even today when I start to forget, I take that folded drawing from my wallet, look at her tiny body, clad in that teddy-bear hospital gown, and smile back at that toothless grin that taught me about life, love, and friendship.

~Suzanne Timmons

The Dress

The test of our progress is not whether we add more to the abundance of those who have much; it is whether we provide enough for those who have too little.
~Franklin D. Roosevelt

The security clerk pretended to check tickets on the dress rack nearest the door. Her eyes carefully scanned a woman who stood hesitatingly just inside the boutique door. The clerk took a quick mental snapshot — old shoes with run-over heels, a small run in her right stocking, out-of-style leather handbag, crinkly black nylon dress at least fifteen years old and straggly hair. Not the image of this store's usual clientele. She approached the woman, asking the mundane, "May I help you?"

The elderly woman smiled and whispered, "Yes, I need a dress." The surprised security clerk quickly signaled a nearby salesperson who hurried over to the waiting customer. Store policy toward the less desirable was, "Wait on them quickly; get them out of sight."

"How may I help you?" the salesclerk asked. This would only take a moment, and then she could go on her morning break.

"My only granddaughter is getting married. I need a complete outfit for the wedding. I want her to be proud of me. Just tell me what I should wear."

"You mean you want to see a bridal consultant?" the clerk asked incredulously. The woman nodded her head and followed the clerk to a small oval room filled with fancy clothes.

"Why did you bring her in here?" the consultant whispered angrily.

"She wants to be outfitted for a wedding," the clerk said as she laughed and walked away.

The bridal consultant had been a model in her younger years and still affected the haughty look she believed implied sophistication. She asked the woman to sit down at the small desk opposite her and took out a pad and pen.

"First, I must know how much you are prepared to spend," she asked. She was eager to get this over with and might as well cut to the chase.

"I have been saving my money for this outfit ever since their engagement was announced last spring. Annie sent me an airplane ticket so I can spend it all on something nice to wear." Her slightly palsied hand pulled the envelope from her handbag. "I think there is seventy dollars here. You may count it if you like. I can spend it all if need be."

The consultant quickly counted the money. "Actually, there are seventy-two dollars. Perhaps you should visit our basement thrift shop. They have a few dresses for around fifty dollars."

"I went there first. They suggested I come to see you," she said smiling. "They said you would be glad to help me."

(*Oh, that Miriam. She loves a good joke. Wait until I get the chance. I will pay her back for this,* the haughty one thought to herself.)

Just then the elderly woman spotted a powder blue dress on a nearby rack. She stood and walked quickly toward it. Before the consultant could stop her, she held the dress before her in a mirror. "Now, this one I like. It is beautiful, but not too showy." It was a plain dress with a long-sleeved jacket edged with just a touch of matching lace. "I should have matching shoes, of course. I will wear my strand of pearls. Afterward, I will give them to the bride as a wedding present. They belonged to my grandmother. Look, the dress is just my size."

The consultant gulped. She was suddenly feeling a mix of frustration, sympathy and anger. How could she tell this sweet old lady that the price of the dress she wanted was three hundred dollars? Matching shoes would be another seventy-five dollars. Sometimes life just wasn't fair.

A young, beautifully dressed bride-to-be stood nearby watching the scene. She had just picked up the custom veil she had ordered for her own wedding next week. Her family was well-off and had told her to spend whatever she wished on her wedding. She interrupted the consultant before she could speak to the grandmother about the dress.

"Excuse me a moment," she said as she led the consultant aside and whispered. "Let her have the dress, shoes, whatever else she needs. Just add it to my bill. Tell her they are on sale. Just take fifty dollars of her money. That will leave her with a little spending money — and her pride."

"But why?" the consultant asked. "You don't even know her."

"Just call it a wedding present to myself. I never knew either of my grandmothers. As I walk down the aisle, I will think of her and pretend she is my grandmother, too."

~Lee Hargus Hunter

McDonald's

Remember that the happiest people are not those getting more,
but those giving more.
~H. Jackson Brown, Jr.

Most of my friends are what society would call "punks." We are the teenagers who hang out at the coffee shops or the movies for lack of anything better to do. But being punks doesn't mean much.

One evening, after a day of not doing much, we were sitting in McDonald's when a guy in our group whom I had just met that day walked in. Brian was the typical punk teenager, dressed in black with the dyed hair. Right before he stepped inside, he yelled something outside to a man walking down the street. I just hoped he wasn't trying to start trouble. He sat down and a minute later, a burly homeless man stuck his head in and looked at Brian.

"Did you say something to me?" the man demanded, and I thought I saw a mean glint in his eyes. I shrank back, thinking that if Brian had tried to pick a fight, this was the wrong guy to do it with. I had seen too many people and places kick teenagers like us out for pulling stuff.

While the rest of us were looking for a place to back into, Brian got up and walked up to him. "Yeah... would you like something to eat?"

The relief was almost audible, and the man smiled and walked in.

After a large meal of hamburgers, fries and dessert, the man left, and even the staff waved good-bye to him. When we asked Brian about it, he explained how he had money that he didn't need and the man had none, so it was only right.

~Shelly Miller

Measuring Miracles by Leaps and Bounds

It's the constant and determined effort that breaks down all resistance and sweeps away all obstacles.
~Claude M. Bristol

am no stranger to being different and challenged. It took a while, but I finally got used to people asking, "So, how did you lose your arm?"

Losing my arm to cancer when I was only eleven was a hard way to learn what it means to be handicapped. Doctors discovered a tumor the size of an apple when I broke my left arm in three places. It cost me my arm and shoulder, and because I lost my shoulder, I can't wear a prosthesis. Trying to join in sports was an exercise in frustration for me: I was always picked last, or not at all. So my first challenge was adjusting to life as the "one-armed" kid. When I got over the shock, I determined to be the best I could be at everything I tried. This cancer wouldn't stop me!

I discovered vaulting at Cal-Poly when I was working on a degree in animal science. Vaulting is gymnastics on a moving horse, sort of like Cossack horsemen or circus performers. It is definitely a two-armed sport. The more I watched the Cal-Poly team, the more I knew I wanted to vault. Quite an ambition for a young man with one arm. The school said, "You can't vault… you only have one arm." Well, telling me "can't" is like guaranteeing my success. As the first disabled competitive vaulter, I became a bronze medalist. I was even part of a special demonstration at the 1984 Olympics.

After college I got a job as a vaulting coach working with the handicapped in a therapeutic program. That's where I met my wife, Virginia. Just when things were going well, the non-handicapped program was discontinued, but I was not going to give up my dream of creating the first team of handicapped and non-handicapped vaulters who would compete in mainstream competition. Virginia and I took the vaulters who wanted to continue in the program, and with more determination than money, we formed Valley View Vaulters. Virginia became the manager and longeur (the person who controls the horse by holding the lunge line, which is attached to the bridle of the horse as it moves in a circle), and I coached the vaulters of all ages and abilities.

We were so broke we couldn't even afford one horse. We set up a practice barrel in Virginia's backyard for our integrated team of seven (one-third handicapped and two-thirds non-handicapped), and as we entered competitions, people who believed in what we were doing would lend us their horses.

We knew that our fledgling team would raise the bar for the handicapped, achieve success, and share in the joy of one another's accomplishments. Since 1980 I've coached thousands of kids and young adults. In 1993 we began winning competitions, and in 2002 we captured the Trot Team National Championship, a remarkable accomplishment, considering our overall team remained one-third handicapped and all of our competitive teams included members with handicaps. Our team was winning time after time without any special considerations.

We have helped kids who have cerebral palsy, autism, Down syndrome, spinal bifida, schizophrenia, ADD, vision or hearing loss, acute arthritis, and more have a better quality of life. They believe and they achieve. When they look at me doing what I do with one arm, they figure, if I can do it, they can, too.

At the 1996 Nationals, the American Vaulting Association

acknowledged our program's amazing successes, and for the first time in their history, a demonstration class for disabled vaulters was included. Thirty-three-year-old Jeffrey, who only four years earlier had been confined to a wheelchair, performed in a special exhibition class for more severely handicapped vaulters. He was one of five participating Valley View Vaulters whose disabilities ranged from cerebral palsy to autism. Raising himself up from a chair in the arena, Jeffrey walked without help to our big white horse and mounted, assisted only by me giving him a leg up. His face glowed with achievement as he stood upright on the horse's back and flawlessly executed a series of intricate compulsory exercises before facing backward and dismounting by swinging off the horse. He walked back to his chair unassisted. Thunderous applause from teary-eyed spectators filled the arena. There is no way to place a value on his accomplishment.

After Jeffrey's performance, his father reminded us, "When Jeff started, he could barely get his legs apart. Remember, Rick? It took four men to lift him onto the horse. You not only helped him physically… you helped his socialization. Now he wants hugs from everyone. You and Virginia gave him that kind of freedom."

As Virginia often says, some of our kids don't do well in school. They are not in the top of their classes — for the most part, they are really struggling and don't feel good about themselves. With vaulting they get in touch with life, go forward, and gain self-esteem.

Our profits can't be tracked on a balance sheet, because we are always struggling to stay out of the red, but they are greater than most would ever hope for. Since raising enough money to fund the team is a constant struggle, we measure our profits in achievements of the students and the loving support network that has been formed by all of the vaulters and their families.

I don't know who gets more out of the programs — those with disabilities or those without. The kids who don't have physical or psychological problems learn what it means to care and be sensitive to those who do. But they don't see the difference as a curiosity; it just means their friend and teammate needs a little more help or time. It gives them wonderful values. When we watch determined youngsters with challenges successfully accomplish what should be impossible, those are our riches. No one could ever hope for more.

~Rick Hawthorne as told to Morgan St. James

Chapter
6

Create Your Best Future

Embracing Differences

The Truck

Be content with what you have; rejoice in the way things are.
When you realize there is nothing lacking, the whole world
belongs to you.
~Lao Tzu

Being ten years older than my brother Sammy, I played a huge role in his care and have always shared an unbreakable bond with him. When he was an infant, I would marvel at him while he slept, in awe of how little and perfect he was. I admired this little being with all my heart and daydreamed about what he would be like when he was my age. When Sammy was diagnosed with autism around three years old, my world crumbled. I remember feeling angry, confused and afraid for him. For days after his diagnosis, I could not look at my little brother without a flood of tears. My greatest concern was how he would be accepted by others. I wanted people to see Sammy just as I did, not labeled by autism.

One day, shortly after his fourth birthday, Sammy walked over to me with a new toy truck in both hands and said, "Break it!" He handed me the small toy truck.

My grandfather walked up to us and with a screwdriver in hand said, "Give it to me, he wants us to break it for him." I looked at them both with confusion. My grandfather then said, "He's been having me break all of his toys. I think that's how he understands them. How they're built, what they're made of." I handed him the truck and watched as my grandfather unscrewed the pieces. When he got to the parts with wheels and gears, Sammy's eyes lit up with wonder. His gaze was focused on the pieces coming off the truck one by one. He took each piece in his hands as it came off and examined it thoroughly. It was clear to me now that my brother saw things so differently than I did. He knew that the pieces worked together harmoniously, but also that each part was unique. He saw that each part had its own special purpose.

It occurred to me that just like the truck, all of the "pieces" that fit together to make Sammy were pieces placed together perfectly for him. Each piece together created my brother, who sees the world in a different light than anyone I have ever known. His actions at four years old helped me to understand that we are all fit together in a different way for our own specific purpose. I now see the beauty in these differences.

Now, whether he is telling me about math and numbers, presidents, or demonstrating his exceptional memory, the many special qualities my brother has inspire me. Since his diagnosis I no longer cry when I look at my little brother — I smile. I don't see a scary thing called autism. What I see is my brilliant brother Sammy who lights up my darkest days and teaches me new things every day.

~Olivia Mitchell

One Click

Life is partly what we make it, and partly what it is made by
the friends whom we choose.

~Tehyi Hsieh

Students of every color and rung on the socioeconomic
ladder came together to receive a faith-based education at
my high school. Many of my St. Ignatius classmates were
the Spanish-speaking children of immigrant parents. We
had a higher percentage of African Americans than any other private
high school in Chicago, and our valedictorian lived in Chinatown with
her grandparents, who barely spoke English. In addition, a large percentage of students were awarded full-tuition scholarships or substantial
financial aid. I was happy to go to a school with a diverse community,
and graduated with the belief that never again would I learn among
students of such differing backgrounds.

My first year at Boston University forced me to reassess my definition of diversity. I realized with shock that I had never attended a
school with a large Jewish population. In fact, my experience with the
religion was limited to a two-week unit in high school religion and
frequent ingestion of Jewish deli food. Somehow I doubted my affinity
for potato latkes made me any more culturally adept.

During the chaos that is freshman year move-in, my dad, ever
the chatterbox, discovered that one of my Claflin Hall floor-mates,
Danielle Chelminsky, had spent the past year living in Israel, during

which she voluntarily went through basic training for the Israeli army. I had been a BU student for less than twenty-four hours, and already I couldn't believe that while I had been hanging candy canes on a Christmas tree, my future best friend was learning how to shoot an AK-47 in a Middle Eastern desert.

A few weeks into the year, Danielle introduced me to her friend Thalia Rybar, who, despite growing up in predominately Catholic Guatemala, was also Jewish. Although she speaks fluent English, her first language is Spanish. Grabbing dinner in the dining hall with Thalia, Danielle, and other "Latin Jews" at BU was always riveting. Perhaps my major, journalism, played a part in my intense curiosity—for the longest time, I took on the role of Dinner Interrogator. I wanted to know everything.

Thalia and her friends never ceased to entertain me with tales of growing up in developing countries. I learned that while there are a sizeable number of Latin Jews around the world, each country's individual community tends to stick together. The low cost of living means nearly all Latin Jews employ a full-time staff that includes maids, drivers, landscapers, and sometimes bodyguards. The maids, non-Jewish natives, must learn to prepare kosher meals. The bodyguards protect the families from kidnappers, who take wealthy members of the community for ransom. Sharon Malca, from Colombia, endured six months without her mother when she was taken hostage in the Colombian mountains.

Junior year, I moved into an apartment with Thalia, Danielle, and another friend, Pamela. By this time, aspects of Judaism that had once seemed foreign now felt commonplace. I learned the difference between Ashkenazi and Sephardic Jews, the proceedings of a Bar or Bat Mitzvah, countless Yiddish terms (*chutzpah* is a favorite), and the important role of Israel in the Jewish community. I attended Passover Seder at Danielle's house twice. Her family invited me to read the *haggadah*, or book containing the Passover story. Normally I would feel like an idiot stumbling over Hebrew words, but the overwhelming sense of encouragement I felt made me realize what an honor it was to be included in the tradition.

Thalia and her Latin friends often talked about their weekly get-togethers, which they call "Latin Shabbat." Shabbat, the Hebrew word for rest, takes place each Friday, and includes a special dinner. At Latin Shabbat, all the college-aged, Spanish-speaking Jews in Boston congregate for a huge meal. When Thalia invited me and Danielle, I had no clue what to expect—I had never been to any Shabbat dinner, much less a bilingual Shabbat.

If you think you've seen it all, work up an appetite for challah bread and attend Latin Shabbat. When I say I felt like a foreigner, I mean it. I was the only natural blonde, I don't speak Spanish, I didn't know the etiquette, the night's schedule, the words to the prayers, the lyrics to the songs, or even how to toast. I couldn't believe I was a mere hundred yards from my own apartment.

Hanging tentatively behind Thalia and Danielle, I entered the apartment. Immediately, the unfamiliar bombarded each of my senses: the strong scent of just-out-of-the-oven brisket mixed with red wine and expensive European perfumes and colognes. Loud, loud, Spanish, my *gringa* cheek being pressed against those of strangers in the customary Latin air kiss greeting. Thalia's stiletto-clad friends quickly maneuvered around folding chairs and tables to welcome me. What did I want to drink? Could they take my coat? My purse? I barely had time to respond before I was being ushered by five glamazons to meet David, the host.

Thalia, Sharon, and two other friends, Karina, and Sarah, spent the next ten minutes teaching me to salsa. I am admittedly a pathetic dancer—the type who bops to the right when everyone else is boogieing to the left—but I was a novelty to these girls, a project. We salsa-ed until we were all on the floor with tears in our eyes.

The dancing, the Spanglish banter, the delicious smells—I was having the time of my life, and for the first time in my life, I was the minority.

I left Latin Shabbat feeling exhilarated and full of energy, liberated at such newness. That night and many days after, I thought about what had been most special about that night, and why I had reacted so strongly. It took several days to realize that my amazement stemmed from the reverence and seriousness with which this group protected their religion, traditions, and culture.

Amidst the eating, the games, the goofing off, the drinking, and more eating, David stood at the head of the table. Instantly, the group silenced. In English, David earnestly thanked everyone for coming, specifically praising the girls, Thalia included, who had spent all day cooking the massive trays of brisket, potatoes, rice, chicken, salad, and desserts. I knew Thalia and her friends cooked for Shabbat every week, but I hadn't realized the extent of the meal. Like their mothers and grandmothers at home in Guatemala, Mexico, or Peru, and great-grandmothers in Eastern Europe and Israel, my friends were maintaining a tradition, and taking on a role. It was beautiful to see a group of modern, well-educated young women embrace their history.

Next, David read a prayer in Hebrew. It was flawless, not only in his delivery, but in his sincerity. I attended Catholic school for twelve years and had not once been to a gathering in which someone my age stood and recited a prayer. I can't even think of one friend who brought a Bible to school, let alone read from it on a regular basis. David's reading, and the subsequent explanation of its meaning, made me reassess the importance of organized religion. I have, at times, been skeptical of Catholicism. Suddenly, I felt compelled to embrace it.

Opening myself to the experience of another religion and culture has been the single greatest decision of my college experience. There is so much to learn, so much to absorb, so much to take away. Living with Thalia and Danielle was the result of a simple click on the housing website. That one click altered my worldview forever.

~Molly Fedick

My Best Friend Mike

A friend is one who knows you and loves you just the same.
~Elbert Hubbard

"Hi. It's Mike..."

"Hi, Mike, what's the matter?" Mike had been going through a lot lately, and it was not unusual for him to sound upset.

"I need to tell you something, but I'm not sure if I should," he said. Curiosity got the best of me, and I convinced him to let me in on his big secret. "I can't tell you on the phone. Come over." I walked for five minutes around the block, rang his doorbell and followed his mother's instructions to go up to his room.

Mike had been my best friend for the past two years. At first I thought he was weird. We met during our freshman year of high school and soon became inseparable. The summer after that year was the highlight of our friendship. I never had more fun with any other person. We spent every night and every day together. Time flies when you are having fun, however, and we soon found ourselves back in school. I began to notice a change in Mike. The fun ceased, and I felt a strain in our friendship.

Mike was suffering from depression, and I could not understand why. He seemed to have everything going for him. He was doing well in school, there were no problems at home, and he had many friends who loved him. I soon found myself spending every weekend in his bedroom, trying to convince him to cheer up. Nothing seemed to work. His parents became worried and decided to seek professional help.

Mike began to take medication to counteract his depression, and things seemed a little better, but they were not what they used to be. I was still clueless as to what had been causing this change in his behavior. I did not want to give up on my true best friend, so I continued spending painful hours trying to drag him out of his house.

It was one of those weekends, and there I was, sitting on his bed, waiting to hear what he had to say. I had a sense that he was about to tell me something serious. There was a strange look in his eyes, and he would not focus them on me. The silence was overbearing. He finally looked up at me.

"I'm gay." It hit me like a bolt of lightning. I was shocked. "Okay" was all I managed to utter. Silence followed for minutes afterward.

It took some getting used to, but I decided right then and there that I was not going to lose my best friend over it. Mike seems to be back to his normal self these days. We're seniors now, and I still spend a large portion of my time with him and his friends.

A smile comes to my face every time I think back to the first day we met, and the first thought that came to my mind as I approached the bus stop that day: *Who is that weird kid?* That weird kid is my true best friend, Mike, and there is nothing weird about him.

~Brian Leykum

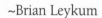

At the Foot of the Bed

To be one, to be united is a great thing. But to respect the right
to be different is maybe even greater.
~Bono

During my daily rounds at the hospital, I came across a room where I could immediately tell by looking through the glass doorway that the man inside, though his back was to me, was visibly disturbed. He was anxiously sitting up on the far side of the bed with his feet hanging off while he pulled repeatedly at the unkempt sheets.

Knocking on the door frame, I announced myself: "Hello, I'm Chaplain Jon. Is everything all right in here?"

Pointing to the wall at the foot of the bed, the man replied, "No, there is a crucifix." I sighed as I examined the wall, knowing full well what was there, and I quickly looked at my census list to verify the patient information and faith tradition. I found the room number and the only word I needed to see: *Hindu.*

As a Protestant chaplain serving at a Catholic hospital in the multicultural and interfaith environment of Los Angeles, it was not infrequent for me to find patients perturbed by the presence of a crucifix on their wall. Trying to be diplomatic and defuse the situation, I explained, "If you are offended by the crucifix, I can make arrangements for it to be removed during your stay here." The truth, more accurately, is that some of the more zealous of the Catholic faith had learned of this practice of accommodating people of other faith traditions, and had most of the crucifixes permanently installed on the wall, so the best effort to accommodate patients often was to drape a cloth over the offending relic.

The Hindu patient left me dumbfounded by what he told me next. Turning more toward me and pulling one knee onto the bed, his face wrinkling from being misunderstood, he explained, "I am not offended by the crucifix. I am disturbed that it is at the foot of my bed, which is a place of dishonor in my culture. Every time I lie down, I feel as if I am disrespecting the God of this hospital."

The teacher had just become the student. I was overwhelmed with how much respect this man had for a faith not his own. I couldn't help but think that I had just glimpsed a nugget of human unity whose offspring surely is peace.

~Reverend Jon Arnold

Go in Good Health

No one ever becomes poor through the giving of charity.
~Maimonides

Even in the 1930s when the Great Depression left no family untouched, *tzedakah* and tolerance were twin morals in our home. Alongside the candlesticks my mother had brought from Europe stood the Jewish National Fund box, into which my mother dropped her weekly spare change, and spare it was.

We lived in a middle-sized city in Western Canada. In our home, we lived in a world of Judaism and Orthodoxy. Outside, everyone, no matter what their heritage, was labeled "English." At home, observance of the Sabbath and the Jewish holidays dominated our lives. My father attended synagogue services daily, and several times a week a teacher came in to give Hebrew lessons to us five children. At school and on the playground we mixed, sang Christmas carols and ended the day with the Lord's Prayer.

The outside world to us also consisted of many churches. My own firsthand experience with churches began when we were very young and my parents bought a home across the street from a Roman Catholic church and parochial school. We used to hear the church bells ring all day, and we learned to set our clocks by them. From our screened verandah we would see the nuns and priests walk from building to building, their hands tucked into their long gowns. In the summer, we would hear the bells ring out their glad tidings on Saturday afternoons, when young happy couples would park their Model Ts in front of their church, and with their huge families, would gather for their weddings. With my "English" friends I would run to the open church door in time to see a bride and groom walk up the long aisle to the altar. After the guests were seated we would steal quietly into the last pew. There, before the crucifix of Christ, their Lord, the couple would kneel and promise never to break their solemn vows. To a young child, the organ, the choir, the stained glass windows (no-no's in our little clapboard synagogue), plus the candles burning in the little red glasses and the lavishly embroidered robes made a lasting impression.

Later I would watch the hooded sisters and the long-robed brothers stand in the doorway to greet and give their blessings to the newlyweds. I saw in these devout faces a radiant love that only they knew, and I wondered how being married to God could fill their lives so well.

Living on the same street and watching them go by daily, they became to me something mysterious, a mystique that I could feel and yet not touch, that I could see and yet not know. They were different, and they lived in a world very alien to my very orthodox home; and yet their constant smiles as they passed our house gave me a feeling of kinship. I used to walk by their residence and wonder about them as I gazed childlike at the black shades in their windows, wishing I could know more about how they lived and felt and worshipped their God. One winter, when I was ten, was a particularly cold one. It seemed as if the snow would never stop falling and the wind would never stop blowing. Christmas drew near, and the Depression seemed endless. We began to feel the tightness of money all around us. There were large heating bills, warmer clothing to buy for five children, and more and more food seemed to disappear from our table. But, one by one, the Christmas lights began to glitter in our neighbor's windows, and the fortunate Gentiles who had evergreens in their front yards shook off the snow and put up a few lights to welcome the holiday. In our home, Hanukkah came and went. We lit the candles, one more every nightfall. Uncles came and gave us Hanukkah *gelt* [money]. My father taught us *"Oi Hanukkah, Oi Hanukkah, a yontif a shaineh"* (a holiday, a pretty one) and then we ate Hanukkah-latkes and dreamed of better times next year.

One evening, a week before Christmas, the doorbell rang. When I opened it, two nuns stood on our front porch. "Merry Christmas!" they exclaimed.

I stared at them in wonder. Never before had I been so close to nuns. Their white stiffly starched bibs and cowls looked like the icicles that hung from our eaves. One rang a small bell, and the other held a brass plate.

"Mama," I called breathless. "There is someone here!"

My mother came from the kitchen, her hands covered with flour. She was in the midst of making apple strudel. A wisp of hair was falling over her face, and as she came to the door she moved the back of her hand slowly over her forehead. Then she noticed the visitors, and in Yiddish said to me, "Tell them to come in. It's cold out there."

I looked again at the callers and then at my mother, and was not quite sure I had heard right. Then my mother opened the door with her floured hand and said, "*Kimtaran. Sis kolt.*" (Come in. It's cold.) The nuns pushed the storm door open and entered.

"Merry Christmas," they said again. "We are collecting for the poor. Would you like to donate?"

My mother could speak very little English, and understood less, but the plate spoke for itself. "Go," she said to me in Yiddish. "Get me my purse."

Still stunned by the strangeness of the presence of nuns in our home, I dashed upstairs. From under the corner of my mother's mattress, I brought out the little black leather pouch that held the precious and very scarce money that had to clothe and feed seven people. Then I stood on the bottom step and leaned over the banister and watched as my mother dropped two dimes and a nickel into the plate. Twenty-five cents! It was a fortune to me. It could then buy two quarts of milk, two loaves of bread and a whole bagful of rock candy.

The nuns, their faces devoid of makeup but wreathed in smiles, were profuse in their thanks. "Thank you, and God bless you!" they repeated several times.

"*Geht gezinter hait*" (Go in good health) my mother told them.

As she opened the door and said again how cold it was, her voice showed real concern. The sisters seemed to understand her. "Oh, that's all right," they said, their voices quiet and peaceful. "God takes care of His children." Then they were gone.

My mother closed the door and went back to her baking. I followed her into the kitchen, wanting to ask a million questions, but all I managed was, "Why?"

"They're good people," my mother told me, rolling her dough. "Very good. They do good things for others. It's their holiday, but we must help."

"What do they do?"

"I don't know all they do. But they have hospitals, and children's homes, and help the poor, and we should help them. Some day you will understand." As the years went by we continued to set our clocks by the church bells. The sisters came each Christmas to collect alms for the poor. My mother continued to drop change into the brass plates. My sisters and brother married and moved away.

During most of those years my father was very ill and was in and out of hospitals many times. During his last illness he was in a Catholic hospital.

One morning my mother received a call that my father was in critical condition and that she was to come at once. I received a message at work that I was to come immediately and I rushed to the hospital. When I arrived there a sister met me at the door of my father's room. "Your father passed away ten minutes ago," she told me.

My concern now was for my mother. She had been all alone with my father at his death, with no one to comfort her. The sister led me to another room, where she had given my mother a sedative. I was amazed to find my mother so calm in her grief, and I kept repeating, "You were all alone! If only I had gotten here on time!'

My mother shook her head. "I wasn't alone," she assured me. "The sister was with me."

"But someone in the family should have been with you," I cried.

"No one is ever alone in this world," my mother told me. "I said the prayer for the dying person, and when the sister heard me she put her arm around me and said the prayer with me." Then, as my mother and I wept together in our grief, the sister put her arms around both of us, and as we all prayed together, I recalled my mother's words of long ago, "They do good, and we must help them."

~Lottie Robins

No Words

What matters most is not "what" you are, but "who" you are.
~DaShanne Stokes

T.J. struggles with the pencil in his left hand, pushing it carefully up and down on the notepad that sits in his lap. My middle sister, Kellie, has asked him to write the word "Mommy" on the paper to show my younger sister and me what he has recently learned in school. The pencil stops moving. T.J. yells "Mommy!" and turns the notepad around to show us the scribbled letters M-O-M on the paper. We all clap and cheer at his accomplishment, and we watch as a proud smile spreads across his face. This may seem like an insignificant feat, but for T.J., it is a milestone. He has just learned how to spell "Mom," and he is ten years old.

My little brother, T.J., was born on my first day of high school. My parents were in their early forties at the time, and it was a surprising situation for all of us to have a new baby in the house. My dad, Tom, was the most excited of all, since he finally had a boy to balance out his houseful of women.

When he was three, my family discovered that T.J. was not developing language skills at a normal rate. The doctors did not have any answers as to what could be causing the delay. T.J.'s disorder put a strain on my family, and our household could be a tense place to live during some of the years that followed. As my brother got older, it became more apparent that his disabilities reached beyond simple language skills.

My mom spent a lot of her time trying to find a solution. My dad reacted in a very different way. He embraced his chance to be a father to his son. They would go for haircuts, hang out at the mall, or just drive around listening to sports radio in the car. T.J. loves these outings with our dad, and the minute he returns from work, my brother pulls on his shoes and waits by the door. He and my dad have developed a bond that goes beyond my brother's "problem," and have become buddies who struggle every day to maintain a semblance of normalcy.

There was one day in particular when I realized that my father had fully accepted T.J. for who he is, and it was this same moment in which I saw the true depth of my father's love for my brother. We were sitting on a bench by the lake — the three of us — and my dad was making funny faces to make my brother laugh. In the midst of the laughter, T.J. stopped and reached up to softly touch our father's face. My dad looked down at him and said almost so softly that I couldn't hear, "Well, kiddo, it looks like it's you and me for the rest of my life." There wasn't a sense of sadness or burden in my father's voice, only acceptance and unconditional love for the little boy who sat beside him. It seemed that T.J. understood this, too, in his own way, and he smiled and touched our father's face again.

T.J.'s condition has yet to be fully diagnosed. My parents continue to help T.J. express himself with words, pictures, and sounds. My dad and T.J., however, have become a duo, and when it's time for them to go "cruising" in Dad's car, we all know that it is strictly boys' night out. The women in our house know that T.J. loves all of us, each in a different way, but the love he has for his dad is written in a language only he understands. All of us have the privilege of speech, but only the two of them speak *their* language, and it requires no words.

~Stacy Flood

A Ray of Peace

The Torah was given to the world in order to establish peace.
~Midrash

I was talking with a young field service engineer, who I was working with on a perplexing computer-related problem. We were discussing Steven Spielberg's movie, *Saving Private Ryan,* and I mentioned that it had brought up too many real memories about battle. He agreed, and asked me, "Where did you get hurt?"

"Over there, in Israel," I said.

"Me, too."

He then revealed that he was a Palestinian. My new friend, whom I shall call "Riyadh" (not his real name) then told me how he came to be in the United States. The following story is his, as he told it to me.

Riyadh was born in the Old City of Jerusalem, one of four children. He had an older brother and two sisters. His father, a successful environmental engineer, moved his growing family out to the suburbs when Riyadh was a toddler, and he remembers his childhood in Ramallah fondly. In a very matter-of-fact way he told me that one day in 1982, while on his way home from school, he had been shot by an Israeli soldier. There had been a street demonstration going on at the time, people were running all over the place and there was a lot of confusion. Passersby rushed the wounded youth, bleeding profusely, to his parents' home. He was seen by a local Palestinian doctor, who was unable to do more than apply a field dressing to stop the bleeding.

But the doctor quickly arranged for him to be transported in a Red Cross car through the mountains to a hospital in Jordan, where he was assessed to be in critical condition. Once stabilized, Riyadh was flown out of the country secretly to a hospital in Turkey. Because of the difficult situation in his homeland, and the fact that he had departed illegally, he could not return. And so, sponsored by a Palestinian doctor in Texas, he sought political asylum and was admitted to the United States.

After recovering from his wounds, the local Palestinian community placed him in a boarding school, near a university in Texas. Now older and alone, and half a world away from home, Riyadh entered the world of American teenagers. Differences in language and customs made his first year in school difficult, but he learned very quickly.

After time in school, Riyadh faced an uncertain future. His parents urged him to stay in the United States until the situation at home calmed down. Though his visa was for only a short duration, he applied for admission to a school of engineering in Texas.

About a week after being admitted, he received a letter summoning him to a meeting with the dean of students. Riyadh was worried, wondering what the dean could possibly want with him. He was quite uncomfortable during the meeting. The dean stared at him, but also acted in a very fatherly and concerned way, inquiring whether he was happy there, and whether there was anything he could do for him.

"Well, my visa is very short," Riyadh told the dean.

"No problem, I will get it extended for the full four-year term of university," replied the dean. "Is there anything else you need?"

Riyadh alluded to his financial situation, and was then surprised by an offer of a full scholarship. After further prompting by the dean, Riyadh admitted that he didn't really have any place to live, and he had no income. On the spot, the dean offered him a position as a systems administrator, which would afford him a place to live and a small stipend.

With his college years thus assured, yet completely baffled as to how it had all happened, Riyadh began his higher education.

After two months, the dean again sent for him, making it clear that he had something he had to tell Riyadh.

Once Riyadh was in his office, the dean told him that he knew him; he knew who he was, he had recognized his name from his application to the university.

Riyadh was puzzled. The dean knew him? Recognized his name? How could that be possible?"

"Riyadh," said the dean, "I am the soldier who shot you."

As Riyadh, amazed and stunned, listened, the dean went on to relate his own story to the student. Joel (not his real name) was born in Brooklyn, and had emigrated with his parents to Israel as a child.

When he was grown, he signed up for his period of duty in the Israeli army. When he and his fellow soldiers were sent to restore order after a demonstration had turned violent, he found himself in a very dangerous situation. Rocks were being thrown, and the situation was getting out of hand. He fired his rifle in what he believed was an act of self-defense. Fate decreed that the bullet hit young Riyadh.

When Joel learned later that he had shot a young Palestinian boy, he was deeply distressed. His fellow soldiers tried to console him, saying that sometimes unfortunate things do happen in violent street confrontations, as well as in war. He should not blame himself.

But Joel needed to find out what had happened to the kid he shot. Once he learned Riyadh's name, he went straight to his parents' home to inquire about him, and to apologize. Riyadh's parents were very old-fashioned, and would not even speak to Joel; his father threw him out of the house.

Joel continued to feel personal anguish over what he had done, even though he still believed he was at the time acting in self-defense. But that didn't make any difference. After some time, he and his family decided to return to the country of his birth and make a new start.

Back in the United States, Joel went on to complete his graduate degree, and find a job with a college in Texas.

As he listened to the amazing story unfold, Riyadh felt a mixture of emotions: hate, love, loneliness. He thought of an old expression in Arabic, describing someone who slaps you with his right hand and straightens your hat with his left hand.

When Joel had finished his story, the Palestinian and the former Israeli soldier, now colleagues at an American university in Texas, looked at each other for a moment. Then they reached out, shook hands and embraced in an act of reconciliation and friendship. In an instant, that terrible moment when a stray Israeli bullet ripped into a Palestinian boy was redeemed. Time had wound its full circle, what was sundered had been united, and a ray of peace beamed out to the Holy Land from a far-off country called America.

~Rabbi Harvey Abramowitz

Road to Reconciliation

A journey is best measured in friends rather than miles.
~Tim Cahill

I was in Vietnam from 1970 to 1971. I was a nineteen-year-old grunt — a foot soldier. I spent most of my time in the field scrounging through the jungle and rice paddies, looking for the "enemy." In February 1971, barely six months after my arrival, my platoon was out on a reconnaissance in the central highlands. I saw a clump of grass on the road and in the millionth of a second it took me to say to myself, *Hmm, I better not step on that,* I stepped on it. The next thing I remember I was on the ground screaming and writhing in pain.

I had placed my foot on what we called a "toe popper," an anti-personnel land mine. I lost my right foot and part of my right calf. Although it was a very traumatic experience, I also felt tremendous relief and happiness — I knew it was my plane ticket home.

Back in the States, I was fitted with an artificial leg and I threw away all my souvenirs of Vietnam — my photographs, my uniform and my Purple Heart. They had no value to me. They reminded me of something of which I wasn't really proud and I had one constant reminder: one artificial leg.

Twenty-six years passed, and I never once thought about returning to Vietnam — until I received a newsletter from an organization called World T.E.A.M. Sports. In it, they announced their upcoming Vietnam Challenge. I had never heard of it before.

A team of Americans, Australians and North Vietnamese veterans and civilians would ride bicycles down Vietnam's main freeway, freeway One, from the north to the south, a distance of twelve-hundred miles. Being a cyclist and a fan of a good challenge, I knew that I wanted to go, and I applied.

I was accepted and a flood of emotions filled my heart and soul. Wonder and excitement. Hesitation and fear.

The possibility of meeting a former North Vietnamese soldier fascinated me. Maybe, just maybe, we shared similar feelings. Thrown into war, how did he feel when he was being attacked? What was it like fighting us?

I was also curious about my fellow veterans. I had had nothing to do with Vietnam veterans for twenty-six years. What would it be like to travel with a whole group of them?

Four months later, I found myself on a plane with more than thirty team members heading back to a place I knew only as a war, not a real country with real people. As I looked at the faces of the other veterans, I wondered if that's how I must have looked. How would the North Vietnamese people react? How would we react?

Upon our arrival, we were warmly greeted by open arms, flowers and gracious smiles at Hanoi's airport. After a few days in the capital, we were ready to hit the road.

On the first day of January 1998, I was riding out of Hanoi with my eighty American and Vietnamese war veteran teammates. The energy in the air was ecstatic. Before I knew it, I was waving to hundreds of cheering Vietnamese citizens, holding hands with a former North Vietnamese soldier.

His name was Tran Van Son. He was my age, and like me, Tran had also lost his right leg to a mine. But unlike me, he also lost six immediate family members in the bombing raids on Hanoi. He said he used to be filled with hate for Americans, and he nearly lost his spirit hundreds of times.

As Tran opened up to me, I felt my own heart unfolding. One day, I heard that he had slipped in the shower, and his leg was hurting him. I offered him some gel liners and stump cushions to ease his pain. He put them on and gave me a "thumbs up." He smiled his magnificent smile. And that was enough.

We had a connection, a special connection. As language was a barrier, we often relied on a smile or a hug to convey our camaraderie. Over the miles, we found that we could just let go, relax and enjoy each other's company, even without words.

In Vietnam's national cemetery in Hue, Tran and I were talking about his prosthesis. I knew that he could benefit from some of the new technology that was available and I was doubting the capability of his artificial leg. He mentioned that he had run the New York City Marathon twice. I was amazed. He obviously loved running as much as I did, and if a new leg could bring him a fraction of the joy I felt, then maybe I could arrange for a new prosthesis for him.

As I pondered the possibilities, he asked me, "Are you a fast runner?"

"Yes," I replied. Then he said, "I do one hundred meters in fifteen seconds." "You gotta be kidding." I was shocked. He shot back, "You, me, race right now." And so we did.

We staged a little one-hundred-meter race in Vietnam's equivalent of Arlington National Cemetery. We sprinted neck-and-neck down the improvised course, to the cheers of veterans from both sides. It was a tie, and at the finish line we hugged each other in a spirited moment that cut across history and brought much-needed healing.

In that instant, I mentioned to Tran that maybe someday he would be able to come to the United States, and we could run the New York City Marathon together. We smiled at the possibility and knew that somehow we would make that dream come true.

From that day on, Tran and I "talked" daily. I couldn't help but feel awed that twenty-eight years ago Tran and I might have tried to kill each other. And we were fast becoming the best of friends. I felt like I was the luckiest person alive.

When I returned home I talked with my friend Jim, who owned the company where my prosthesis was made. I told him about Tran Son and how he should have a new prosthesis and running foot. Jim agreed, and we started making calls that night.

In April of 1998, it was Tran's turn to travel to my country. My family and I waited for him at the airport in Sioux Falls, South Dakota, and my heart fluttered when I saw the face of my smiling friend come through the gate. I realized that I actually knew this man. He was my friend. This Vietnamese man was my friend, and now our friendship would continue over here.

We got Tran a new prosthetic leg and lightweight flex foot. Seeing him on his state-of-the-art leg brought tears to my eyes. Tran had given me so much, and now I was happy to give something back to him... and, in many ways, to his country, Vietnam. In three short days, Tran and I were once again running together, more comfortably, and this time in my hometown.

It was an honor for us to have Tran Son staying at our house. My wife Robin and I noticed how Tran brought out the best in our two teenage daughters. They seemed to blossom when Tran was with us. He had three daughters of his own, and across the miles, he treated mine as his own. We were his American family.

He spoke eloquently at our daughters' school about forgiveness. Despite all that had happened between our two countries, despite all of his loss, he found the place in his heart to forgive. We were so proud to know this man who had traveled so far to be with us and share his gentle sense of dignity and grace.

In November, Tran flew back to the United States, this time to New York City. But this time he was there to meet me when I arrived at the airport. When he saw me walking through the gate, he ran to greet me, his head bopping up and down, that ever-present smile on his face.

Together, we ran the New York City Marathon. Through five boroughs and a little over twenty-six miles, we cherished each other's company and recalled our journey through his country. After all the horrific and heartrending moments we had endured, a marathon was somehow the easy part.

As we headed toward the finish line in Central Park, Tran's innocence prevailed. Even though it's not permitted, he stopped to ask an official if she would take our picture below the banner. She couldn't refuse his beaming face. And so my new friend and I finished our race, triumphant hand in triumphant hand, just as we had started our journey in Hanoi so many months before.

~Daniel Jensen

Chapter
7

Create Your
Best Future

Accepting and
Asking for Help

The Walk That Changed Our Lives

*It can be hard to break the friendship code of secrecy and make
your friend mad at you, but you must do what you feel in your
heart is right.*

~Amanda Ford

The closer we came to the counselor's office, the more obvious it became that this walk would be one of the most important of our lives. It was one of the last days before school got out for the summer, and eighth grade was coming to an end. My friends and I were all thrilled. Everyone, that is, except our friend, Hannah.

It had started the previous summer, when Hannah had begun to keep to herself a lot. Whenever we would go out, she would insist on staying home by herself just to sit around. In fact, a lot of changes had come over Hannah ever since we had entered junior high. She obsessed about her weight, her complexion and how unpopular she was. She never seemed to focus on the good things she had to offer; it was always about what she didn't have or what she was lacking. We were all concerned that something was very wrong, but at thirteen we didn't exactly understand it or know what we could do to help her. Hannah seemed to be getting worse every day. She hated herself, and it was tearing our friendship apart.

Then one morning not long ago, Hannah came to school and told us she had almost committed suicide. She said she had thought about her friends and could not go through with it. We were in shock and had no idea what to do. Since she told no one else — not her parents or her sisters, just us — we tried to figure out what to do ourselves, feeling that no one else would understand. Though we didn't want to stop being there for her, we couldn't carry the burden by ourselves. We knew that if we made one wrong move, it could cost us our friend's life.

We walked into the counselor's office and waited for what seemed like an eternity until they called our names. We held hands as we walked in, each of us holding back tears. The counselor invited us to sit down, and we began to tell him about Hannah and all that had been going on. When we were finished, he told us that we had done the right thing. We waited as he called Hannah's mother. We were overwhelmed with a million questions. What would Hannah say when she found out that we had told? Would her parents be mad at her for not telling anyone sooner? What was going to happen?

When Hannah's mother arrived at school, she had obviously been crying and her face seemed full of questions. She began to ask about Hannah's behavior and what she had told us. It was awful to tell her how Hannah had been alone at home one day testing knives to see if they were sharp enough to take her life. We all cringed at the thought of not having her in our lives today.

We learned later that after we had gone back to class, Hannah had been called down to talk to her mother and her counselor. It turned out she was relieved and grateful that she didn't have to keep her secret any longer. She began counseling and has since gotten better. Since that day we are so grateful to see Hannah's smiling face, or even to simply be able to pass her a note in the hallway between classes.

If we had not taken that long, horrible walk to the counseling office, we may not have been able to share high-school memories with Hannah. I know now that when we took that walk, it gave us the ability to give her the greatest gift of all... her life.

~Maggie McCarthy

A Student Teacher Who Made a Difference

A teacher affects eternity.
~Henry Adams

At the beginning of my senior year in high school, I had no intention of applying to college. Honestly, I thought that people like me didn't attend college, for many reasons. I am a Mexican American who was born and raised in an "under-served" urban community with limited educational resources. I attended the local community high school where college wasn't encouraged for the average student like me. The scholarships and college-related events were offered to the honor students.

The only contact that I had with my high school counselor was to choose my courses. As far as family, no one had ever attended college, and I had no idea where to start, and if I could even afford it. My thought process was that I would graduate from high school and get a job. My father had suffered a back injury while working in a factory and was unemployed for many years.

I felt that it was my responsibility to help provide for my family and contribute financially to the household. Besides, I could never envision myself as a college student completing a degree. It just wasn't for me.

Although I viewed myself as just an average student with average grades, I never realized that some key people at my school did notice my potential. I clearly remember the day that my psychology teacher abruptly interrupted my English class with some interesting news. She was excited about sharing some news with the English instructor as well as the entire class. She had just graded a research paper from one of her classes. Before she began reading it to the class, she stated, "I want to share a brief passage from this well-written paper that has college material written all over it."

It took me a while to realize that the paper she was reading belonged to me. Me, college material? No way. I blushed in front of my peers as she recognized my work. Of course, after a while I thought to myself, I got lucky. Although I enjoyed expressing myself through writing, I never thought that I was actually good at it.

The end of the first semester was coming to an end and I heard many of the honor students talking about being admitted into the college of their choice as well as scholarships that they had received. I knew it was too late for me to start anything. I figured there was no point since I was so far behind.

It's funny how fate works, because all it took was one ordinary day that became the turning point in my academic life. It was a Friday morning during my English class. Our student teacher invited the entire class to attend a youth expo at Navy Pier. The expo would take place the next day, which was a Saturday. I took a permission slip home and had my father's permission to attend. The plan was to meet my student teacher at the train station and go from there.

When I arrived at the train station that Saturday morning I noticed that my student teacher was waiting by herself, and no other students were in sight. She greeted me and we chatted for a while as we waited. Fifteen minutes passed, and no one showed up. We decided to go anyway. Throughout the train ride and the field trip my teacher talked to me about her college experience and how she was excited that I would soon experience college too.

I told her that I was too late and that I would not attend. She was genuinely surprised and disappointed. She was completing her

Education degree at the University of Illinois at Chicago and she mentioned that I should apply. I didn't know much about this university but I gave it some thought. She also mentioned that she felt that I was a good writer and that I would do very well in college. I enjoyed hearing these words very much.

On Monday morning, I built up the courage to pay a visit to my guidance counselor to inquire about the whole college process. I remember feeling very nervous about the whole thing, but thinking it was something I had to do. I walked into my counselor's office and asked about applying to UIC. My counselor looked at me and handed me the application with no further explanation. The meeting was over. Being that I was a very timid student, I didn't bother to ask additional questions.

I decided to approach another guidance counselor about the application process. The next counselor took the time to sit with me, and basically informed me that UIC was too much of a school for me and that I should apply to a city college instead. She looked at my ACT score and warned me that the university would not be a fit for someone like me. I can still recall the warm feeling rushing through my face and my heart pounding in my chest. I felt rejected and like a failure.

I informed my student teacher about my experiences with both guidance counselors. She brushed it off and said to me, "Don't worry about it, I will help you out." She helped me with the application and registration process. A few months later I proudly informed her that I was accepted to the university and received financial aid to cover tuition and fees. I also decided to apply for several scholarships that I can proudly say I received. I obtained one for four years consecutively. At one point, upon receipt of a scholarship, I was invited to read my scholarship essay during the recipient ceremony, in front of over 300 people.

Overall, college was such a great experience and I learned the value of perseverance and self-confidence. I decided to take on a new challenge and completed a Master's Degree in Educational Leadership. I am currently in the process of applying to a doctoral program in Policy Studies in Urban Education at UIC. These achievements are still surreal to me.

As I reflect on my educational journey, I am grateful to that one individual who not only believed in me, but guided me through a crucial point during my senior year in high school. Thanks for everything, Ms. Tracie.

~Elizabeth Herrera

The Sandals That Saved My Life

Though no one can go back and make a brand new start,
anyone can start from now and make a brand new ending.
~Carl Bard

My junior high days were the darkest and the hardest time in my life. During that time, I didn't feel like I had any friends, except for this one person. This "friend" used to tell me that we would always be "friends forever." Friends are people who care for you and who are there for you whenever you need them. They nurture you when you're down. I never felt that way about her.

We only had one class together, so I didn't see her very often. She was all wrapped up in her own thing— her boyfriend, her social life, all her other friends. When I would walk the halls of junior high by myself, I would see her hand-in-hand with other people and she would just stare at me as I walked by. She never came over to talk to me except in that one class.

One rainy day, I got on the Internet and instant-messaged her. I thought it was the greatest thing in the world that we could talk on the Internet back and forth; it was so cool. We started chatting about school, boys, everything that two normal preteen girls would talk about. I brought up that I had gotten a new movie, and I wanted her to come over and watch it with me. I waited and waited for her reply, and when it came it was like daggers in my heart with unbearable pain.

She said, "Why would I want to come and watch it with you? Every time you get something new, you always have to brag about it to me and it makes me sick. You brag about everything all the time." I apologized to her up and down, that that's not what I meant, and I kept on apologizing.

Then she wrote back, "I am not going to sit here and fight with you about it, even though it is true," and she signed off.

I sat in my chair for ten minutes in a daze, wondering how a person who said she was my friend could say something like that to me. I went into the living room and sat down next to my mom, then burst out crying. She comforted me and reassured me that whatever it was, everything would be okay.

When I went to bed that night, I couldn't sleep. I felt so alone; like no one really loved me and like I was just some person that other people could just use whenever they felt like it. I felt almost invisible. I cried and cried until I finally fell asleep.

The next morning, I woke up around 8:00. My mom came into my room and said that she and my dad had doctor's appointments and that they would be back in a couple of hours. After they left, I sat on my bed and wondered what would be a good way out of this. Then, something came to my mind.

I would kill myself and put everyone out of their misery. That way, they wouldn't have to pretend that they like me, or that they are my friends. My social life wasn't the only reason that I decided to do this. Other things, too, were really bothering me — my grades, for one.

I sat and thought about how I would do it. *Should I shoot myself or take pills, or should I cut my wrists?* I settled on pills. I put the pills on the table next to my bed while I sat and wrote my final words to my family and friends.

I was ready to pop the pills for my final minutes on Earth.

Then the phone rang.

It was my mom calling to see what my shoe size is because she had found the cutest pair of sandals at Old Navy. I said, "Oh… yeah, okay, I wear an eleven."

Then she went on, "What's wrong? Are you feeling okay?"

I was like, "Yeah, Mom, I'm fine."

Then the words that I had longed to hear from *anyone* came out, "I LOVE YOU, and I'll be home in an hour." I hung up the phone. I sat in a daze, with the pills in my hand, thinking, *How could I have forgotten that someone actually does love me?*

When my mom came home, she hugged me and kissed me and said that she loved me a lot. I never told her what I had been thinking about doing.

The next day my "friend" called and said, "I was only kidding about the whole thing." I never told her about it, either. I kept it to myself. To this day, I still haven't told anyone about what I almost did. I have never actually blamed anyone but myself.

I am so blessed that my mom's phone call got through to me. Not only did it make me realize that I really am loved and cared about, but that suicide is never the answer. Maybe I just needed to hear the words "I love you" more often. Maybe we all do. Even when I have problems at school, my family is always there for me and I needed to remember to value that support. I know that I have to be there for them, too.

According to my definition of friendship, my mom's the best friend I'll ever have. My mom doesn't know how really special she is and how much of a hero she is. Thank you, Mom, for loving me so much — and saving me — without even knowing it. You're my forever friend.

~Mallorie Cuevas

Editor's note: If you, or someone you know, is thinking about suicide, call 1-800-SUICIDE or log on to www.save.org.

Feeling Full

Recovery is remembering who you are and using your strengths
to become all that you were meant to be.
~Recovery Innovations

Anxious, obsessive compulsive, and anorexic—had you asked me months ago, I would have told you I was all three. I don't know why then it came as such a shock when the doctor stated I wouldn't be leaving the hospital that morning.

I recognized that I had a problem. But when a medical professional looked at me and said, "You're an anorexic. Your heart, in fact your whole body, is going into failure. You could die," it all suddenly became very real. That diagnosis meant that I couldn't run from it anymore.

I had admitted to my parents that I was suffering from an eating disorder towards the end of tenth grade. What had started as a desire to improve my health rapidly snowballed into a drastically unhealthy change in habits and alarming weight loss. I limited my caloric intake to about 800 calories a day and exercised up to four hours a day. I was consumed with thoughts about my body and how to maintain the "perfect" and completely unattainable goal I had in my mind.

All of this left me with intense emotional distress, physical damage, and a 101-pound devastated body. I had withdrawn and disconnected from my social life. I felt completely hollow and starved of everything in life. I was dying, inside and out.

At the beginning of the summer, after having told the truth about my struggle, my parents immediately did all that they could to help. Sadly, the reality of the matter was that help would be months away. I was put on a waiting list for an eating disorders recovery program, so we were left to face my anorexia as best as we could on our own. Though I still failed to consume an appropriate amount, I did will myself to eat more. And although the constant thoughts of exercise prevented me from concentrating, I did cut my workouts in half. Summer was an uphill battle, but come the end of July, my saving grace was just around the corner.

Camp Kintail was a Presbyterian summer camp near Goderich, Ontario, right off Lake Huron, and also known as my home away from home. That summer was my fifth year at camp, and one of my most profound. Kintail had always been my sanctuary. It was the one place that I could truly be my open and honest self. Every summer, I was graced with beautiful people, scenery, and opportunities to grow as an individual. As a result, I learned that no matter what life threw at me, I could be sure that my time at Kintail could get me through it. That summer I was to spend a month in their leadership program, which ultimately saved my life.

It was my intent to reveal my issue once I got to camp. However, that proved more difficult than I had anticipated. While I had many friends at camp, I felt we'd grown apart. Though I tried, I couldn't bring myself to share my problem. Three days passed and I hadn't told a soul. Then one morning in the lodge, for no reason other than a gut feeling, I approached one of my fellow leaders in training. I knew little more than her name.

"Hayley, can I talk to you?"

Within minutes, tears were pouring down my face as I choked out the truth. To my surprise, she began crying too. She patiently listened to me as I expressed how I felt, but she already knew. When I finished, she looked me in the eyes and said, "One year ago, I was exactly where you are now." Hayley explained that she had overcome her eating disorder the prior summer and firmly believed camp had saved her life. I honestly believe in that very moment she saved mine.

For the rest of camp, Hayley was like my guardian angel. No matter how stressful things got or how difficult I became, she did everything in her power to keep me happy, safe, eating, and feeling supported.

Going home was the hard part, because it meant tests and evaluations, and then waiting until late October for my meeting for the recovery program. But on the third day of school, my stepmom told me that my evaluation had been bumped up. "They saw the result of your preliminary ECG, and they're concerned. They want to see you tomorrow."

With this urgent evaluation came the possibility of admittance into the hospital. It's funny how the world works, because that morning, Hayley (whom I hadn't talked to since camp) contacted me and asked how I was doing. I told her the truth, and she did the same with me. "This is when you have to get better. You're slowly committing suicide. Think about how much you have ahead of you." I honoured her words.

I went to my appointment that morning wearing my kilt and collared top, my hair done, my make-up on. I thought I would be going to school that afternoon. But there I was, sitting in that box of a room, the doctor's words still ringing in my ears. I would not go home for a month.

For quite some time, I blamed myself for this — for the inability to just eat a piece of cake or skip a run. People had reacted strongly upon discovering my illness: "I thought you were smarter than that" and "You've just got to eat." These responses only furthered my self-hatred, and I believed them. Until I started hearing the response from people uncovering the truth: "It's a disease."

It took a lot for me to finally understand that it is a disease. Lying in my hospital bed, devastated and sobbing, I recalled apologizing to my parents for all of the stress I had caused and that I couldn't just be better. They would have none of that. "Would you just tell a cancer patient to get better?" No, I suppose you wouldn't. Thinking that over, I finally accepted that I was sick, and not by my doing. However, getting better would be through my own doing.

My month in that hospital was hands down the hardest month of my life, but I got through it. And I still continue to recover from my disorder. Some days I feel unstoppable, and some days I feel stopped dead in my tracks. Each day, however, I continue to heal and recover, because I have an infinite will to do so.

"I eat. I'm still anorexic."

A friend recovering from her disorder once told me that. It's a statement that explains a lot and holds much truth. I eat, but I still struggle. I'm still ill, and I'm still a long way from being completely better, but that's okay.

It's okay because I have people like Hayley in my life, an incredibly supportive and understanding family, places like Kintail, and a strong drive to recover.

With all of that in mind, I know I'm finally on my way to feeling full again.

~Samantha Molinaro

Freshman Orientation

Many of our fears are tissue-paper-thin, and a single courageous step would carry us clear through them.
~Brendan Francis

"At this time, we ask that parents and students separate into two groups for the remainder of the day. Parents and students will be reunited at the conclusion of the campus tour."

Flocks of incoming freshmen happily abandon their parents upon hearing this announcement. I am less than thrilled at the prospect of starting college, let alone leaving my mother's side to tour the campus with the rest of the wide-eyed incoming freshmen.

"Okay Laur, I'll see you in a few hours, and remember, this is going to be a great experience for you!" Mom says, her big brown eyes alive with enthusiasm. I am amazed by my mother's resilience, considering what my family and I have been through during the past four years.

My mother disappears into a sea of overzealous parents who look as if they have ransacked the campus bookstore; many of the parents, to the embarrassment of their teenagers, are proudly sporting university attire with slogans like, "I'm a Sunny Brook University Dad."

We follow our senior tour guide. The other incoming students chatter and make casual introductions. I drag behind. How could I have believed I was ready for this? After all, it has only been a few months since I was discharged from the hospital. I am feeling better for the first time in years... but college?

My brooding is interrupted by a peppy voice. "Hi, I'm Jennifer."

The voice is attached to a freckle-faced blond girl dressed in what can only be described as hippy-like sports attire. For some strange reason, I like her immediately.

"I'm Lauren," I reply.

"Commuting or dorming?"

I fumble for my words, still caught up in my own thoughts. I would dorm, but I have spent the last four years overcoming a major depressive disorder that nearly claimed my life. I am still readjusting to living back home, in a place where I can come and go without asking for a "pass" or for a staff member to unlock the door to let me outside. I'm not quite sure I'm ready for this right now.

"I, uh, I don't know yet. My parents think I should dorm, but I don't really want to," I say in my most confident voice.

"You should definitely dorm! I'm going to, and I think it will be a lot of fun!"

I can't decide if Jennifer's enthusiasm is annoying or refreshing, but I decide to give her the benefit of the doubt. Before I can utter my less than enthusiastic reply, the tour guide announces that it is time to create our schedules.

We crowd into the Student Activity Center, or as the true, full-blown university students call it, the Sac, a nickname that immediately reminds me of the warm, safe bed at home I wish I were nestled in. We are ushered towards stiff, metal-backed chairs that hungrily await our freshman flesh. Three seniors hand out course bulletins as thick as textbooks, and slap registration forms down on the tables in front of us. All around me, papers crinkle and pencils scribble furiously. These sounds blare like an alarm clock, screaming "Wake up, Lauren!" Students seem to be moving through the process at rapid speed and I have not even opened my course catalog.

Focus, I tell myself. You can do this. Just read through the catalog and find the courses you like and a schedule that works. No big deal.

Intro to Psychology A or B, Foundations of Biology 2, Calculus, Geology 101, English, History, sections 1, 2, 3, 4, 5,6,7… the list goes on, and on, and on.

I begin to panic. How am I supposed to know what to do? I'm just relearning how to live in the real world again, and they want me to make a schedule?!

Other freshmen are handing in their materials, grinning as they rush out to meet their parents.

I cannot breathe, anxiety is coursing through my veins, and my head is pounding.

In moments, I am sobbing.

Other students abandon their tasks to stare at me, making me wish that the earth would open up and swallow me whole. One of the seniors in charge walks over to my table.

"What's the matter?" she asks gruffly.

"I… I can't do this!" I cry.

"All you have to do is make your schedule, just like everybody else," she says, clearly annoyed.

I cry harder. Then, a warm hand on my shoulder… Jennifer.

"Everything is alright," she tells the senior. "I'll help her."

The insensitive upperclassman walks away, and I feel the weight of the dozens of staring eyes lift. The other students quickly lose interest in the spectacle I've created and I can breathe again.

"What's wrong, sweetie?" Jennifer asks.

I am touched by this near stranger's concern. She hardly knows me, but seems to genuinely care.

Jennifer's kindness gives way to new tears. If crying were a major, I would have earned my doctorate in it by now.

"It is just too much; it is just too overwhelming," I say. "I… I have depression and I take medication."

Why did I say that? She probably thinks I am a freak now. But Jennifer puts her arm around me and her words reach out and wrap warmly around my soul.

"I know all about that sort of thing," she says. "My mother has depression. Besides, I think it's pretty normal to feel overwhelmed right now."

And with these words, just like that, the stigma of my mental illness is lifted for a moment and I am just a normal teenage girl with real fears about this exciting but frightening new adventure called "College."

The room is nearly empty now, and I still have no schedule. The pages before me are watermarked with tears.

Jennifer reaches out and gently places her hand on my arm. "Okay, so you said earlier you wanted to be a Psych major, right?"

And with that, this girl who was a stranger to me before this day guides me through the process, step-by-step, until I have everything in place and my schedule is complete. I am amazed at how much more clearly I can see now that the veil of anxiety and tears has lifted. "See," Jennifer tells me softly, "you knew exactly what to do — you just needed to believe in yourself."

That was the beginning of what would blossom into a powerful friendship. With a hug goodbye and a promise to keep in touch, we left Freshman Orientation with much more than our schedules. As I went to meet my mother, I decided that I would give living on campus a try... after all, I had come this far, and with a little help from a new friend, I had been reminded of the strength that existed in me. Four years later, as I graduated from the university with the distinction of Magna Cum Laude, I looked back on Freshman Orientation, on all of my fears and insecurities, and smiled.

~Lauren Nevins

She Already Knew

I would maintain that thanks are the highest form of thought;
and that gratitude is happiness doubled by wonder.
~G.K. Chesterton

I was fourteen. My girlfriend at the time was in southern Georgia while I was in Metro Atlanta, and we had only met online, never in person. We'd gotten into the habit of staying up late on the phone, even falling asleep sometimes, because my sisters or parents would constantly interrupt during the day. Nighttime was the only time we were sure to be unbothered.

I'd gotten comfortable in the routine: my dad would fall asleep on the couch, Mom would help him sleepwalk into their bedroom, my sisters and I would each go to bed, and my mom would turn in for the night after cleaning whatever dishes were left in the kitchen. I'd hear my mom's door shut and immediately text my girlfriend for her to call me.

This particular night, however, my mom was taking a very long time to go to bed. My girlfriend grew impatient, so I let her call but warned her that I would have to whisper until my mom went to bed.

What I didn't know was that my mom was in the living room, on the other side of my bedroom wall, reading a book with no intention of stopping any time soon. Eventually, I got too complacent and loud, and she heard me. My heart jumped out of my chest when she burst through the door, hissing at me to get off the phone and go to sleep. I quietly whispered what had happened to my girlfriend and hung up, burying under the covers so that I wouldn't have to face my mom's glare.

The next day, I was a wreck at school. I knew my mom wanted to talk to me about why I had been up so late, but we wouldn't have a chance to be properly alone until she drove me to orchestra that night. At school, I was constantly expressing my worries to my friends, all of whom already knew I was gay, asking them what I should say. I've always been a generally good kid; I wasn't used to getting in trouble, but there simply wasn't any credible excuse I could give to my mom to explain why I had been up so late without coming out to her.

Then I thought about what my mom's reaction would be if she did know it had been my girlfriend I was on the phone with instead of just a friend, like she'd thought. Her being my girlfriend was the only reason I would stay up with her on the phone, after all. I voiced the idea to my friends. Although they said that it was a brave decision to make on a whim, I had their support in whatever happened.

I wasn't particularly worried about my mom's reaction, necessarily. I'd been thinking about what would happen if I came out to her for a while; I didn't think that she would go so far as to kick me out or anything, but I had absolutely no idea what her opinions were on LGBT issues. I was sure she wouldn't hate me, but that didn't mean she would accept my sexuality.

Usually, I would sing along to the radio when riding in the car, especially when it was just my mom and I. However, that night, the ride to orchestra was spent with me in silence, constantly wondering when she would bring up the late-night phone call. When she dropped me off, she assured me that we would talk on the way back home.

Well, that didn't assure me at all. It only served to make me more nervous, so during rehearsal, I forced myself to get completely lost in the music we were playing so that I wouldn't have to think about what was to come. As soon as I started packing up my violin, though, all the nerves came back. I felt sick to my stomach, wondering what was going to happen once I told my mom that I was gay.

We were five minutes into the car ride when she asked me, "So, what made you think it was okay to be on the phone at two in the morning?"

This was it. This was my chance. I willed for my voice not to crack as I spoke, but it felt as if my heart was trying to claw its way up my throat. "Because she's my girlfriend," I replied.

There was only a half-second pause: "Okay, so why did you think it was okay to be on the phone at two in the morning?"

I was shell-shocked. Out of all of the reactions I'd imagined, I definitely hadn't thought that my mom would simply gloss over my Big Coming Out Moment.

That wasn't the case, however. After chastising me for staying up on the phone and promising me she'd take it away if she caught me again, my mom started asking me about my initial answer. She asked if I was gay, and then how I knew; I told her yes, and that I'd simply never wanted to be with a boy, but girls had always gotten my attention.

She was completely fine with it all. "If I'm being completely honest," she told me, "I kind of already knew." Apparently I'd had a fixation with girls since I was little, be it the pink Power Ranger or my fifth-grade student-teacher. She promised that she didn't love me any less or any differently.

That was nearly six years ago. Since then, my mom has been my support system within the adults of my family. When I came out to my dad and he didn't react very well, she was right there to reassure me that everything would be fine. She asks how my girlfriend is doing when I'm dating someone, and she can always tell when we've broken up. She doesn't question my clothing choices and lets me be who I am.

A lot of people don't get so lucky when they come out to their parents. A lot of teenagers are kicked out onto the street simply because of who they love. My mom has been the most accepting, loving parent I could ever wish for. I knew I was lucky to have her before I came out, and that belief was confirmed once I'd told her the truth.

I know that she'll always be by my side, supporting me in who I am and what I do. She's the best mother I could ask for, and I will never be able to thank her enough for that.

~Ayanna Bryce

English Teaching Wonder

Being honest may not get you many friends but it'll always get you the right ones.
~John Lennon

Mrs. Seley, my seventh-grade English teacher, was the loudest, most obnoxious, put-you-on-the-spot teacher I had ever met. She was crazy, goofy, dramatic, quiet, serious and outrageous, all in the first five minutes of class. No wonder I liked her.

To be honest, I wasn't sure about her at first. She seemed pretty tough, and I didn't do well with particularly tough teachers.

And even though I had been a star student in English in elementary school, my grades in her class fell. I went from low A's to B's, then from low B's down to C's.

But that wasn't the only class I was having trouble in. Due to personal problems at home and a demanding school schedule, I was becoming more and more stressed out. My grades were suffering. I wasn't sleeping well. I was talking back to my family and becoming so irritable that I was spending less time with my friends. Straight As turned into C's, D's and dreaded F's. ("F" I found out, doesn't stand for "Fantastic.") In fact, the only class I was able to keep an A in was science, which for me was nothing more than a daily nap.

One day near the end of the semester, Mrs. Seley pulled me aside.

She explained to me that I needed to get my butt into gear, and that she wasn't afraid of failing me, regardless of how smart I was. She reminded me that the personal goal I had set to read eight books during the semester was a long way from being met. I had read only two. Either I needed to have a serious cram session or Mrs. Seley would see me again next year. She certainly wasn't subtle about it.

When Mrs. Seley had finished explaining that I might need to start making friends with sixth-graders, she asked me a question that I hadn't expected. She wanted to know if what I had written in a previous assignment was true. Two months earlier we had been asked to write about a meaningful time in our lives. Most people wrote about their vacations to Hawaii or the Bahamas or France, but I interpreted the word "meaningful" differently than everyone else. So I didn't write about a vacation. I wrote a story about the problems that were happening in my life right then. When I write, I write from the heart. Nobody wants to hear about some heartfelt trip to Canada.

Tears came when I thought about all the awful things I had written, and then confirmed to her that they were indeed true. Not out of pity, but out of understanding, she decided to help me with my grades. She cut my reading from eight books to four so I had enough time to finish them before grading time came.

I realized then that Mrs. Seley understood what it was like to be a teenager like no other teacher I had ever met. She didn't help me because she felt sorry for me. She did it because she remembered things that happened in her own life. And she wanted to give me a chance.

That chance made all the difference to me. I had to admit that I couldn't rely on myself to do everything that needed to be done. Sometimes I needed help, and with just a little bit of it, I could pick myself back up and start over again. The stress of that time in my life may have long-term effects on my body (I developed lactose intolerance and irritable bowel syndrome, or IBS, and I am still recovering from my "breakdown"), but the long-term effects on my mind were worth it. I learned more than just nouns and verbs in English that year. I learned that I wasn't alone in the world.

~Nicole Poppino

Unconditional Mom

My mother had a great deal of trouble with me, but I think she enjoyed it.

~Mark Twain

I was a rotten teenager. Not your average spoiled, know-it-all, not-going-to-clean-my-room, getting-an-attitude-because-I'm-15 teenager. No, I was a manipulative, lying, acid-tongued monster, who realized early on that I could make things go my way with just a few minor adjustments. The writers for today's hottest soap opera could not have created a worse "villainess." A few nasty comments here, a lie or two there, maybe an evil glare for a finishing touch, and things would be grand. Or so I thought.

For the most part, and on the outside, I was a good kid. A giggly, pug-nose tomboy who liked to play sports and who thrived on competition (a nice way of saying: somewhat pushy and demanding). Which is probably why most people allowed me to squeak by using what I now call "bulldozer behavior tactics," with no regard for anyone I felt to be of value. For a while, anyway.

Since I was perceptive enough to get some people to bend my way, it amazes me how long it took to realize how I was hurting so many others. Not only did I succeed in pushing away many of my closest friends by trying to control them; I also managed to sabotage, time and time again, the most precious relationship in my life: my relationship with my mother.

Even today, almost 10 years since the birth of the new me, my former behavior astonishes me each time I reach into my memories. Hurtful comments that cut and stung the people I cared most about. Acts of confusion and anger that seemed to rule my every move — all to make sure that things went my way.

My mother, who gave birth to me at age 38 against her doctor's wishes, would cry to me, "I waited so long for you, please don't push me away. I want to help you!"

I would reply with my best face of stone, "I didn't ask for you! I never wanted you to care about me! Leave me alone and forget I ever lived!"

My mother began to believe I really meant it. My actions proved nothing less.

I was mean and manipulative, trying to get my way at any cost. Like many young girls in high school, the boys who I knew were off limits were always the first ones I had to date. Sneaking out of the house at all hours of the night just to prove I could do it. Juggling complex lies that were always on the verge of blowing up in my face. Finding any way to draw attention to myself while simultaneously trying to be invisible.

Ironically, I wish I could say I had been heavy into drugs during that period of my life, swallowing mind-altering pills and smoking things that changed my personality, thus accounting for the terrible, razor-sharp words that came flying from my mouth. However, that was not the case. My only addiction was hatred; my only high was inflicting pain.

But then I asked myself why. Why the need to hurt? And why the people I cared about the most? Why the need for all the lies? Why the attacks on my mother? I would drive myself mad with all the whys until one day, it all exploded in a suicidal rage.

Lying awake the following night at the "resort" (my pet name for the hospital), after an unsuccessful, gutless attempt to jump from a vehicle moving at 80 miles per hour, one thing stood out more than my Keds with no shoe laces. I didn't want to die.

And I did not want to inflict any more pain on people to cover up what I was truly trying to hide myself: self-hatred. Self-hatred unleashed on everyone else.

I saw my mother's pained face for the first time in years — warm, tired brown eyes filled with nothing but thanks for her daughter's new lease on life and love for the child she waited 38 years to bear.

My first encounter with unconditional love. What a powerful feeling.

Despite all the lies I had told her, she still loved me. I cried on her lap for hours one afternoon and asked why she still loved me after all the horrible things I did to her. She just looked down at me, brushed the hair out of my face and said frankly, "I don't know."

A kind of smile penetrated her tears as the lines in her tested face told me all that I needed to know. I was her daughter, but more important, she was my mother. Not every rotten child is so lucky. Not every mother can be pushed to the limits I explored time and time again, and venture back with feelings of love.

Unconditional love is the most precious gift we can give. Being forgiven for the past is the most precious gift we can receive. I dare not say we could experience this pure love twice in one lifetime.

I was one of the lucky ones. I know that. I want to extend the gift my mother gave me to all the "rotten teenagers" in the world who are confused.

It's okay to feel pain, to need help, to feel love — just feel it without hiding. Come out from under the protective covers, from behind the rigid walls and the suffocating personas, and take a breath of life.

~Sarah J. Vogt

Accepting and Asking for Help

The Right Thing

Teenagers want to be able to fight for what's right—but finding
out what's right is now 90 percent of the battle.
~Maggie Stiefvater

The counselor was late for our appointment. I sat in one of the hard plastic chairs in her office that, despite a few squirming attempts to rearrange myself, continued to be uncomfortable. I glanced at the boy who sat beside me, my partner in crime. He looked upset and unsure, wounded by the decision that we had finally made out of desperation. Friends for many years, we now offered each other little comfort as we sat lost in our own thoughts and doubt.

My tingling nerves heightened my senses, and I took in everything around me. From the smell of freshly sharpened pencils to the sight of the overly organized desk, the room oozed with the aura of a disciplined junior high school counselor and I found myself again questioning our judgment in choosing this complete stranger to help save our friend.

She entered in a cloud of smiles and apologies for being late. Sitting down across from us, she looked at us expectantly. I felt as if she were waiting for us to announce that she had just won the lottery rather than tell the story of pain and frustration we had both been holding in for so long.

I was overcome for a moment by the fear that had nested in my stomach. It was hard to imagine how my best friend Suzie would react when she found out that the two people she had trusted most in the world had betrayed her. But selfishly, I was also concerned about how this betrayal would affect me. *Would she hate me? Would she even speak to me?* As much as the pain that she would feel, I contemplated whether or not I would have a best friend the next day.

"Why don't you begin, Kelly, by telling me why you're here?" the counselor suggested. I cast one more glance at my friend; his sad eyes confirmed that we were doing the right thing.

As I began to tell Suzie's story, my uncertainty gave way to a feeling of relief. Carrying the emotional burden of a friend who was slowly killing herself was a lot for a fourteen-year-old to handle, and more than I could stand any longer. Like an exhausted runner, I was passing on the baton for someone else to carry.

By way of my emotional and broken telling, Suzie's story came out. How we laughed at her strange habit of breaking all her food into tiny little pieces, not realizing that by splitting her food up, she could take more time to eat less. How we went along with her self-deprecating jokes about how overweight she was, without realizing that deep inside, she wasn't joking.

The guilt rose in my throat as I related fact after fact, knowing now that all these things should have made us aware months earlier that Suzie actually had a very serious problem. We had pushed it away as she had deteriorated a little at a time. It wasn't until it was almost too late that we had finally understood the big picture.

I explained that the depression that typically walked hand-in-hand with anorexia had closed in on Suzie a few weeks earlier. I had sat by her side, avoiding the sight of her dark-circled eyes and gaunt cheekbones as she told me that she now ate practically nothing at all, and that for no explainable reason, she would often cry for hours.

It was then that I too began to cry. I couldn't stop my tears as I explained how I hadn't known how to stop my friend's tears, either. She had reached a point that terrified me, and the terror in my voice was plain as I revealed the last thing I knew, the thing that had cemented my determination to tell someone: She was looking for an escape from the pain, sadness and feelings of inadequacy that were now constant for her. She thought that killing herself might be that way out.

My part completed, I sat back in disbelief. I had just poured out secret after secret that I had been told with the understanding that I would never speak them again. I had shattered the most sacred aspect of our friendship: trust. A trust that had taken time, love, and good and bad experiences to build had just been destroyed in ten minutes, broken out of helplessness, desperation and the burden that I could no longer bear. I felt weak. I hated myself at that moment.

So did Suzie.

She needed no explanation when she was called to the office. She looked at me, at her boyfriend sitting at my side, at the concerned look of the counselor. The tears of fury that welled up in her eyes said that she understood. As she began to cry out of anger and relief, the counselor gently sent Aaron and me back to class, shutting the door behind us.

I didn't go back to class right away, but instead walked the hallways of the school trying to make sense of the emotional ramblings going through my head. Though I had just possibly saved my friend's life, I felt less than heroic.

I still can recall the overwhelming sadness and fear that surrounded me, as I was sure that my actions had just cost me one of the best friends I'd ever had. But an hour later, Suzie returned from the counseling office, and with tears in her eyes, headed straight into my arms for a hug that I, perhaps even more than she, needed.

It was then that I realized that no matter how angry she was at me, she would still need her best friend to help her get through what was going to be a very difficult journey. I had just learned one of my first lessons of growing up and being a true friend — that it can be hard, and even terrifying, to do what you know is the right thing.

A year later, Suzie handed me my copy of her school picture. In it, she had color in her cheeks again, and the smile that I had missed for so long spread across her face.

And on the back, this message:

Kel,

You were always there for me, whether I wanted you to be or not. Thank you. There's no getting rid of me now — you're stuck with me!

I love you,

Suzie

~Kelly Garnett

Making My Day

Hope is patience with the lamp lit.
~Tertullian

f life was a journey, then I, at age thirteen, had given up. On the outside, I was perfect. Talented, athletic, and prim, I was the girl who teachers counted on and parents asked their daughters to invite over. I befriended new students and cleaned my friends' rooms after sleepovers. I never said a word of gossip and had won countless "student of the month" awards.

Yet I was haunted by demons. I held a secret from the world, a secret I rarely let out. I was smart and calculating, and I never showed chinks in my armor. But my flawless demeanor is what eventually did me in.

Depression is difficult to describe to someone who isn't familiar with it. It shows itself in many ways: anger, emotional detachment, fatigue, loss of interest. Or it may simply be a crushing, unexplainable sense of failure. Simply put, it's not finding inner strength to live.

That's where I found myself at age thirteen. Hopeless. I was seeing a therapist after my mother had finally gotten tired of the fake smiles and black moods, but even with Kim's sensible advice and years of experience, something was deeply missing. I simply could not go on.

One dreary day in January, I leaned heavily against my school locker as the lunch bell rang. I had received a homework assignment from Kim the day before: to write a list of my best friends and why

I liked them. My problem with this task was that I couldn't think of people for my list. I had companions, but at that point in my life I couldn't bring myself to care much about anyone, including myself.

I slammed my locker and faced the throng of seventh graders on their way to lunch. I ran through them in my head, wondering who I could possibly include on my list. So many different faces passed, but none that I would die without. I sighed. It was official: I was going to flunk therapy.

"Hey," said a small voice to my right. I looked down and saw Luz, a girl in my grade. Luz was short and soft-spoken with something good to say about everybody. Her big eyes held a sweet soul that made her quite well liked. I had always had a fondness for Luz, but had never known her very well. Even so, looking at her accepting smile lifted my spirits a bit.

"Hey, Luz," I greeted. "How are you?"

"Great. Say, you got a haircut!"

I fingered my short hair, genuinely pleased that she had taken notice of me.

"Yeah," I murmured.

"You look really, really pretty," Luz exclaimed. "You're gorgeous!"

I blinked twice.

"Really?"

"Totally."

"Luz!" a voice called from down the hall.

"Got to go," Luz said. "Bye!"

She trotted down the hall.

"Gorgeous," I whispered to myself. "I'm gorgeous."

Watching Luz scamper down the school hallway, I had a bit of a revelation. I wasn't happy. In fact, I was clinically depressed. Each day was going to be a struggle, and ultimately I might lose. But seeing a person who was so good to the core shook me a bit. It reminded me, however briefly, of the happiness in the world. It gave me hope.

"Luz!" I yelled.

You see, happiness, at least for me, is slow to come and quick to leave. Life is a journey, but the pursuit of that precious thing we call happiness is more than a journey. It's a challenge that some, like Luz, seem to have already conquered. Like her name, Luz, which means light, she lit up the darkness for me.

As I opened my mouth, I took that light that Luz had unknowingly offered.

"Luz!" I called again.

My new friend turned. There was so much I wanted to say. Thank you. You're prettier than I could ever be, inside and out. God bless you.

What I said instead came straight from the heart.

"Luz, wait up. I'm coming with you."

~Monica Quijano

Chapter
8

Create Your Best Future

Powering Through Challenges

USA vs. My Mom

*The turning point in the process of growing up is when you
discover the core of strength within you that survives all hurt.*

~Max Lerner

n 2012, 1,276,099 people were arrested for possession of a controlled substance in the United States, according to one website
that I researched. My mother was one of them. I would have
never thought my mom would end up in prison over prescription
medication. I didn't know you could get addicted to something a doctor
prescribed. But ever since my parents separated in 2007, my mom had
abused her prescription medication.

Mom has been diagnosed with a number of things, including
scoliosis and depression. Along with those diagnoses came several
medicines: Oxycontin, Percocet, and Xanax are a few that come to
mind. These are highly addictive medications. I believe her addiction
started when I was in sixth grade. Her friends would come over, and
she'd tell me to go to my room because they were having "adult talk." I
wasn't ignorant as to what was really going on; I knew she abused her
medicine. She crushed up her pills and used a straw or a broken pen
to snort them. Once I asked why she didn't just take them by mouth
and she replied that they worked faster when she snorted them.
I didn't really understand why she needed the medicine.

Mom had a new boyfriend when I was in seventh grade. He paid
for our apartment, bought her a car, and always made sure we had

food and necessities. He seemed like an okay guy, but then I found out that he abused prescription medication too. They were both looking for a better life and somehow they thought that abusing drugs was the answer. They were always nodding off. Holding a conversation with them was nearly impossible. They would drool and mumble things to themselves. Their eyes would roll back and their bodies were lifeless at all hours of the day. If they even started to come down from their high, they would do more drugs.

My mom wasn't my mom anymore. I became angry; I was tired of watching her do that to herself. It was as if she had just forgotten about me, like she didn't care about me anymore. I would come home from school and find her passed out. I would run to her with tears rolling down my face because I thought she was dead.

Then my mom and her boyfriend started to sell prescription medications. A guy would give them a certain amount to sell, and they would bring the money back to him and get a piece of it. They claimed it was just "easy money" until they got back on their feet and got real jobs. We always had random people coming and going at our house. This happened throughout the day and even during the night.

Sometime after they started dealing, my mom and her boyfriend began making trips with groups of people to Florida. In Florida, they would all visit multiple doctors' offices as new patients, get prescriptions, and then go to multiple pharmacies to get the scripts filled. My mom made these trips several times a year. She was trafficking drugs across state lines, a federal offense. In 2011, a group of six people, including my mom, split up into two vehicles and drove down to Florida. On their return, the Georgia State Police pulled over one of the vehicles — one that my mom wasn't in.

I don't know exactly what happened, but they were released and drove back to Kentucky. About a month later, they were arrested in Somerset, Kentucky and held in Pulaski County Detention Center. The police offered them a deal — if they named the others involved in the drug activity, they would get reduced sentences. So, they spoke out against my mom and the others involved. On January 31, 2012, a U.S. Marshall found my mother and arrested her. I found out via text message that my mother had been taken to jail. It was the worst day of my life.

I would go to Pulaski County Detention Center about twice a week to see my mom. You were only allowed thirty-minute visits, and you had to sit behind a glass window and talk through a nasty telephone that didn't work half the time. Most of our visits ended in tears or fights.

My mom went before the judge on September 11, 2012 and pleaded guilty to the drug charges. I went with my grandmother to watch the trial. We sat in the last row and saw my mom enter through the side door in handcuffs and foot cuffs, as if she were a dangerous criminal. She started crying when she saw me, and I did too. I will never forget when the judge asked her if she had anything else to say. Despite the judge's warning not to look into the seats behind her, my mom turned to face me. With tears rolling down her cheeks, she apologized and told me how much she loved me. It absolutely broke my heart.

The judge sentenced her to fifty-seven to seventy-one months in prison, due to the counts and her criminal history. At first it didn't hit me that it would be a long time until my mom was back in my life. But now, two years into her sentence, I realize how much time together we have lost; time that we will never get back.

My mom used to be a powerful, independent, lovely woman. She was a single mom, had a job and a house. She was even thinking about going to college to further her education in childcare. Now, she is residing in a federal prison camp, about eight hours away from me. We usually get five-minute phone calls once a week. I haven't seen my mom in over a year. I haven't hugged my mom since January 1, 2012.

I can't help but wonder what our lives could have been like if she hadn't used prescription drugs. I watched her ruin her life with prescription medication, and because of that, I will never have a normal life. My mom hasn't had a chance to see me go to my high school proms. She hasn't been there to help me through the most important times in a teenage girl's life. I graduated high school in May of 2014, and my mom wasn't able to see it. I started college in August of 2014, and she missed that too.

It has had a huge impact on me, but I have come out on top of this situation. I took AP classes in high school, while also holding down a part-time job and participating in extracurricular school activities. My family has told me that they don't know how I'm living with this, that they would break if they were put in my position. But in all reality, you can't stop living when you have a life-changing experience. Life goes on, and someday it's going to get better. I don't feel sorry for myself. I accomplish a lot more that way.

~McKenzie Vaught

A Hand Up

The only thing that overcomes hard luck is hard work.
~Harry Golden

"There was a fire yesterday." My mother's voice was matter of fact. "The shop and the apartment are in pretty bad shape. You can't come home. There's no place to come to right now and we don't have money to pay for you to stay in college. So you have to decide what to do."

Stunned, I asked a few questions, hung up the phone and fled to the Resident Advisor's room in tears.

I was nineteen years old, in my sophomore spring at the University of Michigan, 600 miles from my New Jersey home. A home that no longer had a place for me.

"No one died," the RA soothed. "It's only stuff. In two months the semester is done. Then you can figure out what's next." At about twenty-two or twenty-three years old, she probably hadn't dealt with anything more traumatic from her undergraduate charges than a breakup with a boyfriend or disagreements between roommates.

No one died, except I felt my dream of a degree from this university slipping away. And I was on my own to keep it alive.

Since I'd been twelve, the third daughter of a family in a blue-collar mill town, my father had supported my dream to pursue a science degree at a big university. Less than a quarter of the students from our local high school went on to college. Most who did stayed nearby and became teachers, nurses, learned a trade, or took a factory job. A mere handful of the two hundred in my senior class ventured away from their roots, yet Dad never questioned my decision to leave the state for a campus I'd not even seen, and he promised to help as much as he could.

As soon as I was old enough I'd worked at jobs ranging from writing a newspaper column, sales clerking at department stores, dispensing ice cream at Dairy Queen, and lifeguarding at the Y, socking away as much as I could toward my goal. I also graduated as valedictorian with an assortment of small scholarship awards. That, plus what Dad could send me from month to month, had gotten me to that April of the second year, and that phone call.

I confided my plight to a favorite professor, one who really took time with students who shared his passion for biological sciences. "Go to the Dean of Women," he advised.

The Dean of Women? In a huge university, what was one undergrad in the grand scheme of things?

To my surprise, she was approachable and sympathetic, but skeptical. "Unless you want to drop out and put off finishing a degree until you are in a more stable situation, I'd advise you to enroll in summer school. You don't need to stay in the dorm; you might find a cheap apartment. I don't know how you're going to make it."

"I can't drop out. I have nowhere to go and I'd still need to find a job and a place to live. And I'm afraid if I quit now, starting again will be even harder." Threaded through my desperate anxiety I heard my father's voice from all the times life had thrown us a curve: "We'll always manage." And we did.

"Okay," the Dean said. "Here's a deal. If you can get yourself through summer classes, I'll give you a tuition grant for the fall and allow you to move to an approved rooming house. You'll pay rent, but can probably economize on meals and piece together some jobs."

Piece together jobs and study? Economize? That sounded familiar from the prior six years of my life. I was flooded with gratitude for the chance to continue toward a degree and I understood her clever challenge. If I could manage the next four months myself I'd have earned her faith in me plus the grant-in-aid she held out as a reward in the autumn.

"Deal," I said. "I'll make it somehow."

After final exams that June I took the train for a brief trip to New Jersey. My dad's one-man glass and picture frame business had indeed been heavily damaged. But true to his nature, he'd cleaned up the debris and taken out a bank loan to replace the inventory, which was not insured, then hired carpenters to make the apartment livable. My younger sister had moved in with the family of a high school friend in exchange for babysitting and housework. I'd have to replace the summer clothes that weren't with me in Ann Arbor, and years later I came to the strange realization that I had almost no documented past. No high school yearbook, no family pictures, keepsakes, artwork, or award-winning essays.

Back in Ann Arbor that summer, I housesat in the basement apartment of a professor on sabbatical — rent-free — worked in the cafeteria at my former dormitory, took classes, and scoured the bulletin boards on campus for psychology experiments paying subjects twenty dollars in any study concocted by a grad student.

Also, for the rest of my college career, I sold my blood once a month for thirty dollars to a medical research team who needed fresh, not bank, blood. And, of course, I borrowed money.

College wasn't the fun time for me that it is for so many young people. When I feel a tinge of regret, it passes when I measure it against what I gained in maturity and determination, self-reliance and ingenuity, which served me well when later employed in research. Those years were invaluable in coping with life's later difficulties. And they imbued me with a belief about what can be accomplished if you truly want it badly enough to work for it.

Recently, my husband and I endowed a modest scholarship granted each year, not to a high school senior, but to a student entering the final year toward any degree, one who has a student loan. This unusual scholarship reflects the Dean of Women's challenge to me that awful spring of the fire. It also reflects the attitude of my father and my husband.

"First show me how much you will do to attain what you say you want, then I'll help you."

~Ann Vitale

Redefining
Limitations

Life shrinks or expands in proportion to one's courage.
~Anaïs Nin

I sat in the guidance counselor's office my senior year of high school, bright eyed about the possibilities of college. The counselor sighed and pushed her glasses onto her head. "Are you sure you want to go to college?" she asked. "It will be difficult with your limitations, you know." My limitation, as she called it, was diabetes. I was in three AP classes, a varsity athlete on the track and field team, and nationally ranked in Speech and Debate. But according to her, I was limited.

"Well," I hesitated, unsure of how to respond to her question. Was I sure? Yes, I was absolutely sure that I wanted to go to college. But I started to feel a gnawing monster in my belly, questioning my ability to succeed. Later that night at home, I helped my mom fold laundry in the living room. "What would you think if I just went to community college for a while and figured it out?" I asked her.

She looked at me, confused. My mother had left school to start a family. "What do you mean, figure it out?" I told her about my meeting with the guidance counselor, and watched her face change from confusion to anger. I was glad my mom was by my side for this battle, because I had a feeling it would turn into full-on war.

I talked to the admissions counselor at the school I really wanted to go to. All I was missing was my official high school transcript. I promised to have it in the mail the next day, and took a stamped envelope with my forms to the guidance office. Two weeks later, I received a rejection letter, and I called the admissions counselor in tears. "You promised!" I sobbed into the phone, disconsolate about what I perceived to be my dream school. Soothing me over the phone, she pulled up my file, and told me that they never received my official transcript. I never saw anger in color until that afternoon. I called my high school and demanded answers. I sat for hours in the guidance suite, and brought a ferocious mama bear with me. We couldn't prove anything, and my counselor's simpering smile totally and utterly defeated me.

I was burning. I knew that I could not lie down and accept defeat because then my "limitation" would win. I revamped my college efforts, and eventually accepted a track scholarship to Cabrini College, where I spent four magnificent years growing into a woman that I can be proud of. After the track team was cut for budgetary reasons, I focused on social justice, a specialty of Cabrini. I had started insulin pump therapy my freshman year, which gave me an entirely new outlook on living with diabetes. I was able to throw myself into the service of others.

During January of my senior year, I went on a life-changing mission trip called Rostro de Cristo to a small town called Durán in Ecuador. The week I spent there with my classmates and the wonderful residents of that town created memories that I will never forget. The people, the places, the food—they all hold a special place in my heart.

As I sat on the concrete ground of a schoolyard in Ecuador that week, with a child on each knee, I thought about how lucky I was to have had that guidance counselor in my life. The devastation of what she did to me propelled me to do my best and pursue my passions. As José fingered the tubing coming out of my pocket, I gently explained to him in broken Spanish that it was for my diabetes. He hugged me tightly, taking my breath away, and stood at the gate each day to hug me as we came into the school.

That mission trip lit a fire in me for helping others, and when I got back to the States, I filled out applications for yearlong service opportunities. I graduated in 2012 with two bachelor degrees and my teaching certification, along with high honors and accolades from the honors college. I was accepted by the Mercy Volunteer Corps and went to serve at the Navajo Nation Indian Reservation in rural Arizona. I spent the year after graduation teaching high school U.S. Government and Psychology, and working as a part-time secretary. Now, I am in grad school full-time and working in a high school in North Philadelphia as I study to become a reading specialist.

I still have diabetes, and unless there is a breakthrough, I will always have diabetes. What I don't have are limitations. My ability to serve others and to teach — that's something diabetes cannot take away from me. They are something an out-of-touch counselor cannot take away from me. My biggest "limitation" was not my endocrine system, but my inability to believe in myself. Once I overcame that fear, I realized nothing could stop me from reaching for the stars.

From the streets of Ecuador, to the hogans of the Navajo Nation, to my cluttered classroom in Philadelphia, nothing can limit me. Have insulin pump, will travel.

~Jamie Tadrzynski

Celebrate Life

Life presents as many opportunities for happiness as it does for tragedy.

~Rudolph Giuliani

Last night I attended a bar mitzvah that would have been inspirational at any time, but for the three-hundred-plus who attended in the aftermath of the events of September 11, 2001, it was an amazing, life-affirming experience. I am sharing this story because I believe that many will find comfort from the stories shared with our congregation by a thirteen-year-old boy.

Like many citizens across the nation, my husband and I felt the need to be with people immediately following September 11, and planned to attend the Friday night Shabbat service at the Birmingham Temple of Farmington Hills, Michigan. During the drive, I read from the temple bulletin that a bar mitzvah would be celebrated. I was surprised and hoped it would be postponed, preferring the focus of the evening to be on making sense of the week's events. Tragically, the adult son of a favorite temple friend had been on the ninety-fourth floor of the World Trade Center, and I knew it would be a sad night as we all struggled to digest this personal and national tragedy.

We arrived to find the parking lot filled and the temple crowded. Many apparently felt the need to come together. The service began with beautiful, mournful music. Then Rabbi Sherwin Wine spoke at length about the horrors of the terrorist attacks. He stated that we had two purposes for being there this night. The first was to mourn the victims, including the son of Skip Rosenthal, Joshua Rosenthal, a fine man who had grown up worshipping at the temple and was well known to many present. The second purpose was to thwart the terrorists' desire to demoralize us by continuing to celebrate life-cycle events—in this case, a bar mitzvah, the "coming of age" of a Jewish boy.

Next, family members of the bar mitzvah boy read passages about milestones, family, dignity, power and peace.

Then Rabbi Wine introduced Jackson, the bar mitzvah boy. At our Humanistic Judaism temple, it is the custom of bar and bat mitzvah students to spend the year prior to their thirteenth birthday researching the life of a Jewish hero or heroine, and apply lessons from their hero's actions to their own life. Tonight, the Rabbi stated, Jackson would be our teacher.

Jackson climbed the box placed behind the podium and faced the packed room, grinning. Proudly he announced that he had chosen to share the story of the life of Solly Gonor. Jackson had read his book, *Light One Candle: A Survivor's Tale from Lithuania to Jerusalem*, about how, as a twelve-year-old boy in Germany, Solly had endured unspeakable hardships to keep himself and his father alive during the Nazi regime. Jackson had managed to locate Solly, now a seventy-four-year-old living in Israel, and began a year-long e-mail correspondence.

Jackson told us how Solly, as a twelve-year-old himself, enjoyed sports and hanging out with friends, when suddenly he was no longer free and was in danger because of his Jewish identity. Solly's family missed a chance to leave the country, and after they were forced from their home, hid briefly with five other families in a barn. In the middle of the night, Solly's father woke them and led them out of the barn just as soldiers arrived. The family watched in horror as everyone in hiding was forced out, forced to dig their own graves, and shot, one by one.

Jackson shared a story about how the Gonor family lived for a period in the Kaunas ghetto, where Solly endured hunger and cold.

Solly was bravely able to retrieve food thrown over the ghetto wall by a boy who had been a friend before the war, each risking his life to make a midnight run to the barbed-wire fence when the guards were not looking. Boredom was another hardship, as the Germans banned one of the Jews' last remaining pleasures by ordering the collection and destruction of all books. Knowing he risked his life, Solly and a friend hid books in a forbidden part of the ghetto. Solly grieved when his former math teacher was found with a book and shot. Solly attributes his ability to stay alive in the ghetto to his friendships with two other teens, both of whom later died in concentration camps.

Solly's family was sent from the ghetto to a work camp, and then to a concentration camp. It was there that he was separated from his mother, and promised that he would keep his father alive. Jackson told us about Solly's heart-wrenching experiences at the camp, but also about how Solly used his wits to keep himself and his father fed and clothed.

Finally, the Germans had an idea that the Jewish prisoners would build them a fort, and sent them on a death march through miles of snow-covered roads. Here Solly, in his fatigue, lost track of his father. Eventually, Solly collapsed beside a tree, where he truly believed he would die. He fell asleep. A Japanese American soldier, who awakened him and lifted him out of the snow, told him he was free. Solly was later reunited with his father, who had been taken to a hospital. Just five years ago, Solly was reunited with the soldier who found him in Israel. This reunion brought back many memories that Solly had long suppressed, and that was when he began to write his book. Jackson stated that he had committed himself to telling Solly's story of courage.

When Jackson finished speaking, the entire congregation stood and loudly applauded his moving presentation. As the clapping finally slowed, Jackson announced that he had one more part to his bar mitzvah. He stated that, "Due to the closing of the airports this week, none of the out-of-towners has been able to come in for this night, except for one. That person is… Solly Gonor!" A gasp went through the entire room. Jackson proceeded, "Since Mr. Gonor was not able to celebrate his bar mitzvah when he was thirteen, I would like him to join me now."

A white-haired man in the front row stood and slowly made his way up to the podium next to Jackson. The crowd stood and applauded wildly. For several minutes, Mr. Gonor stood with his hand over his eyes, struggling to regain his composure. Then Jackson and Mr. Gonor read together, first in Hebrew, then in English.

After the reading Mr. Gonor addressed us, stating that he never expected that his experiences would one day be an inspiration to a thirteen-year-old boy. He stated that he was glad he had been able to make the journey from Israel and meet his e-mail pen pal.

Mr. Gonor's story reminded us that evil in the world is not new, but that the human spirit and will to survive is strong. At a time when many of us were asking how we could bear the sadness of the days following September 11, we were reminded of those who suffered through years of Nazi cruelty, as well as people in countries all over the world where terrorism is a way of life. We were reminded by thirteen-year-old Jackson that we must, indeed, continue to celebrate life.

Our evening ended by standing together and singing "Ayfo Oree." The words, translated from Hebrew, are as follows:

Where is my light? My light is in me.
Where is my hope? My hope is in me.
Where is my strength? My strength is in me.
And in you.

~Caroline Broida Trapp

Life Rolls On

In three words I can sum up everything I've learned about life.
It goes on.
~Robert Frost

was about nine the first time I got on a board. Something inside of me connected to surfing unlike any other sport. I had played a bunch of different sports, like baseball, soccer and hockey, but surfing became my true life passion. I never regretted walking away from all other sports in the pursuit of surfing.

By the time I was eleven or twelve, I began to compete in surfing. Before long, I was rated number one in the Juniors level of the Pacific Surf Series. I was featured in surfing articles and magazines, and companies began sponsoring me.

I began traveling to surfing competitions to some of the most beautiful places in the world. Things were really looking up. My lifelong dream of becoming a professional surfer was finally on the verge of becoming a reality. Then came the day when my life changed forever.

I woke up like on any other day. I watched a little bit of a surf movie to pump myself up for my surf session. I was excited; the waves were going to be so good. I called my friends. When I pulled up to the beach at Zuma, the waves looked great. I put my wetsuit on and surfed for a while; then I caught this one perfect south swell peak. I stood up backside and pulled in the barrel. As I came out of the tube, the wave hit me in my back so fast that I didn't have time to put my hands up. I hit my head on a sandbar beneath the surface of the water. My whole body went numb and tingly, then I was floating face down — unable to move. When the next wave flipped me over, I yelled for help. At first nobody came to help me, then finally my best friend, Brad, came over to me. I told him, "You gotta keep my head out of the water or I'm gonna drown!"

With the help of another friend, Brett, Brad was able to get me out of the water and onto the beach. I *knew* I was paralyzed. As I lay on my back, my dreams of becoming a pro surfer, of having a wife and kids, and my hopes of being in a big surf movie flashed in front of my eyes. *What was going to happen to me? What kind of a life would I have if I was paralyzed forever? This can't happen to me!* Guess what? It did.

I was taken by helicopter to UCLA Medical Center where it was determined that I had suffered a severe spinal cord injury, just like Christopher Reeve. With the flip of a wave, I had become a quadriplegic with no sensation or movement below my mid-chest. In that split second, my surfing days as I had known them were over. With only limited use of my arms and hands, I spent most of my time in intensive care units and rehab hospitals instead of in the water surfing. My worst nightmare had come true, and I was forced to deal with it.

As bad as it was, and it was very bad sometimes, I surprised myself by maintaining the will to live. I can't really say what made me go from not wanting to live if I couldn't surf — to embracing life without surfing — but by some miracle, it happened. Instead of being angry or afraid, I realized how fortunate I had been the first seventeen years of my life. I realized that I was still better off and more fortunate than some others. I had surfed the world — more than many could ever say.

That fall, I returned to school. I was elected Homecoming King, which was pretty cool, and ended up graduating on time. Shortly after my high school graduation, I enrolled at San Diego State University, stayed as busy as I was before the accident and graduated. I've got to say that I'm living my life to the fullest.

Every year, I speak to thousands of students in schools across the country. I really want kids to know that dreams can change and life can turn out different from what we sometimes expect. At the start of an assembly, I show a video of me surfing in competitions, rippin' on the waves and everything. They expect to see this high-profile surfer coming to speak to them, and then I come out in a wheelchair. They just don't anticipate that at all. I talk about the fact that my life has really just begun. I explain to them about the importance of family and friends. I tell them about how, since the accident, I've gone out on wave runners, gone waterskiing and inner tubing, played wheelchair tennis and ping pong, competed in a billiards tournament — playing pool with the best of them — and have even jumped out of an airplane skydiving!

I've traveled to places like Australia, France, Mexico, Spain, Italy and all over the United States. So many people have gotten behind me. Celebrities have helped me raise public awareness of the need to find a cure for spinal injuries, and I've also hung out with some very cool, great musicians.

But the highlight of my life since my injury came nearly four years after that fateful day. It took surfers like world champions Rob Machado, Kelly Slater and my brother Josh, and the guys from the Paskowitz Surfing Camp to figure out just how to get me back on a board again — and they did it.

I finally got back in the water that I had missed so much — on a surfboard. They rigged a board so that I could hold on to something and ride the waves. I ride lying down, more like a body boarder would, but hey, it's still surfing to me. It's different — but I'm in the water.

Some people kind of freak out, thinking about me out in the water surfing again, but I don't even think about the danger. I've got a lot of trust in my abilities and the people around me. I make my own path, my own decisions. I'm the last one who wants to get hurt. Still, if it weren't for the help of my buds, I might not have ever had the chance to get back out there. I don't know of another quadriplegic in the world who surfs.

I believe that someday I'll regain some use of my paralyzed limbs. It is no longer a question of if, but *when*. I'll be ready, when the time comes, to take advantage of the breakthroughs in modern medicine. I know I'll never achieve my dream of being the world's greatest surfer, but dreams are abundant. I still have so many that are just as worthy and exciting — so many dreams that I have yet to achieve. I know that I've got a lot of living left to do. Life rolls on, waves continue to roll on and I'm rollin' and surfing right along with it all.

~Jesse Billauer

Editor's note: To find out more about Jesse and his organization, Life Rolls On, log on to www.liferollson.org.

Seeing the Real Me

Nothing splendid has ever been achieved except by those who dared believe that something inside of them was superior to circumstance.

~Bruce Barton

During the first part of my life, I was a victim of circumstance. I was born, one of three blind or legally blind children, to a blind mother and to an angry, alcoholic father. I became a shy, withdrawn, and frightened young girl who pretended to be invisible as the stress of my home life became unbearable. My father was abusive and although my mother was loving and kind, she was not strong enough to protect her young children from this angry alcoholic who held us prisoner.

To escape this fearful environment, I would run away to my grandparents' home where I would stay for the warmth and safety. When we attended church, I recall a man standing in the pulpit, yelling, screaming, and banging his fists. This frightened me even more and I withdrew further. I learned that God was a strong, punishing God and we had better be good, or else.

My grandparents loved me very much and became overprotective. I allowed them to do everything for me — they tied my shoes, dressed me — and I became dependent on them. Fearful to tell anyone of the anger and physical abuse at the hands of my father, I became non-verbal. When I went to school I was diagnosed as "uneducatably retarded" and sent to a mental facility. I felt like a true misfit.

Luckily, I had a kind and loving caregiver who saw something special in me. One day while she brushed my hair, I started talking to her. She soon realized my brain was not the problem, but my limited vision. She fought and successfully lobbied on my behalf to have me placed in a special classroom for the visually impaired called the "sight-saving class." I started to feel more comfortable, and with time, fit into the program. I realized that I could read the letters if they were big and black. I liked learning, and liked the positive attention I received when I did good work.

I began to let go of some of my fears. I struggled socially, but learned to reject fear and to challenge myself. At first when I was bullied and teased I ran away because that's what I had always done. Then, with some encouragement, I began to reject the bullying and teasing. I faced the bullies with determination and courage, and did not run away. Finally, they stopped teasing me and left me alone.

Then they came to tell me that I would be going to a regular high school in the fall! What? Were they crazy? Me, attend a regular high school with "normal students"? All of the old fears returned and I became a shy, frightened, and withdrawn child again. But with support and encouragement, I did attend high school that fall.

The first year was horrible. I was teased and bullied about my limited vision. I felt ugly. The pushing, bumping into me, and the name-calling all became too much and I ran away.

A special uncle invited me to visit and stay with him on the family farm. There, I found a whole new freedom. I could fall down and get back up, all by myself. Isn't this what life is all about? I had the freedom to play and laugh. I hid in the hayloft and began to discover the true me. Also, I had the love and encouragement to try everything. Among other things, I found a whole new Lynn emerging.

As I learned to get around the farm using my other senses, I grew more independent. I was opening up and blossoming into a beautiful young woman. I started to believe in myself. In high school, I worked hard at my studies and other students wanted to be my friend. I finally felt normal and accepted as part of the group. At first I thought I had to be a people-pleaser for others to like me. But that was not true. Eventually, I started making good friendships, dating, and found that people liked me for me!

When I graduated from high school, I went on to York University in Toronto, Ontario and participated in the social work program. I worked part-time at Sunnybrook Hospital as an admittance clerk, moved out of the dorm, and shared an apartment with my cousin Diane. One day we went shopping together. I bravely started to look at a few racks of clothes by myself. As I ran my hands over a few blouses I turned and wanted to go on to the next rack of clothes. All of a sudden someone walked right in front of me. I excused myself and moved to the left. Again the person stepped right in front of me. Giggling a bit, I excused myself again and moved to the right. Again the person moved right in front of me. Someone teasing me. As I raised my hand to give the person a little push to get out of the way, I realized I was arguing with a reflection of myself in a full-length mirror. How embarrassing! My cousin Diane was laughing hysterically! Instead of running away and hiding, I also laughed and learned it is okay to do dumb things and laugh about them. Humour is a wonderful part of life.

Eventually I got married and became a wife, mother, grandmother, and a very successful businesswoman in my community. And, like a beautiful butterfly, I emerged as the bold, sassy and independent woman that I am today. I am an entrepreneur with my own business, and I am a professional speaker, author, teacher, and mentor/coach. I believe my mission is to share my story and learning experiences so that other people can overcome their fears and obstacles to achieve their dreams and goals. Life is worth living and you need to take charge of your own destiny. Dreams do come true!

I did not allow my circumstances to stop me. I did not allow my disability to block me. Nor, did I allow fear to prevent me from suc-ceeding and becoming the person I am today. Neither should you! "Don't allow anyone or anything to keep you down."

~Lynn Fitzsimmons

Turning "I Can't" into "How Can I?"

Optimism is the foundation of courage.
~Nicholas Murray Butler

Because I was born with severe cerebral palsy, my parents—eager to find help for my condition—moved us from Iran to the United States when I was only eighteen months old. And if that were not challenge enough, I would later discover that for most of my life, I had been stalked by two killers. But first, some background.

I grew up attending schools where having a handicapped student was novel, but that never proved to be a problem for me. I always felt accepted by my classmates and everyone at school. From my wheelchair vantage point, going through grade school and high school was fun and fulfilling.

Growing up, I assumed I could never move out of my parents' supportive home and have the kind of college experience most teens do. You see, I'd always relied on my parents for the most basic of tasks. Every morning, they would help me get out of bed and stumble to the bathroom, then assist me with showering, brushing my teeth, and so on. Then they'd help me get dressed and ease me into my ever-present wheelchair—not to mention feed me, gather my books, and get me off to school.

Doing things teenagers normally do—rebelling, demanding freedom, taking risks—was a wistful, daunting proposition for me, because I depended on my parents so much. I believed nobody else would help me. So I ignored and suppressed my desire to go off to university. After I completed two years at a nearby community college, I thought I'd have to attend a university within driving distance of my parents' house, get dropped off for classes, picked up afterwards—the same old drill. What choice did I have?

As I watched my classmates finish community college and move on, I felt empty inside. And angry. I wanted to be moving on with them. Sure, I should be happy making the Dean's List and getting good grades. But countless times, I got stuck in the thought, "If I weren't handicapped, I'd be living on my own and creating a great life at college like my peers."

Then one day, my humanities professor at the community college suggested I move out of the house and apply to the University of Southern California. "You're nuts," I wanted to tell him. "How could you possibly understand the effort and intricacy it takes for me to meet my basic needs every day—let alone live away from home?"

But I must admit, because someone else could see the possibility, I was inspired. Why should I weigh myself down with limited thinking? Why stop my creative mind from exploring possibilities and solving challenges that living on campus would present? In asking these questions, I realized the powerful difference between saying "I can't" and asking "how can I?"

By saying "I can't," I was already beaten; by asking "how can I?" my brain would automatically churn out possible solutions. I figured that since my brain is just like any other muscle, the more I used it, the stronger it would get. So when my professor planted the thought that I really could achieve my dream of living independently on campus, my desire came alive.

Don't get me wrong. My deciding to go to USC wasn't as simple as packing my bags, telling Mom and Dad to "just send money," and wheeling myself out the door. It became a long, grueling journey fueled by research, sacrifice, and problem-solving along the way. I had to explore all kinds of things, such as getting assistants to help me, not only with attending classes and taking tests, but also with meals and getting me ready in the morning and at night. Could I possibly find one person to do all of this? Could I chop up the tasks among several people? What could I realistically handle on my own without assistance? Simply asking questions helped me formulate solutions short of requiring my parents to drive back and forth every day to help me. That would defeat the whole purpose.

Not long after starting my search, I found a roommate willing to help me in the mornings and at night, so I got that part covered. Then, in my classes, I figured out that by making friends, I could ask for assistance with issues that came up like helping me type papers. I had to arrange taking tests with staff members in the office of disability; they would provide me with someone to fill in my answers on the tests. On a regular basis, I'd have to meet a friend or hire an assistant to help me at lunch and dinner. Getting these arrangements set up meant I could enjoy a fabulous new experience — living on campus for two years.

If orchestrating all of this seems like a big chore, believe me, it was. Imagine having to coordinate every "mundane" task around the schedules of several other people. No way can I say having to jump through so many hoops was "fair." But long before this, I had decided I could sit back with a "life's not fair" attitude and wallow in "being right," or I could accept my situation and figure out ways to even the playing field going forward.

Yes, it sounds corny to say it out loud, but I truly believe life is what we make of it. I'm proud to say I relied on my positive thinking and made living on my own at university happen. No, my disability didn't go away. I didn't "overcome" cerebral palsy. I can assure you I still have it. But I discovered the identity of those two killers I mentioned, the ones who had been dogging me, and so many other people. They're dream killers — negative thinking and reduced expectations. They add a highly destructive element to the world. Yet no one has to accept these deal breakers, no matter what disability comes with the package.

Sure, it may be okay for some to settle for a "safe" job with a "decent" mate and say they're happy because they're "secure" in this world. But like negative thinking, reduced expectations and safe choices destroy the essence of life.

Don't get me wrong. I don't suggest rashly rushing into new things. On the contrary, having cerebral palsy has given me the ability to patiently assess situations before ever moving forward. That's how I methodically and sensibly achieved my dream of living on campus while earning a marketing degree.

Today, I run my own business as a professional speaker, business consultant, and award-winning author. And what keeps me going is constantly asking—and answering—these two questions: How can I do what seems impossible? And how can I love my life just the way it is?

~Sourena Vasseghi

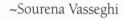

The Greatest Gift

Never does the human soul appear so strong as when it foregoes
revenge and dares to forgive an injury.
~Edwin Hubbell Chapin

Whenever a stranger hears my accent and asks where I'm from, I want to answer: I was born in Paradise. For me, growing up in Rwanda *was* paradise.

My tiny African homeland is so breathtakingly beautiful it's impossible not to see God's hand in her mist-shrouded mountains, lush green hills and sparkling lakes. But it was the beauty of the people that made Rwanda so idyllic to my young heart.

Everyone in our little village got along like a big, happy family. As a youngster I wasn't even aware our country had two tribes — the majority Hutu (then numbering 7 million of Rwanda's 8.2 million inhabitants) and the minority Tutsi, of which I was a member.

I never felt unsafe or threatened when I was out playing and was the happiest girl in the world at home surrounded by the warmth and affection of my three doting brothers and the most loving, protective parents imaginable.

My parents were teachers and looked up to in the community. There was always a place at our table for anyone in need, and people traveled from miles around to seek my parents' advice and counsel.

But things were not as they seemed. My parents had shielded me from the simmering ethnic tensions in our land. When I was twenty-four years old those tensions erupted in a storm of violence that forever swept away the paradise I knew as a child.

On April 7th, 1994, the Rwandan's president's plane was shot down and extremist Hutu politicians unleashed a diabolic plot. All commerce was shut down and it was announced on the radio that the business of the nation would be killing Tutsis. Seven million Hutus were commanded to pick up a machete and carry out the following orders: *Kill every Tutsi you know, kill every Tutsi you see, kill every Tutsi man, woman, child, and infant — kill them all, leave none alive.*

Hatred enveloped the hearts of people I had known and trusted all my life — neighbors, teachers, schoolmates and friends.

When the killing began, hundreds of terrified Tutsi families swarmed to our home seeking sanctuary. But when my father saw the heavily armed government militia surrounding our property, he feared the worst and hurriedly pressed his rosary into my hand.

"Run to the pastor's house," he urged, "he is Hutu, but he is a good man and will hide you. Go, Immaculée… go *now!*"

I spent the next three months crammed into a 4 by 3-foot bathroom with seven other terrified Tutsi women as the slaughter raged outside. I heard the screams of those being hacked to death just beyond the bathroom walls.

I lived in constant fear of death — or worse. I prayed day and night with my father's rosary pleading for God to spare my life, but I would learn there was a difference between being spared and being saved. Hatred began taking hold of my heart, just as it had in the killers. I wished them dead; I wanted them to suffer like they were making so many others suffer. Had someone given me a loaded gun, I might have crawled out of my hiding place and tried to kill them all.

When I said The Lord's Prayer, the words "forgive those who trespass against us" simply would not form on my lips. How could I forgive the unforgivable, forgive those I wanted to kill myself?

The sickening thirst for revenge was foreign to me; my parents raised me to love my neighbor and live according to the Golden Rule. I grew more terrified of what was happening to my soul than what the killers might do to my body — I did not want to survive the slaughter if it meant living with a spiteful heart incapable of love.

I prayed for God to show me how to forgive those I had grown to hate. Suddenly, I saw an image of Jesus in the moments before his death, crying out to God to forgive those who were crucifying him.

In that instant, I realized the killers were children of God who had lost their way. I prayed: "Forgive them Father, they know not what they do." The hatred drained from me and my heart flooded with God's love. For the first time I was aware of the power of forgiveness to heal and transform—it was the greatest gift I have ever received.

When the killers were finally driven from the country, I emerged from hiding and learned of my family's fate. Thank God my eldest brother survived because he was studying abroad. My father had been shot protecting the families who had come to him for help, my mother was hacked to death on the street when she ran out of hiding to help a child, and my youngest brother was machine-gunned to death with thousands of other unarmed Tutsis corralled in a sports stadium. My elder brother had his head chopped open by family friends; I heard that before he died he forgave his killers.

In all, more than a million innocent souls were murdered during that bloody nightmare.

Discovering the details of my family's murder reignited my struggle to prevent anger and hatred from taking hold of my heart, but I had also discovered the one way to win that struggle was through forgiveness… and I knew what I had to do.

Several months after the genocide, a politician friend arranged for me to meet the man who led the murders of my mother and elder brother.

When I arrived at the jail I was stunned by what greeted me. A sick and disheveled old man in chains was shoved onto the floor at my feet.

"Félicien!" I cried out. He had been a successful Hutu businessman whose children I'd played with in primary school. Back then, he was tall, proud, and handsome—with impeccable manners. In front of me now, he was a hollowed-eyed specter in rags covered in running sores. His hatred had robbed him of his life.

The jailor kicked him in the ribs yelling, "Stand up, Hutu! Stand up you pig and tell this girl why you murdered her mother and butchered her brother!"

Félicien remained on the floor, hiding his face from me in shame. My heart swelled with pity. I crouched down beside him and placed my hand on his. Our eyes met briefly and I said what I had come to say: *I forgive you.*

Relief swept over me, and a sigh of gratitude slipped through Félicien's parched lips.

"What the hell was that about, Immaculee?" the furious jailor demanded as Félicien was dragged away. "That man murdered your family! I brought him here so you could spit on him. But you forgave him! How could you do that?"

"Because hatred has taken everything I ever loved from me," I said, "Forgiveness is all I have left to offer."

I turned and walked out of that prison free of anger and hatred and I have lived as a free woman ever since.

~Immaculée Ilibagiza with Steve Erwin

Believing Anna

If you don't like something, change it; if you can't change it,
change the way you think about it.
~Mary Engelbreit

used to feel like I was carrying a terrible secret, always afraid that if I said the wrong thing I'd give myself away and people would know. I say I'd give myself away because this disorder was a part of me and had always been, even though it hadn't surfaced until my third year in college. I had spent my childhood and adolescence blissfully unaware of my schizophrenia. Like some hideous monster, it had lurked within the dark maze of my mind, finally reaching the end of the labyrinth and manifesting itself just before my twentieth birthday.

For the longest time I feared having another breakdown and being sent back to the hospital. I had been a psych patient at several hospitals. Every time I was released from in-patient treatment, I vowed I would never go back. I would actively monitor my thoughts for signs that I was relapsing. As ridiculous as it sounded when my doctor would ask me these questions, I posed them seriously to myself: Was I having racing thoughts? Was I obsessing about numbers? Was I seeing or hearing things that others didn't? I asked myself these questions, foolishly believing that I could somehow outrun a monster that already had me as its prisoner.

My very first breakdown happened like anything truly awful does, without warning. I remember not sleeping for I don't know how many nights on end. I must have been acting strange because my friends noticed. Which is saying a lot, because I'm usually the quiet one who people overlook.

I remember having some pretty strange thoughts at the time, mostly about God and myself—I think my doctor called them "grandiose delusions." I had always been an imaginative person, it's true, but before my first breakdown I had always had a firm grip on reality. I honestly don't remember when I actually snapped, or if it can even be pinned down to one specific moment. I do know that I was experiencing what psychiatrists refer to as a manic phase. I had so much energy and so many thoughts racing inside my head that I couldn't sleep. I also know that these bouts of extreme energy gave way to some bizarre thought patterns.

I thought I was receiving messages from God. I thought that God had a special secret mission for me. I thought that the world had ended and God was coming for me. I thought that I was God. I can't explain how my brain created these ideas, or why I actually believed them. I was acting out a chemical imbalance. I was not in my right mind.

During this time, I hallucinated quite a bit. I can't decide which hallucinations scared me more, the ones I saw or the ones I heard. Familiar faces became sinister and warped, like frightening caricatures. Sometimes I saw bright flashes of light and other times I couldn't escape the shadows that only I could see. I heard strange clicking metallic animal voices, the likes of which reminded me of the sounds I heard when I was swimming underwater and the pool was being vacuumed. Only, I wasn't swimming and the sounds were all in my head.

It used to make me physically sick to talk or even think about things I had done under my delusions. For a long time, I tried so hard to pretend that everything was okay, that I was normal. I couldn't face what I had done.

I took a ride in a stranger's van. I walked the middle white line of the highway with cars swerving to avoid hitting me. I believed the voices in my head that told me, "God wants you to kill yourself." I didn't trust the kind faces of those I loved; I hit my father and pushed my best friend down. I threw water at nurses and went to court hearings in handcuffs. I did so many things I would never ordinarily do. The ones who understood the nature of schizophrenia told me it wasn't my fault and that I shouldn't blame myself.

It was a hard line to swallow, though. I couldn't reconcile that with my long established ideology that I could overcome any obstacle if I wanted to, that my life was the product of my own actions and therefore of my own making. I didn't understand the nature of mental disorders nor did I understand people who suffered from them. I used to believe that people could overcome anything if they tried hard enough. I might have kept up this unrealistic notion had I not had another breakdown.

It was my third hospitalization and it was where I met Martin. Martin was a balding middle-aged man with bright blue eyes and a sad face. He had checked himself in because he was suffering from severe depression. He usually kept to himself and only came out of his room for meals and the occasional Group or Occupational Therapy session. Seeing him sitting by himself looking at his hospital tray with disinterest, I decided in a rare moment of bravery to join him.

"Gotta love this slop they call food," I said in an attempt at humor. He looked up at me and gave a feeble smile.

"Yeah," he mumbled.

I asked him how he was doing, expecting the usual (and often phony) "good" response. He was so close-mouthed in Group that I was surprised when he actually answered honestly.

He told me he was depressed and didn't know why. He said depression was a different kind of sadness, one that no amount of tears could alleviate. That it was an intense feeling of hopelessness and isolation, that it was a struggle to get out of bed in the morning, an immense burden to summon the will to go to work or to shower or even to eat. That there was this intensity of feeling and yet a powerful numbness at the same time, as if he was somehow still breathing but not really alive.

Out of candor, naïveté, or just plain stupidity, I asked him why didn't he just find something that made him happy and do that.

He stood up, anger in his piercing blue eyes, and said, "You just don't understand. This isn't something I can just will away!"

And that was when I finally understood. I couldn't just will my schizophrenia away. I had to recognize that my illness was beyond my control. I could manage it with therapy sessions and medication, but it would always be a part of me. I had to forgive myself for what I had done and face the memories I had blocked out for so long.

I began to talk to Martin and some of the other patients and I shared with them all that I had gone through. Talking to them, I remembered how to laugh again and cry again, I remembered how much I loved art and music, how I wanted to be a writer. I remembered who I used to be before my diagnosis. And I remembered who I could still be, in spite of it.

I began to paint again. I expressed my memories through brush-strokes, describing the frightening world I had lived in during each mental collapse. It was more cathartic than painting a pretty yellow birdhouse.

But I created happy things too; I made birthday cards with rainbow-maned unicorns for a male patient's young daughters and did a portrait sketch of a female patient named Darla. "You made me beautiful," she said when she saw it, and I told her she was. I enjoyed therapy and the colorful community it gave me. I laughed when a patient named John dubbed arts and crafts "Total BS" and elected to roll homemade cigarettes instead, saying the cigarettes would make him happier than a picture made of macaroni, but could he make a ceramic ashtray?

On my last day at Lakeview, a girl named Anna, who had jumped off a bridge, stopped me to say goodbye. "I'm glad I met you, Abby," she said. "I know that I'm going to be okay now."

Wondering how someone could be certain of something like that, I asked Anna how she knew.

She said, "Because you're going to be okay."

I made my way outside the hospital with my mom holding my hand for probably the first time since I was seven. I smiled at the brilliant summer sunshine, knowing I could believe what Anna had said.

~Abigail Hoeft

Happiness Through Forgiveness

Forgiveness does not change the past, but it does enlarge the future.

~Paul Boese

t was raining the day I found out. Not just a light sprinkle, but a heavy, foggy, cold February downpour. I had spent a lazy day at Color-Me-Mine painting a teddy bear with my friends. I was twelve years old. I was starting to fit in at school. I was happy. But little did I know that was all about to change.

I came home to my ten-year-old brother watching TV and playing a video game. Just past the television was a sliding glass door leading to our patio. My dad was standing outside on the phone with his back turned towards us.

"Dad's mad," my brother said, not even bothering to look up from his Game Boy. I was in such a good mood from spending the day with friends that I didn't even care to know why. I went into my bedroom and sat down at my computer, ready to spend the rest of my Saturday online. Not even two minutes later, my dad walked into the bedroom my brother and I shared, sat down, and said, "Nicole, we need to have a family meeting." He called for my brother to come into the bedroom, and as we waited for him, my mind raced, trying to think of anything I might have done to get in trouble. It was never a good sign when he called me Nicole. My brother finally shuffled in and sat down on the bed next to my father.

Without any warning at all, he looked at me and said, "Your mom's gone." I didn't understand what he meant. I didn't want to. Everything went silent. I could hear only my own breath echoing in my ears like a bad horror movie, and I watched my dad and my brother hold each other and cry.

"You're lying," I said, starting to laugh. Why was I laughing? I knew they weren't lying. My father was sitting in front of me bawling his eyes out—a grown man crying like a toddler. But I couldn't believe him. My mother was my best friend. He handed me his cell phone and told me to call my grandmother, and that she would tell me everything I wanted to know.

I ran outside and I stood in the rain and I listened as my grandma cried and told me that my mother, my role model, my favorite person in the world, had killed herself. I was devastated. I wanted to cry, but the tears just wouldn't come. They built themselves up in my chest forming a heavy anchor, but they would not come. I hung up the phone and walked inside. My brother was back at the television; my father was outside on the phone again. Everything looked normal. It didn't appear as if the world had just rolled over on its back. I returned to my bedroom, and did what any twelve-year-old girl would do in a situation like this: I updated my AIM status—"RIP Mom."

And finally, the next day, I woke up crying. I cried for two weeks straight. I didn't eat or go to school. I left the house once: for the funeral. I was guilty. I felt like I should have been a better daughter, gotten her a better birthday gift, done more chores around the house. I couldn't stand to look at myself. Suddenly, every little thing I used to do seemed like another cause of her suicide. She killed herself because I never did what she asked. She did it because I wasn't who she wanted me to be.

I beat myself up until there was nothing left to beat. I broke myself down so far that I could think of nothing else to do but hate myself. And that led to hating her. I hated her for leaving me. For making me feel worthless. For leaving me to take on the role of mother, of woman of the house. I was twelve years old. I needed her. How did she expect me to be raised by just my dad? Every girl needs her mother! She couldn't just leave when things got hard! Isn't the point of having children to be completely selfless and only think of them? I had endless thoughts, endless questions.

After two weeks, my father made me go back to school and promised me that everything would be fine. But he was wrong. Everyone knew what had happened. My friends could barely look at me. People I didn't even know pointed at me when I walked through the halls. I couldn't deal with the pain of everyone staring, asking questions I didn't know how to answer. So I turned away from my friends and spent all of my time alone. I was miserable.

My mother had gone from being my best friend to my worst enemy. This was all her fault. I hated her and I hated myself.

But the problem with hatred is that it eats you up. It burrows inside every little pore in your body. It drains you of all your energy. Living with hatred is an incredibly difficult thing to do. So I started working at forgiving. Because when it comes to forgiveness, sometimes it helps you more than the person you are forgiving. My mom will never know that I forgave her. I will never be able to go up to her, look her in the eye, and say, "I forgive you." But now, I can look myself in the mirror, and know that sometimes people are selfish. People are stupid and act without thinking. People are people and we all do things we regret, but if we are never forgiven and never forgive, we will never be able to move on in our own lives.

I took all the anger that I was feeling and I channeled it into forgiveness and understanding. Everyone deserves a second chance no matter how hard they have hurt you. I may never know the reason why she hurt me the way she did, but I don't need to. I have forgiven her, and because of that, I can be happy.

~Nicole Guiltinan

Broken Wing

You were born with wings. Why prefer to crawl through life?
~Rumi

Some people are just doomed to be failures. That's the way some adults look at troubled kids. Maybe you've heard the saying, "A bird with a broken wing will never fly as high." I'm sure that T. J. Ware was made to feel this way almost every day in school.

By high school, T. J. was the most celebrated troublemaker in his town. Teachers literally cringed when they saw his name posted on their classroom lists for the next semester. He wasn't very talkative, didn't answer questions and got into lots of fights. He had flunked almost every class by the time he entered his senior year, yet was being passed on each year to a higher grade level. Teachers didn't want to have him again the following year. T. J. was moving on, but definitely not moving up.

I met T. J. for the first time at a weekend leadership retreat. All the students at school had been invited to sign up for ACE training, a program designed to have students become more involved in their communities. T. J. was one of 405 students who signed up. When I showed up to lead their first retreat, the community leaders gave me this overview of the attending students: "We have a total spectrum represented today, from the student body president to T. J. Ware, the boy with the longest arrest record in the history of town." Somehow, I knew that I wasn't the first to hear about T. J.'s darker side as the first words of introduction.

At the start of the retreat, T. J. was literally standing outside the circle of students, against the back wall, with that "go ahead, impress me" look on his face. He didn't readily join the discussion groups, didn't seem to have much to say. But slowly, the interactive games drew him in. The ice really melted when the groups started building a list of positive and negative things that had occurred at school that year. T. J. had some definite thoughts on those situations. The other students in T. J.'s group welcomed his comments. All of a sudden T. J. felt like a part of the group, and before long he was being treated like a leader. He was saying things that made a lot of sense, and everyone was listening. T. J. was a smart guy and he had some great ideas.

The next day, T. J. was very active in all the sessions. By the end of the retreat, he had joined the Homeless Project team. He knew something about poverty, hunger and hopelessness. The other students on the team were impressed with his passionate concern and ideas. They elected T. J. co-chairman of the team. The student council president would be taking his instruction from T. J. Ware.

When T. J. showed up at school on Monday morning, he arrived to a firestorm. A group of teachers were protesting to the school principal about his being elected co-chairman. The very first communitywide service project was to be a giant food drive, organized by the Homeless Project team. These teachers couldn't believe that the principal would allow this crucial beginning to a prestigious, three-year action plan to stay in the incapable hands of T. J. Ware. They reminded the principal, "He has an arrest record as long as your arm. He'll probably steal half the food." Mr. Coggshall reminded them that the purpose of the ACE program was to uncover any positive passion that a student had and reinforce its practice until true change can take place. The teachers left the meeting shaking their heads in disgust, firmly convinced that failure was imminent.

Two weeks later, T. J. and his friends led a group of 70 students in a drive to collect food. They collected a school record: 2,854 cans of food in just two hours. It was enough to fill the empty shelves in two neighborhood centers, and the food took care of needy families in the area for 75 days. The local newspaper covered the event with a full-page article the next day. That newspaper story was posted on the main bulletin board at school, where everyone could see it. T. J.'s picture was up there for doing something great, for leading a record-setting food drive. Every day he was reminded about what he did. He was being acknowledged as leadership material.

T. J. started showing up at school every day and answered questions from teachers for the first time. He led a second project, collecting 300 blankets and 1,000 pairs of shoes for the homeless shelter. The event he started now yields 9,000 cans of food in one day, taking care of 70 percent of the need for food for one year.

T. J. reminds us that a bird with a broken wing only needs mending. But once it has healed, it can fly higher than the rest. T. J. got a job. He became productive. He is flying quite nicely these days.

~Jim Hullihan

Just a Kid

*A hero is an ordinary individual who finds the strength to
persevere and endure in spite of overwhelming obstacles.*
~Christopher Reeve

"Van, I can't move. Please get me off the ice."
"I wish I could Travis, but we need to stay
here until the ambulance arrives." And then
we waited. "Of all nights for a snowstorm,
why tonight?" I thought to myself as we waited what seemed like an
eternity for the ambulance.

Hockey connects many different groups of people — players,
referees, coaches, and even the off-ice officials. Sometimes there are
events that draw together all of these participants as well as others
from outside of the arena.

This story, although tragic, is a story of inspiration. In the 2000–
2001 season I was coaching the Assumption Crusaders senior boys
hockey team, a high school team from Burlington, Ontario. We were
an average team that had shared some above average experiences. The
previous spring we travelled to the Czech Republic, Germany, and
Austria to play a series of games against European teams. This trip also
enabled the boys to experience other cultures and take in the incredible
sites of the Austrian Alps and surrounding regions. In the fall of
2000, we travelled by bus cross-country to play in a tournament in

Dartmouth, Nova Scotia. The boys were a close team, a group of players bound together by hours spent in dressing rooms, working hard at practice, and competing in games, not to mention hours hanging out together outside of the arena.

In December of 2000 we were playing another local high school team. They were the dominant team in our league, and we knew we had our hands full just trying to keep the score close. Through two periods of play the score was 4–0. During the intermission our conversation was light as our coaching staff reminded the team that they were playing well and were only a "field goal" away from tying it.

At the start of the third period, our captain, Travis Colley-Zorrilla, broke in from the side boards at the blue line and went in on a partial breakaway. He made a wonderful move pulling the puck from his backhand to his forehand before shooting the puck past the outstretched glove of the goalie and into the back of the net.

What happened next took only seconds but its impact would last forever. Travis caught his foot on the goalie, and that, coupled with the weight of an opposing player who landed on him after the goal, changed the direction of his fall from a gentle slide into the corner to an abrupt crash into the end boards. Not able to get his arms up to protect himself, the impact was absorbed by his head and led to a variety of horrific injuries including three broken vertebrae in his neck; specifically C4, C5, and C7. The most significant and sustaining injury was the crushed spinal cord that led to the paralysis of his arms and legs.

There are so many feelings and thoughts that went through me when I heard the doctor describe the extent of his injuries. Disbelief, shock, sadness, devastation, numbness, even anger. Travis, on the other hand, elected to be strong, resilient, optimistic, and uplifting to all who came to visit. While he remained in the ward recovering from his injuries and numerous surgeries, he never once questioned "why me?" or demonstrated any sign of self-pity. Early on he even commented, "I am glad that this happened to me and not anyone else, because I know I can handle this."

Travis was just a kid but he simply took this enormous challenge in stride and talked of walking again, going to college or university, and accomplishing all of his dreams in spite of this setback. I watched other patients in the ward who also suffered spinal cord trauma try to cope with the staggering news. They all had such sad stories of one wrong turn, or one bad decision, or being in the wrong place at the wrong time. Not all of them shared his strength of mind.

While Travis remained in the hospital, so many people in the school community pulled together to help. No one knew quite what to do, but we all tried to do something. Classmates, teachers, and parents all chipped in to prepare meals for his family, car pool for visits, and help out around the house to somehow make life easier for his family. In the meantime a committee was organized to fundraise. The reality of an injury like this is that modifications are required to all aspects of the home: kitchen counters need to be lowered, bathrooms need easier access, floor plans need to be altered, and all aspects of day-to-day living require greater accommodation. Transportation is another issue all together; a new van would be required to accommodate a wheelchair.

We decided a dinner-dance with a silent auction would provide the greatest return. Our committee reached out to everyone we could think of — local politicians, school community, local parish, celebrities, local businesses. We used our school as a depot for auctionable items. The outpouring of items was overwhelming. Sports memorabilia such as signed NHL jerseys and sticks came from teams across North America; Don Cherry provided all sorts of items but especially his genuine care and interest; PGA golfers like Fred Couples sent golf equipment and clothes to auction. We raised more than $100,000 through the generosity of our community — not just our local municipality but the hockey and sports community at large.

In addition to raising money, the local fire department stepped forward and offered to provide all the labour to customize Travis's house. A local building supplier (Home Depot) matched our efforts by providing an equal value in required building materials to every dollar spent in the store. It was a labour of love as every day a team of people showed up with tools and went to work on Travis's home.

In total more than 100 workers would come over to the house, some immediately after their own twelve-hour shifts. The entire community was one big example of positive thinking and can-do attitudes.

It's been more than ten years since the accident. In that time Travis has dedicated much of his time to giving back to the community. He speaks to children in the community, both as an individual and for the Shoot For A Cure campaign, never shy about describing, in detail, his injuries and how his life has changed since that fateful game. He served as an ambassador for other fundraising ventures such as Wheels in Motion. He, along with friends and former teammates Chris Warren and Colm Rea, served as coach of the Crusaders lacrosse team for three years — teaching, instructing, motivating, and passing on skills that he is more than capable of providing.

Travis and I have always had a very close relationship, but in these past ten years we have become genuine friends. We live only blocks apart and find time as often as we can to catch a Leafs game on TV, travel to Cornell University to watch the Big Red battle away in the Lynah Rink, wheel around Glen Abbey Golf course and watch Fred Couples and other PGA tour stars shoot incredible scores trying to win our Canadian Open.

There are times when people will ask me how Travis is doing; I can't even get through a sentence without acknowledging that he's the bravest person I know, that he's my hero, and that he has demonstrated what it means to be a champion. A captain is expected to be a role model: mature, responsible, hard working, and dedicated to the goals of the team. Travis has maintained those qualities for life. Travis is truly an inspiration to all who know of his story and what he has overcome since that snowy December afternoon.

~Carl Van Landschoot

Chapter
9

Create Your Best Future

Reaching Out to Others

The Smile

Smile at each other, smile at your wife, smile at your husband, smile at your children, smile at each other — it doesn't matter who it is — and that will help you to grow up in greater love for each other.

~Mother Teresa

Many Americans are familiar with *The Little Prince*, a wonderful book by Antoine de Saint-Exupéry. This is a whimsical and fabulous book and works as a children's story as well as a thought-provoking adult fable. Far fewer are aware of Saint-Exupéry's other writings, novels and short stories.

Saint-Exupéry was a fighter pilot who fought against the Nazis and was killed in action. Before World War II, he fought in the Spanish Civil War against the fascists. He wrote a fascinating story based on that experience entitled *The Smile (Le Sourire)*. It isn't clear whether or not he meant this to be autobiographical or fiction. I choose to believe it is the former.

He said that he was captured by the enemy and thrown into a jail cell. He was sure from the contemptuous looks and rough treatment he received from his jailers that he would be executed the next day. From here, I'll tell the story as I remember it in my own words.

"I was sure that I was to be killed. I became terribly nervous and distraught. I fumbled in my pockets to see if there were any cigarettes that had escaped their search. I found one and because of my shaking hands, I could barely get it to my lips. But I had no matches; they had taken those.

"I looked through the bars at my jailer. He did not make eye contact with me. After all, one does not make eye contact with a thing, a corpse. I called out to him 'Have you got a light, *por favor?*' He looked at me, shrugged and came over to light my cigarette.

"As he came close and lit the match, his eyes inadvertently locked with mine. At that moment, I smiled. I don't know why I did that. Perhaps it was nervousness, perhaps it was because, when you get very close, one to another, it is very hard not to smile. In any case, I smiled. In that instant, it was as though a spark jumped across the gap between our two hearts, our two human souls. I know he didn't want to, but my smile leaped through the bars and generated a smile on his lips, too. He lit my cigarette but stayed near, looking at me directly in the eyes and continuing to smile.

"I kept smiling at him, now aware of him as a person and not just a jailer. And his looking at me seemed to have a new dimension, too. 'Do you have kids?' he asked.

"'Yes, here, here.' I took out my wallet and nervously fumbled for the pictures of my family. He, too, took out the pictures of his *niños* and began to talk about his plans and hopes for them. My eyes filled with tears. I said that I feared that I'd never see my family again, never have the chance to see them grow up. Tears came to his eyes, too.

"Suddenly, without another word, he unlocked my cell and silently led me out. Out of the jail, quietly and by back routes, out of the town. There, at the edge of town, he released me. And without another word, he turned back toward the town.

"My life was saved by a smile."

Yes, the smile—the unaffected, unplanned, natural connection between people. I tell this story in my work because I'd like people to consider that underneath all the layers we construct to protect ourselves, our dignity, our titles, our degrees, our status and our need to be seen in certain ways—underneath all that, remains the authentic, essential self. I'm not afraid to call it the soul. I really believe that if that part of you and that part of me could recognize each other, we wouldn't be enemies. We couldn't have hate or envy or fear. I sadly conclude that all those other layers, which we so carefully construct through our lives, distance and insulate us from truly contacting others. Saint-Exupéry's story speaks of that magic moment when two souls recognize each other.

I've had just a few moments like that. Falling in love is one example. And looking at a baby. Why do we smile when we see a baby? Perhaps it's because we see someone without all the defensive layers, someone whose smile for us we know to be fully genuine and without guile. And that baby-soul inside us smiles wistfully in recognition.

~Hanoch McCarty

Gramma's Good China

The truth is, unless you let go, unless you forgive yourself,
unless you forgive the situation, unless you realize that the
situation is over, you cannot move forward.
~Steve Maraboli

For years, every Saturday afternoon my family—Mom, my stepfather and I—had dinner at Gramma's house. We watched sporting events on TV, played *Yahtzee* and enjoyed a home-cooked meal: spaghetti and meatballs, pot roast, chicken and biscuits… you get the idea.

Anna Marie, or Gramma as we all call her, is seventy-nine years old and very set in her ways. She attends church every Sunday, never misses an episode of *60 Minutes*, completes the daily crossword puzzle in the newspaper, makes apple pie for every holiday and refuses to ever take the good china out of the cabinet because her regular dinnerware is "good enough."

However, one Saturday at the end of October things were different. My mom, my stepdad and I stayed home because my father was coming to visit. My biological father, that is, who I hadn't seen since he left town sixteen years earlier. He called asking to visit, saying he wanted to see me.

I was dreading it.

Saturday afternoon when the doorbell chimed, I peered through the blinds at my father on the porch. He looked older, heavier, grayer.

For some reason, I expected him to look exactly as he did in the single photo I had of him — the two of us at the lake when I was seven. I kept the picture in my sock drawer.

My father, mom and stepfather were politely exchanging pleasantries when I stepped into the entryway. My father extended his hand to shake mine. "David," he said, smiling. "It's great to see you, son."

I knew what I should do, but I couldn't. My arm, my hand was immobile.

This man had walked out on us. He had never been there. He missed every Christmas and birthday, my basketball games, my college graduation; why would I shake his hand?

I nodded, grunted and sat on the couch.

Mom told him about her job and the vacation cruise that she and my stepdad had taken, then motioned towards me. "David's been busy lately with his job and finishing his thesis, haven't you, honey?"

I nodded. "Yeah, high school, college, getting a job. A lot can happen in sixteen years."

"David," Mom grumbled through clenched teeth.

My father held up his hands. "It's okay. I understand. You're not thrilled to see me. This was a stupid idea, but I wanted to see you."

"You've seen me." I shrugged.

"Why don't we have dinner?" Mom suggested. "I made meatloaf."

"Thanks anyway. I'm not hungry." I got up and headed for the door.

My father called after me. "I'd really like you to stay."

"But, honey, you haven't eaten," said Mom.

I walked out the door.

And that's how I left it. I didn't say another word about it. My father didn't call again. The following Saturday we went to Gramma's as usual.

Secretly, I stewed about my father, daydreamed about him, lay awake at night, replaying the visit. What should I have said or done? Why did he leave? Why did he return? Did he know how much he hurt me? Did he even care? I was angry. I couldn't let it go.

Two weeks after my father's visit, I took Gramma grocery shopping for Thanksgiving. When we returned home, I put the groceries away while Gramma sat at the kitchen table reviewing her shopping list.

"Green beans; got it," she mumbled, checking off items. "Potatoes; got it. What have I forgotten?"

I set the bag of onions on the countertop.

"Oh, the apples," Gramma said. "I forgot apples for pie."

"Okay," I replied.

Gramma reached out and caught my sleeve. "What's wrong, David?"

"I'll get apples tomorrow."

"Not apples," answered Gramma. "What's wrong with you?"

I shrugged. "I'm fine."

"You're not fine," Gramma said. "In this family, food is serious business. If I'm talking about pie and all you say is 'okay', then you're not fine."

"I'm putting groceries away."

"I know what this is about," Gramma announced. "It's about your father."

I turned away and slid two jars of olives into the cupboard.

"Your whole attitude has changed," Gramma said. "Ever since he came to visit, you're not the same."

"This isn't the time," I told her, grabbing another grocery bag off the floor.

"This is the perfect time," she replied. "You finish with the groceries. I'll make coffee."

Ten minutes later we sat at the dining room table, facing each other over a plate of brownies.

Gramma sipped her coffee. "Tell me about this."

"I'm mad," I replied. "He left us and hasn't bothered to keep in touch. Why has he come back?"

"Your father wants to make peace."

"Well, I don't want peace. I don't want to see him."

Gramma pointed at me. "This isn't good. You're tearing yourself up. And you're making life miserable for everybody else being such a grumble-bug."

I couldn't help smiling when she mentioned the name she had called me since I was a baby whenever I got upset. "My father is making me a grumble-bug."

"No." She shook her head. "You're *allowing* your father to make you a grumble-bug. You're making yourself miserable and you know what? Your anger isn't affecting your father a bit. He doesn't know you're a grumble-bug."

I rolled my eyes.

"Look at it this way," Gramma explained. "Anger is like taking that beautiful turkey we bought and leaving it on the counter until it spoils and smells bad. Then, to really show your father how angry you are, you cook the spoiled turkey and you eat it yourself hoping your father gets sick."

"That doesn't make sense," I said.

"Exactly," replied Gramma. "Neither does the way you're handling this situation. Your father goes off to live his life — you stay sick with anger. You're only hurting yourself."

I shrugged. "What do you suggest?"

"Forgive him."

"No way, Gramma." I folded his arms. "Why should I?"

"Forgiveness isn't always something you do for the other person," Gramma explained. "Sometimes you can forgive to help yourself feel better."

"What do I do?" I asked.

"Invite your father for Thanksgiving."

I shook my head. "Do you know how uncomfortable that would be?"

"I never said it would be easy," Gramma answered. "But it's better than eating spoiled turkey the rest of your life."

"Okay," I agreed. "I'll invite him to dinner, but on one condition."

"What condition?"

I pointed to the cabinet in the corner. "It'll be a special occasion. The regular dinnerware won't do. You'll need to use… the good china."

So, the following Thursday, we had Thanksgiving with my father and the good china.

"Are we actually going to eat off it?" Mom asked, stroking a plate with her fingertips.

It wasn't my best Thanksgiving, but it wasn't nearly as bad as I had imagined. We had a good meal and my father joined in the conversations. My father and I played *Yahtzee* after dinner. I discovered we both were Dallas Cowboys fans. After the apple pie, I walked my father out to his car.

"I'd like to get together again sometime, David," my father said. "I have a lot to tell you. And I'd like your forgiveness."

I nodded. "I've got your phone number. I'd like to hear what you have to say. I'll call you."

My father held out his right hand.

This time I did shake his hand. It wasn't easy, but I knew if Gramma could use the good china, I could do this. I was starting to feel better already.

~David Hull

These Things Take Time

In some families, please is described as the magic word. In our house, however, it was sorry.

~Margaret Laurence

I came to motherhood late in life and all at once. One moment I was thirty-six and single, and the next I was married with three stepchildren, ages thirteen, seven, and five. For many reasons, this was destined to be a somewhat fractious situation because the kids lived predominately with their mother 3,000 miles away. Except for two separate yearlong interludes, we saw them only during summers and the rare Christmas holiday. Even so, and despite my gross lack of experience as a parent, the kids and I managed to forge a mostly amicable relationship.

My stepson Anthony was an affectionate child who delighted in art, reading, and superheroes. We became particularly close, but this began to change as he grew from an endearing five-year-old into a truculent teenager. Hindsight, of course, is 20-20, but at the time neither my husband nor I realized the many issues that plagued him. All we knew was that our immensely likeable son had seemingly turned overnight into the Terminator — difficult to talk to, impossible to reach, and combative over the least little issue. Our relationship degenerated into a tense, battle-ridden landscape of sullen silence broken by argument and confrontation.

Everything came to a head one Christmas. Anthony was living with us at the time, but according to the terms of the parenting agreement, he flew to be with his mother for the holiday. No sooner did he get there than he called to say he wasn't coming back. We were stunned. My husband talked with him at length, but he was adamant. I also spoke with him, apologizing for my behavior and lack of patience, acknowledging my part in our difficulties and asking him to come home so we could work together to find a way back to where we'd been. He refused. At that point, I'm afraid I did one of the worst things a parent can do — I gave up on him. Although Anthony and his father stayed in guarded contact, he and I didn't speak again for six years.

Then one night my husband came to me and said, "Anthony's on the phone and wants to talk to you." Cautiously, I took the receiver and said hello. "I just want you to know I'm sending you a letter," was all he said before hanging up. I wondered what hate-filled message I was about to receive, but when it arrived, the opening words read: "First of all, I want to say I'm sorry." By the end of the letter, I was crying. When I got myself under control, I picked up the phone.

It took enormous courage and a willingness to risk rejection for Anthony to reach out to me after so long. It took immense trust in our past relationship and the belief that we could reconnect for the two of us to begin again. Slowly, we worked through our issues, coming to a clearer understanding of not only each other, but of ourselves.

Over the past ten years, our relationship has grown into something wondrous. Not only are we mother and son, but we're good friends as well — maybe even best friends — calling to share details of our day, a joke, or to offer support during difficult times. In a way, those years of silence worked to our advantage. But we would never have reached where we are today if it hadn't been for Anthony's bravery and desire to begin again and regain what we had lost.

~Melissa Crandall

Destroying the Bully

You cannot shake hands with a clenched fist.
~Indira Gandhi

If intentionally hurting another soul is part of human nature, then it is a concept I will never fully understand. Many bullies do not take the time to think about those they are hurting, or about what goes on behind the closed doors of their victims' lives. One thing that I have happily discovered is that the ideal bully hates nothing more than if the victim is not shaken by attempts to harass and intimidate. A bully's reason for existing is to be mean, and it is a shock to receive kindness in response. A bully does not understand friendship, but it is one of the most important aspects of life. By spreading kindness you can make friends out of even the worst enemies.

I experienced one of the worst forms of bullying: sneaky bullying. Fortunately for my bully — let's call her Kristy — she was loved by adults who were easily fooled by her false compliments. I met Kristy the first day of art class. I loved art, but as excited as I was, Kristy quickly made me dread it.

When I entered that art room for the first time, I spotted the last open seat in the room and sat next to Kristy. Before I even had a chance to introduce myself, she looked at her friend and said, "Let's move." Assuming there must be something drastically wrong with the table, I followed. She looked at me oddly, and I assumed that it was because she didn't know who I was, so I politely said, "Hi, I'm Ann." She cracked a sly smile and replied, "Well, Ann, I'm Kristy, and my friend and I moved tables because we didn't want to be near you." That was the first snakebite.

For the next few days, I tried to avoid Kristy, but that only worked for a while. She began to poke fun at everything about me: my hair, what I wore, the way I talked, and how I created my art. I told my friends and family, and they offered some ideas like changing classes or talking to the school counselor, but even she loved Kristy. So I decided to attempt the impossible — I was going to make Kristy my friend.

"Kind words are short and easy to speak, but their echoes are truly endless," Mother Teresa once said, and I only wish I had known this when I first met Kristy because it would have made my solution much more obvious. I began to respond politely whenever Kristy threw a nasty comment my way. Instead of the silence or hurt face she expected, Kristy got a compliment thrown back at her. This inflamed her with more fury, and for a short time she criticized me even more, a sign that my plan was working. The conversation usually went something like this:

"Ann, I have to tell you, that is the ugliest picture I have ever seen. I mean, what is it? Another snakebite?"

"Well, Kristy, I think it's really beautiful, and this blue paint I am using reminds me of that pretty shirt you wore yesterday."

Eventually, my kind comments got to her, and she asked, "What is with you, Ann? Why are you being so nice to me?"

I responded, "Well, because I want you to be nice to me." What happened next was amazing. It was like Kristy's whole world flipped upside-down. Even her friend looked shocked by my courageous statement. The snakebites would soon end.

For a few days, the three of us sat in silence during art class, but it was Kristy who made the next move, saying, "Ann, I really like your shirt. Where is it from?" After that, the next conversation was easier, and the one after that even seemed natural. Eventually, Kristy and I knew all about each other's lives and what boys we liked. I had destroyed the bully side of Kristy by making her my friend.

Kristy and I remained friends for a few years after our rough start and had some good times that led to even better memories. Although Kristy eventually moved away, she taught me a lot about myself and what matters most in life. Friendship and kindness are so important in life, and after my experience with Kristy, I know I will always have a friend no matter where I go, even if she at first appears to be a bully.

~Ann Virgo

The Birth of an Adult

*The ultimate measure of a man is not where he stands in
moments of comfort and convenience, but where he stands at
times of challenge and controversy.*
~Martin Luther King, Jr.

The doctors started to rush into the room. The delivery was
going smoothly, but to me it felt like hysteria. The walls
were a chalky gray like the wall of a jail cell. It wasn't the
best setting for Jamie's labor, but it would have to do. Jamie
was only a seventeen-year-old junior in high school. And now she was
giving birth. She lay back in pain. Her only movements consisted of
shaking her head from side to side, in an effort to escape the pain.

I took Jamie's hand, comforting her and trying to soothe her agony.
Her eyes opened, and she looked at me. Our eyes met, and suddenly
I felt every emotion I have ever known. I always knew Jamie would
challenge me to better myself; however, I didn't think it would entail
being her sidekick during her pregnancy.

All this began on the afternoon of New Year's Eve, 1997. I sat in
Jamie's basement awaiting the urgent news she had to tell me. She
collapsed onto the couch and told me how she had broken up with
her boyfriend, Eric, who had left the country to study abroad. This
came as something of a relief, although I did my best not to show
it. I didn't think Eric, or any other guy she had dated, was good
enough for her. Okay, I'll admit it, I was — how should I put it —

a little jealous. But I'd convinced myself we were better off as friends, anyway. And now she needed one.

Then the real news came: She was six weeks pregnant. Tears rolled down her face as she told me. I sat in shock and disbelief. The words were not registering in my head. She reached out and gave me a hug, which must have lasted only a few seconds but seemed like hours. My arms were still at my sides. We talked for a little while, and then I left her house and drove around in my car. I was in shock. I was upset about her lack of birth control because this whole ordeal could have been prevented. I was too young to deal with her pregnancy. Being a seventeen-year-old and a junior in high school was confusing enough without dealing with my own real-life afterschool special.

That evening I arrived at a party to drink my worries away. The air was filled with smoke and the partygoers reeked of alcohol. I could not take the atmosphere for long, so I left. I went to Jamie's house and stood on her front porch staring at the front door. *What should I do?* I asked myself. My foot started to turn from the door, but my hand reached out and pushed the doorbell. I wanted to run and go back to the party. I wanted to have fun this New Year's Eve. Suddenly, the door opened and Jamie stood in the doorway with her head down. "You can't spend New Year's Eve by yourself," I blurted out. She smiled, and we hugged in the doorway. This symbolized the beginning of the new journey that lay ahead for us. That night, we sat and laughed like usual while watching Dick Clark ring in the New Year. After that night, my life would change. I wouldn't be a crazy teenager anymore. I would become a young adult.

Weeks passed, and Jamie told her parents about the pregnancy. She and her parents made the decision to go through with the pregnancy, but to give the baby up for adoption. My parents talked with her parents and offered their support, almost like they were discussing our marriage; Jamie and I were growing and maturing together.

During her first trimester, I found myself at Jamie's house every day after school giving her a foot massage while she relaxed and watched her soap opera. She wasn't able to walk very much. I made snacks for her and enough food runs to Taco Bell to last us both a lifetime.

My friends were not considerate about what I was going through. While I was busy helping a friend, they were busy making fun of me. They would call Jamie's house wondering what I was doing. They already knew, but they just wanted to poke fun. At school, the jokes surfaced like, "Gonna be a good daddy?" and "What are you doing this weekend... Lamaze class?" I shrugged them off and ignored them. I went on with my daily chores and focused on Jamie. I tried to make her life as easy as possible.

Later, one Saturday afternoon as I was catching up on sleep, Jamie called.

"Did you want to do something today?" she asked. "What did you have in mind?" I replied. "I want you to help me choose the baby's family," she said.

My ears turned hot, and I felt uneasy. But I told her I would pick her up. As I drove to her house, I thought about how much I had changed. I was more responsible, but I still considered myself a child. I felt I had no business choosing a path for an unborn baby. I groaned and doubted myself. I arrived at her house and helped her into the car. As we were driving to the adoption agency, Jamie pointed out to me, "You're not speeding."

It occurred to me that I was no longer a crazy driver, thinking about how quickly I could get from one place to the other. I was now responsible for making sure we got there safely.

"I'm driving for three people now," I told her.

We arrived at the agency and were seated in a conference room. Fifty manila folders lay on the table, each containing a couple. One of these folders would be the lucky one. One of these couples would be the parents of Jamie's baby. The counselor and Jamie and I went through each folder discussing their spiritual, psychological, financial, genealogical and emotional backgrounds. I began browsing through one folder, which read "Jennifer and Ben." The folder was more like a booklet chronicling their life with pictures of where they'd been, who they are and who they wanted to become. Their explanation of why they wanted a baby caught my attention. This couple intrigued me. We kept narrowing down the couples, until we were down to two couples: Jennifer and Ben and Jamie's pick. We discussed both couples, finally agreeing on Jennifer and Ben.

As we were getting ready to leave, I took a picture of Jennifer and Ben out of the folder and slipped it into my jacket pocket without Jamie noticing. I wanted to have a record of them before their life was to be changed forever. I put on my jacket, and we left the agency.

It was a miserably cold spring day. After helping Jamie into the car, I walked around the car and a warm breeze struck me. I stood by the trunk of my car feeling the summer draft. I couldn't understand it. It was a cold day, but the wind was warmer than an August breeze. It felt like a sign, an anonymous thank you. We drove away and I thought about the decision we made. I thought about the families we didn't pick. How much longer would it take for them to receive the gift of a child?

A few weeks later we met Jennifer and Ben for the first time. They impressed me. They were a close couple, and I knew they would apply the love they had for each other to their child. Jamie told them that I urged her to pick them, which made this meeting even more overwhelming for me. I tried not to show it, though, as we bonded almost immediately. They urged Jamie to take a childbirth class so she would be ready for all of the upcoming events. She needed a partner for the class, so I agreed. She signed up for a class, and every Tuesday night Jamie and I attended together.

The first class was awkward. I had never felt so out of place in my entire life. Jamie and I sat down together, trying to ignore the seven married couples staring at us. We were too young and too ignorant to be going through a pregnancy and a birthing class. Nevertheless, Jamie had to do it, and I would not let her be alone. After time, we all began to bond and develop a tremendous amount of respect for each other. Everyone realized what a struggle it was for us to get this far.

During the "Mom Time," the dads and I sat outside talking about the babies' futures. The dads talked about peewee football, mutual funds and insurance. I talked about Shakespeare and Geometry. I was out of place, for sure, but I realized there is more to giving birth than nine months and a doctor. So much freedom was sacrificed, replaced with a huge amount of responsibility. The dads respected me and praised me for my humanity towards a friend, not to mention my maturity. I still just couldn't believe I was sitting around talking about babies. I wanted to be innocent again. I wanted to drive my car fast and go to parties, but more important responsibilities called me. I was maturing.

I was getting ready for school one morning when Jamie called me from the hospital. "Um, do you want to get over here?" she asked.

"It's only another sonogram. Besides, I can't miss class," I said.

"Well, I think you might want to get over here, 'cause I'm having the baby!" she shouted.

I ran out of the house and darted to the hospital. At the hospital, the nurse handed me scrubs and I entered her room. She lay there as I sat next to her.

"Well this is it," she said. "Nine months, and it's finally here." She grimaced with pain and moved her head back and forth. Doctors were in and out of her room every two seconds with medication. She was about to give birth. After a few hours of getting Jamie settled, she was fully dilated.

"Okay, here we go. When I say 'push,' you push," the doctor said.

She acknowledged him while grabbing my hands and nodding her head quickly several times. Jamie gave three pushes of strength and, with one final push, she breathed life into a new baby. The doctors cut the umbilical cord and cleaned the baby off. I sat in awe. Every possible human emotion struck me like a freight train.

"It's a boy," they exclaimed.

I smiled, and tears of joy ran down my cheek. No more fear, no more chores, just pure happiness. The baby was handed to Jamie, and she spent the first moments of the baby's life holding him in her arms. She looked up at me, and I looked at her.

"You did it, kiddo," I whispered in her ear.

The doctors left with the baby to run tests and weigh him. Jennifer and Ben came in with the birth certificate. "What's his name?" Ben asked. Jamie motioned for him to come closer, and she whispered in his ear. Ben smiled and went into a different room. I walked outside to get a drink. I came back in a few minutes and saw the completed birth certificate. It read Blake Jonathan.

I smiled and cried. The doctors brought Blake back in. They passed Blake to me, and I held new life in my hands. I thought about the dads in birth class. Then I thought about Blake's future. His first steps, peewee football games, the first day of school and his first broken heart. All the dads' talk finally caught up with me. Jennifer and Ben looked at me and smiled. Tears rolled down their cheeks. I gave Blake to Ben and received a gracious hug from Jennifer. They were his parents now. They were his keepers. Jamie still lay there, crying but filled with delight. I went over to her and gave her a big hug.

"Everything okay?" she asked.

"Fine. Absolutely fine," I whispered, and kissed her softly on her forehead. I would never be the same.

~Jonathan Krasnoff

Nice Timing

*Life is the game of boomerangs. Our thoughts, words and deeds
return to us — sooner or later — with astounding accuracy.*
~Florence Shinn

I had spent over five grueling years on my dissertation for my Ph.D. and was frantically preparing for my oral boards. The boards were to be held in California, and I had scheduled a flight through Minneapolis, where I was to change planes and get to John Wayne Airport. My incoming flight was very late, and I was soon in an all-out sprint to catch my flight to California. Very few people were left in the concourse. I had to stop to catch my breath on a moving sidewalk when I noticed a woman in her fifties struggling with a carry-on bag.

I don't know why, but I looked at her face and blurted out, "Are you going on flight 567 to California?"

She responded, "Yes."

"So am I," I responded. "Give me your bag. I'll run ahead and tell them to wait for you." I took her bag and started sprinting again.

I raced onto the plane and told a flight attendant that one more passenger was behind me and to please hold the plane for her. I seated myself with her bag, and a few moments later she arrived and was the last person on the plane before they closed the doors and took off. After the plane leveled off, I presented the bag to her, and she smiled at me and thanked me.

I didn't sleep a wink in the hotel that I stayed at before my oral boards and arrived at the university at seven o'clock in the morning. The board kept me waiting for an hour in a room before the defense of my dissertation began. I walked into the boardroom and was initially intimidated by all the professors in their regal robes. As I slowly glanced at the faces of all the board members, I noticed the bright face of a woman directly in the center of the board. She looked at me, gave me a flirtatious smile like a young schoolgirl and winked at me. It was the same woman whose bag I had carried ahead the night before. Needless to say, whenever I stumbled on any questions, she did a great job of extricating me.

~Thomas De Paoli

Finding Dad

Forgiveness is a mystical act, not a reasonable one.
~Caroline Myss

I was thirteen years old and had never even seen a picture of my father, when suddenly the invisible character of my childhood had a face. I don't know what woke me up on that cold Michigan night, but my eyes popped open with a sense of urgency at the very second a CNN news anchor was announcing the results of the 1988 gubernatorial election in Rhode Island.

"It was a close one in the Ocean State for Bruce Sundlun," she announced. She talked about how this war hero/business tycoon-turned politician almost beat the incumbent, Governor Edward DiPrete.

My mom had always said, "Your biological father is a man named Bruce Sundlun." But now, for the first time, he was real and staring back at me. On TV. My real father was no longer just the faceless man who broke my mother's heart. The news anchor proved his existence to me with a picture and a story. That night, Mom and I were sleeping in a hotel room, bone tired from a long day of moving to a new house, when I reached over and shook her. "Mom, wake up! Is that him?" I shrieked.

Bleary eyed, she looked up and answered me in a scratchy, shocked voice. "He must have gone back to Rhode Island, where he's from."

I wanted to press "rewind" and freeze his picture. Did I really look just like him, like Mom had always told me?

My creators met in the glamorous world of aviation in the 70s when flying was still about the coolest thing you could do on earth. He was the handsome World War II bomber pilot turned airline CEO, and Mom was his chief flight attendant. She fell madly in love with my father, but when she became pregnant with me, there was nothing but turbulence ahead. There was no DNA test in 1975, and he refused to claim me. Mom knew I was his, but she yielded to his big time lawyers and settled out of court for thirty-five thousand dollars to pay for my life, and a promise not to contact him again or let me use his very important surname.

At that moment, staring at him on TV, none of that mattered. I was a girl who had just found her father — or almost. The Universe woke me up in the middle of the night, awakening a primal need to know the other half of me. And nothing was going to stop me.

My quest wouldn't be easy. My father was eventually elected Governor of Rhode Island in 1991, and he ignored the letters I wrote to the State House asking to meet him. Finally, we hired a lawyer, and I managed to get a secret meeting and a DNA test that proved I really was his daughter. I was positive that once he knew I was really his, he would open his heart and welcome me into his life. But, instead, he did nothing. I was heartbroken. Again. How could he do this to me? What happened to my happy ending?

I really wanted him to be a dad, but if he wouldn't, then I felt he should at least help us pay for college since Mom had been struggling to do it all on her own for so long. I filed a paternity suit at the age of seventeen, and a media frenzy erupted. My story started leading the evening news, and the nation's newspapers printed headlines like "Gov Child" above my picture. Even under the scrutiny of spotlights, my war hero dad was still fighting me. Why couldn't he just be a dad? My soul ached for his acceptance.

I could have given up, but somewhere deep inside me, a little voice told me to have faith, that he would come around. "It's all meant to be," I told myself. I'm sure it sounded like wishful thinking, but it wasn't. My dad shocked the world when, in the middle of the media frenzy, he agreed to pay for my college tuition and invited me to come live with him so we could "get to know each other." I didn't know if I could trust him, but I packed my bags and left everything I knew to uncover my other half. I welcomed his offer of acceptance. My identity was worth the risk.

The same part of me that told me to have faith also demanded that I forgive my father for all the rejection, pain, and anger he had caused me. When I showed up on his doorstep to cross the threshold of my new life, I knew I had to choose to forgive if I wanted the happy ending my soul had been yearning for so long. So I did. I gave my father a chance at redemption, and he ran with it.

There was no long, maudlin apology. Instead, we started to heal the past by living in the present. We discovered we were a lot alike, right down to our love of Oreo cookies and chocolate ice cream sodas. The daily doses of love we shared from simple joys together settled sweetly in my core, and I started to heal the cracks of abandonment in my foundation. My wounds gave way to wisdom, and on the journey to find my father I found my true self. I learned that it's never too late to heal; my father became Dad, and then Poppy to my children. I knew my father one year longer than I did not know him when he passed away at the age of ninety-one, in my arms, surrounded by the family I had always dreamed of. Forgiveness is the closest thing I have found to a fairy godmother. Its energy has the magical power to transform us and create the happy ending we so badly want.

We often teach what we have to learn, which is why I wrote the book *Finding Dad: From "Love Child" to Daughter*. My story taught me that forgiveness is truly the greatest gift you can give yourself.

~Kara Sundlun

How Sweet the Sound

Take a harp, go about the city; make sweet melody, sing many songs, that thou may be remembered.
~Isaiah 23:16

The lead should have been mine. All my friends agreed with me. At least, it shouldn't have been Helen's, that strange new girl. She never had a word to say, always looking down at her feet as if her life was too heavy to bear. We thought she was just stuck-up. *Things can't be all that bad for her,* we reasoned, *not with all the great clothes she wears.* She hadn't worn the same thing more than twice in the two months she'd been at our school.

But the worst of it was when she showed up at our tryouts and sang for my part. Everyone knew the lead role was meant for me. After all, I had parts in all our high-school musicals, and this was our senior year.

My friends were waiting for me, so I didn't hang around for Helen's audition. The shock came two days later when we hurried to check the bulletin board for the cast list.

We scanned the sheets looking for my name. When we found it, I stood there in shock. Helen was picked to play the lead! I was to be her mother and her understudy. Understudy? Nobody could believe it.

Rehearsals seemed to go on forever. Helen didn't seem to notice that we were going out of our way to ignore her. I'll admit it, Helen did have a beautiful voice. She was different on stage somehow. Not so much happy as settled and content.

Opening night brought its fair share of jitters. Everyone was quietly bustling around backstage, waiting for the curtain to go up. Everyone but Helen, of course. She seemed contained in her own world

The performance was a hit. Our timing was perfect; our voices blended and soared. Helen and I flowed back and forth, weaving the story between us — I, the ailing mother praying for her wayward daughter, and Helen, the daughter who realizes as her mother dies that there is more to life than this life. The final scene reached its dramatic end. I was laying in the darkened bedroom. The prop bed I was on was uncomfortable, which made it hard to stay still. I was impatient, anxious for Helen's big finish to be over.

She was spotlighted on stage, the grieving daughter beginning to understand the true meaning of the hymn she had been singing as her mother passed away.

"Amazing grace, how sweet the sound…" Her voice lifted over the pain of her mother's death and the joy of God's promises.

"…That saved a wretch like me…" Something real was happening to me as Helen sang. My impatience was gone.

"… I once was lost, but now I'm found…" I started to cry.

"…Was blind but now I see." My spirit began to turn within me, and I turned to God. In that moment, I knew his love, his desire for me. Helen's voice lingered in the prayer of the last note. The curtain dropped.

Complete silence. Not a sound. Helen stood behind the closed curtain, head bowed, gently weeping.

Suddenly, applause and cheers erupted, and when the curtain parted the entire audience was standing.

We all made our final bows. My hugs were genuine. My heart had been opened wide.

Then it was over. The costumes were hung up, makeup tissued off and the lights dimmed. Everyone went off in their usual groupings, congratulating each other.

Everyone but Helen. I stayed because I needed to tell her something.

"Helen, your song… it was so real for me," I hesitated, my feelings intense. I suddenly felt shy. "You sang me into the heart of God."

Helen's eyes met mine.

"That's what my mother said to me the night she died." A tear slipped down her cheek. My heart leapt to hers. "My mother was in such pain. Singing 'Amazing Grace' always comforted her. She told me to remember God would always be good to me, and that his grace would lead her home."

Her face lit up from the inside out, her mother's love shining through. "Just before she died, she whispered, 'Sing me into the heart of God, Helen.' That night and tonight, I sang for my mother."

~Cynthia M. Hamond

Coffee-Shop Kindness

If you can't return a favor, pass it on.

~Louise Brown

My senior year of high school was an extremely hectic one, to say the least. If I wasn't studying and worrying about my grades, I was juggling multiple extra-curricular activities or attempting to make sense of my plans for college. It seemed as if my life had turned into one crazy cloud of confusion, and I was stumbling around blindly, hoping to find some sort of direction.

Finally, as senior year began to wind down, I got a part-time job working at the local coffee shop. I had figured that the job would be easy and, for the most part, stress-free. I pictured myself pouring the best gourmet coffees, making delicious doughnuts and becoming close friends with the regular customers.

What I hadn't counted on were the people with enormous orders who chose to use the drive-thru window, or the women who felt that the coffee was much too creamy, or the men who wanted their iced coffees remade again and again until they reached a certain level of perfection. There were moments when I was exasperated with the human race as a whole, simply because I couldn't seem to please any-one. There was always too much sugar, too little ice and not enough skim milk. Nevertheless, I kept at it.

One miserable rainy day, one of my regular customers came in looking depressed and defeated. My coworker and I asked what the problem was and if we could help, but the customer wouldn't reveal any details. He just said he felt like crawling into bed, pulling the sheets up over his head and staying there for a few years. I knew exactly how he felt.

Before he left, I handed him a bag along with his iced coffee. He looked at me questioningly because he hadn't ordered anything but the coffee. He opened the bag and saw that I had given him his favorite type of doughnut.

"It's on me," I told him. "Have a nice day."

He smiled and thanked me before turning around and heading back out into the rain.

The next day was miserable as well, rain spilling from the sky. Everyone in town seemed to be using the drive-thru window because no one wanted to brave the black skies or the thunder and lightning.

I spent my afternoon hanging out the window, handing people their orders and waiting as they slowly counted their pennies. I tried to smile as the customers complained about the weather, but it was difficult to smile as they sat in their temperature-controlled cars with the windows rolled up, while I dealt with huge droplets of water hanging from my visor, a shirt that was thoroughly soaked around the collar and an air conditioner that blasted out cold air despite sixty-seven-degree weather. On top of that, no one was tipping. Every time I looked into our nearly empty tip jar, I grew more depressed.

Around seven o'clock that evening, I was in the middle of making another pot of vanilla hazelnut decaf when the customer from the day before drove up to the window. But instead of ordering anything, he handed me a single pink rose and a little note. He said that not too many people take the time to care about others, and he was glad there were still people like me in the world. I was speechless and very touched; I nearly forgot yesterday's deed. After a moment, I happily thanked him. He told me I was welcome and, with a friendly wave, drove away.

I waited until I saw his Jeep exit the parking lot, then I ran to the back of the shop and read the note. It read:

Christine,

Thanks for being so sweet, kind and thoughtful yesterday. I was sincerely touched by you. It is so nice to meet someone who's genuinely nice, warm, and sensitive and unselfish. Please don't change your ways because I truly believe that you will excel. Have a great day!

Hank

As the day passed, I had plenty of complaining customers, but any time I felt depressed or frustrated, I thought of Hank and his kindness. I would smile, hold my head up high, clear my throat and politely ask, "How can I help you?"

~Christine Walsh

Understanding Jenny

*If someone listens, or stretches out a hand, or whispers a kind
word of encouragement, or attempts to understand a lonely
person, extraordinary things will begin to happen.*
~Loretta Girzartis

I jumped into my mother's car, threw my cross-country team bag
into the backseat, slammed the car door and fought with my seat
belt.

"I'm so sick of it!" I said and pulled my hair back into its
frizzy ponytail.

"I can see that," my mom answered, then turned on the blinker,
looked over her shoulder and pulled out into the traffic. "I'm guess-
ing this isn't about your hair."

"It's Jenny, playing her mind games again. Training is less tiring
than dealing with her and her feelings."

"Which one is Jenny?" my mom asked.

"She's been here about a month. She lives at the Timmers."

"Oh, yes, Gloria told me they had a new foster kid. Said she's been
moved around, but she's getting decent grades and joining school
activities."

"I just wish she hadn't joined my activity."

"Why's that?" My mom was pretty good about listening to me vent.

"I mean, we've been training for weeks: stretching, running, pacing, lifting weights and making ourselves into a team. Then in strolls

Jenny, the goddess of cross-country or something. A coach's dream. She paces around the course with us, and suddenly she's so far ahead that she makes the loop and is running back towards us like we're standing in place. A smile on her face, her perfect hair swinging behind her."

"So are you upset because your team has someone who can earn you some real points, or because she has a talent that she enjoys or because her hair stays so perfect?" My mom leaned over and pushed my damp-curled bangs out of my face.

"Mom, I'm not that shallow."

"I know, honey. Sorry. Just trying to see the problem here."

"Jenny's the problem. She helps all of us run faster by upping the pace. She cheers us on. She trains harder, and so do we. We were voted co-captains. Then, this week, she cops an attitude. I spent most of my time running after her."

"No pun intended!"

"Mom! Please! This is serious," I sighed and took a drink from my water bottle. "Our first meet is tomorrow. Jenny keeps saying she won't run with the team. She has all sorts of reasons from leg cramps to a headache. I have to beg her. I have to tell her over and over that she can't do that to the rest of the team. It goes on all day, between classes, at lunch, on the way to practice. She wears me out. What's her deal?"

"She ends up running though, right?"

"Yeah, but we're all tired of it. She's so needy."

Mom pulled into our driveway. Instead of rushing into the house to start dinner, she turned and looked at me.

"Cindy, you gave yourself the answer."

Great, I'm pouring it all out, and Mom's going to give me a pop quiz. "Make this easy, would you, Mom?"

"Well, Gloria told me a little about Jenny. She and her little brother have been together all this time in foster care. They're really close. Her caseworker said that Jenny took good care of her little brother. Every time they would move, Jenny would say that as long as they were together, they had a family."

My heart sank. "Please, don't tell me something happened to her little brother."

"No, he's fine. His father, Jenny's stepfather, earned custody of him. He came for him this week. He had gifts and hugs and big plans for their future."

"Really? That's good."

"Yes, but he had nothing for Jenny. She wasn't even a little part of his big plans."

My chest felt tight. "Why?"

"Well, Jenny's mom and stepfather weren't together that long. Jenny and her brother have been in foster care for a while now. I guess he didn't consider Jenny his."

"What about her mom?"

"Her mom wants her drugs and alcohol more than she wants Jenny."

"Poor Jenny, not to have a family." I was close to tears. "Not to feel wanted or needed."

My mother patted my knee. "That's it, honey. You got it."

And I did.

I didn't see Jenny during school the next day. I started to think I had understood too late, that Jenny wasn't going to show at all.

I was the last one to get on the team bus and was glad there were still a few empty rows. I could take up two seats, put on my headsets and get some down time before the meet.

Then I spotted Jenny. She was sitting in the back, alone.

I started down the narrow aisle, causing quite a disruption trying to maneuver myself and my oversized bag to the back. By the time I got to my seat, most of the team was watching my progress.

"Can I sit by you?" I asked Jenny. She shrugged her shoulders. I took it as a yes. "I didn't see you today. I was afraid you weren't going to make it."

"I didn't think anyone would notice if I made it or not."

The girls around us groaned. Here she goes again.

I looked at Jenny. I saw past her attitude because I understood what she was really saying.

"We would've noticed if you weren't here, Jenny. We want you running with us. The team needs you."

Jenny seemed to fill up, to expand.

"Isn't that right, team?" I called. "Let's hear it for Jenny!"

There was silence. *Please*, I thought, *for Jenny's sake, give her what she needs.*

Slowly and then with building momentum, they cheered for their teammate. As they did, the atmosphere changed. They began to care more about Jenny.

Jenny felt it. The defiance drained out of her shoulders. Her face relaxed. She smiled and blushed with pleasure.

We didn't erase all the pain in Jenny's life, but neither had we added to it.

She ran with us that day. She won the individual blue ribbon and lifted our team to third place. She never threatened not to run again, and she led us to our best season record.

Through our simple offering of friendship and her willingness to accept it, we gave Jenny something more important to her than blue ribbons. We gave her what she desired the most: to know she was wanted and needed.

~Cynthia M. Hamond

Angel

Do not wait for extraordinary circumstances to do good action;
try to use ordinary situations.
~Jean Paul Richter

Two days before my birthday, I got an e-mail that would first make me cry and then make me smile.

Patrick was a kid that I knew from 4-H. We became friends when I taught him how to show horses and he showed my horse in the Junior Division at the County Horse Show. We weren't "close" friends, but he was a pretty cool guy. I mean, how many guys like to show horses and will let a *girl* teach them how to do it? Not very many.

After the horse show and his leaving the club, we kind of lost contact. He sent me a Christmas card with his email address in it, but I put off e-mailing him. I thought, *How much stuff would we be able to talk about anyway?*

His e-mail address was in my address book, and when I changed servers, my new address went to everyone on my list. A few days later I got a reply from Patrick. It was brief; he asked me how I was and told me that he had started riding lessons again. He also asked me how Theo, my horse, was and he gave me his e-mail address. He ended with:

Hope you have a nice day. Patrick.

I replied to his e-mail, just small talk, and my e-mail looked something like this:

> *Hi! Nice to hear from you. That's so cool you're taking les-*
> *sons. I'm really sorry that I didn't e-mail you at all during*
> *the winter. School has been really busy for me this year.*
> *Theo is doing good. He still knocks my radio off the stall*
> *door when I have the music on too loud. You'll have to come*
> *out and visit sometime.*

A few more lines ended my e-mail. When his came back, he had some questions for me.

That's cool. What kind of music do you listen to? I like country. Do you like hunting?

Turns out, country music is the only thing I will listen to! And hunting is one of my favorite pastimes. I had no idea we had so much in common. I thought, *This is cool, we actually like the same stuff!*

Those e-mails were the start of a two-month correspondence that covered a wide variety of subjects. Having a lot in common made it easy to just chat. And to tell you the truth, I enjoyed getting his e-mails.

Toward the end of June, I wrote him a reply to an e-mail I had received four days earlier from him. I felt bad about not getting back to him right away and my e-mail wasn't much more than a note, but what I got back from him took my breath away.

Patrick's e-mail was short. He started off by telling me he was going to be on vacation for three weeks and other stuff like that. But the postscript is what got me. It read:

> *P.S. I really wanted to say thank you for talking to me*
> *through e-mail. I'm usually really shy and am afraid to tell*
> *people what my likes are and all, plus I really have been*
> *bored since school let out. E-mailing you, at least I can talk*
> *to someone. You like everything I like so far, and as long as*
> *I have lived I have never met anyone so much like me. I've*
> *been used to a lot of people picking on me, and I've been*
> *pretty down the past few years.*

When I read that people picked on him, my thoughts were, *Why in the world are kids so mean? Don't they realize how they are making him feel?* It broke my heart to hear him say that he had been down the past few years. I actually started crying when I read how the other kids treated him. It was then that I understood that Patrick was a kid who had needed a friend. My taking the time to e-mail him had made him feel important, like someone really cared enough to talk to him instead of just picking on him.

> *I want to thank you again. You like just about everything I like — hunting, cars, country music, horses. To me you're like an angel.*

Those last six words touched my heart. It made me feel so good I just can't explain it! No one had ever said anything that nice to me before, and to be called an "angel" just made my day! When I e-mailed him back, I sincerely thanked him for what he said and told him to hang on.

That day, I learned a lesson that would stay with me for the rest of my life. From now on, I will take the time to do the little things, like replying to an e-mail or card, even if it's just a line or two. You never know how you might help someone and become his or her "angel."

~Jena Pallone

Like People First

The more we know the better we forgive. Whoever feels deeply,
feels for all who live.
~Madame de Staël

Craig, a close friend of mine in graduate school, brought energy and life into any room he entered. He focused his entire attention on you while you were talking, and you felt incredibly important. People loved him.

One sunny autumn day, Craig and I were sitting in our usual study area. I was staring out the window when I noticed one of my professors crossing the parking lot.

"I don't want to run into him," I said.

"Why not?" Craig asked.

I explained that the previous spring semester, the professor and I had parted on bad terms. I had taken offense at some suggestion he had made and had, in turn, given offense in my answer. "Besides," I added, "the guy just doesn't like me."

Craig looked down at the passing figure. "Maybe you've got it wrong," he said. "Maybe you're the one who's turning away—and you're just doing that because you're afraid. He probably thinks you don't like him, so he's not friendly. People like people who like them. If you show an interest in him, he'll be interested in you. Go talk to him."

Craig's words smarted. I walked tentatively down the stairs into the parking lot. I greeted my professor warmly and asked how his summer had been. He looked at me, genuinely surprised. We walked off together talking, and I could imagine Craig watching from the window, smiling broadly.

Craig had explained to me a simple concept, so simple I couldn't believe I'd never known it. Like most young people, I felt unsure of myself and came to all my encounters fearing that others would judge me — when, in fact, they were worrying about how I would judge *them*. From that day on, instead of seeing judgment in the eyes of others, I recognized the need people have to make a connection and to share something about themselves. I discovered a world of people I never would have known otherwise.

Once, for example, on a train going across Canada, I began talking to a man everyone was avoiding because he was weaving and slurring his speech as if drunk. It turned out that he was recovering from a stroke. He had been an engineer on the same line we were riding, and long into the night he revealed to me the history beneath every mile of track: Pile O'Bones Creek, named for the thousands of buffalo skeletons left there by Indian hunters; the legend of Big Jack, a Swedish track-layer who could lift 500-pound steel rails; a conductor named McDonald who kept a rabbit as his traveling companion.

As the morning sun began to tint the horizon, he grabbed my hand and looked into my eyes. "Thanks for listening. Most people wouldn't bother." He didn't have to thank me. The pleasure had been all mine.

On a noisy street corner in Oakland, California, a family who stopped me for directions turned out to be visiting from Australia's isolated northwest coast. I asked them about their life back home. Soon, over coffee, they regaled me with stories of huge saltwater crocodiles "with backs as wide as car hoods."

Each encounter became an adventure, each person a lesson in life. The wealthy, the poor, the powerful and the lonely; all were as full of dreams and doubts as I. And each had a unique story to tell, if only I were willing to hear.

An old, stubble-bearded hobo told me how he'd fed his family during the Depression by firing his shotgun into a pond and gathering up the stunned fish that floated to the surface. A traffic patrolman confided how he'd learned his hand gestures by watching bullfighters and symphony conductors. And a young beautician shared the joy of watching residents in a nursing home smile after receiving a new hairstyle.

How often we allow such opportunities to pass us by. The girl who everyone thinks is homely, the boy with the odd clothes — those people have stories to tell, as surely as you do. And like you, they dream that someone is willing to hear.

This is what Craig knew. Like people first, ask questions later. See if the light you shine on others isn't reflected back on you a hundredfold.

~Kent Nerburn

Asperger's
and Friendship

*A friend is someone who understands your past, believes in
your future, and accepts you just the way you are.*
~Author Unknown

As far back as I can remember I was the odd one out at school, and for me it meant a lack of friends. However, those who were willing to be my friends tried to help me, and I had a core group of friends who stuck with me through the storms of elementary, junior high and high school.

When I was diagnosed with Asperger's syndrome in the ninth grade, I was told that I would have to go to a special school for autistic kids. My resource teacher at that time said it would be a bad idea, and then he asked me if it was okay for him to talk to my class about my diagnosis. For those who do not know what Asperger's syndrome is, it is a high functioning form of autism characterized by a special interest, sensory integration dysfunction, lack of social skills, communications, and executive function.

I thought we were giving them more ammunition with which to tease me. Well, I was mistaken. Instead, they rallied around me, teaching me what was socially acceptable and how to study better.

I wound up being on the Academic Decathlon team for three years; in my senior year I was team captain. I helped lead the team to Most Improved and received the Most Inspirational Participant award. But I will never forget the high point of senior year — I was asked to be a starting player at the senior alum game; when I went on court my peers started to stamp their feet and call out my name. The game was slowed down, and I was passed the ball. When I missed the first shot, my peers stamped harder and called my name louder. I landed the second shot and scored two points. I will never forget the cheering of my peers. I was voted MVP even though I had scored only two points.

When I moved on to college I found another group of friends at the University of La Verne and these friends have been with me now for five years. I will never forget their kindness. As an Aspie, I don't deal well with surprises; I need to rehearse possible scenarios. But on my twenty-second birthday my university friends decorated the door and hallway of my dorm. I was overcome by the surprise, but surprisingly, I didn't have a meltdown from the surprise! They surprised me again on my twenty-fourth birthday.

But the real moment I found happiness, and really understood what was meant by happiness and friendship, was yesterday — April 9, 2011. It was a joint birthday party for me, my cousin who I call my big sister, and her sister's boyfriend. I had invited thirteen people and only five showed up, but the five that came included an old friend from elementary school, a friend and mentor from high school, and two friends from the university. I was nervous and scared because I had no idea what to expect, but when the party was over I had received a true gift. I realized what makes me happy and stronger is having a large group of friends. Just having a friend is highly unusual for someone with Asperger's, but I have a large support group: a core of five friends that have stayed in contact since elementary school; a group from secondary school, and now friends from the university.

I have two other friends with the same diagnosis and they don't have friends like I do—friends who support me, who guide me, and who are not afraid to tell me when I have done something incorrectly. My friends make me happy, and they make my life worth living — because I am rich in friends.

~Richard Nakai

Chapter 10

Create Your Best Future

Counting Your Blessings

Third World Banquet

Poverty can teach lessons that privilege cannot.
~Jack Klugman

One of the greatest lessons I've ever learned, I learned in the sixth grade. My teacher was Mrs. Schmidt, and for years before I reached her class, I couldn't wait to have her. She was the cool, young teacher who really did make learning fun. She taught the same lessons every other teacher did, but her way of doing it was different. Like they say today, she thought "outside of the box."

One afternoon as we were settling into our desk chairs after recess, Mrs. Schmidt presented the outline for our upcoming project: The Third World Banquet. It was a luncheon we were going to put on for the sixth-, seventh- and eighth-grade classes where each student would eat a meal that symbolized food of a first-, second- or third-world country.

For the next month we planned the event, raising money, gathering parents to help, and brainstorming over the details. Before long we had a plan. To make it fair, every student participating would blindly draw a strip of paper from a bowl. If the paper was marked with a one, that lucky student would be eating a first-world style lunch. If it was marked with a two, they'd be eating a second-world style lunch. And if the paper was marked with three, you guessed it, they'd eat a third-world style lunch.

The day of the banquet finally arrived and just before the lunch bell rang, the bowl was making its way around each classroom for the students to choose their fate for the afternoon. Of course everyone hoped to pick a ticket marked with a one.

Moments later, we stood at the doors to the school gym (which served as the dining hall) waiting patiently to be directed to our seats inside. Soon the parents were escorting the first-world kids to rows of tables that were set with tablecloths, napkins, silverware and plates. The second-world kids were led to another group of tables. There were chairs, but no extra comforts like tablecloths or salt and pepper shakers. Lastly, the third-world kids were led to a roped-off area of the floor that was covered in brown paper on which they were to sit.

Very soon after the realities of our banquet were made known, the faces changed. The first-world students of course were beaming, walking around like little kings and queens, slapping high-fives at their good fortune. The third-world kids appeared suddenly forlorn, trying to find comfort on the hard floor beneath them, envious of the classmates who sat in chairs all around them, dreading the moment they would find out their lunch for the day. In the middle were the second-world kids who sat almost expressionless, a little disappointed they weren't quite as lucky as their first-world friends, but certainly glad they weren't on the floor either.

Before long, lunch was served. The first-world students got spaghetti and meatballs with garlic bread, salad and a choice of drink. They were taken care of first, waited on hand and foot, served seconds if they wanted, and given refills when their cups were empty. They even had cake and ice cream for dessert!

The second-world students were served peanut butter and jelly with half pint-size cartons of milk. At those tables, there were no seconds, no endless refills, no dessert at the end. But it wasn't nearly as bad as the third-world kids had had it. And for that, they were grateful.

Inside the roped-off area of floor in the "third world," it was crowded and uncomfortable. As the students situated themselves, nearly on top of one another, a few pitchers of water, cups and small bowls of rice were passed out. But of course there were no forks.

As much as the experience of the banquet on a whole stays with me today, it is a small detail that I remember most clearly, a detail that has a place in my story thanks to an old classmate, Tyler. He was one of the bigger boys in class. From his appearance, one would think he would be rough and tough and interested in causing trouble. He played along and fit in with the rest of the kids but underneath was really a gentle soul. So there we all were all dressed in the same red, white and navy uniforms, but divided by wealth (or lack thereof).

The first-world students sat with one another eating and drinking and laughing in their comfortable "first world," forgetting about the "poverty" that surrounded them—poverty that for some of their best friends had suddenly become a reality. The second-world kids, with whom I sat, had quickly forgotten all about the spaghetti they weren't eating, just thankful they hadn't chosen papers marked three. The third-world students sat on the hard floor, rationing the water and scooping sticky, flavorless rice into their mouths with their bare hands.

It was at the end of the lunch that Tyler, who sat in first world and who, in his everyday humble and kind-hearted shoes, seemed the least affected by his status, sat up in his seat. Something suddenly made him see the lesson Mrs. Schmidt was hoping we would all see. When offered seconds on his dessert he said, "Yes, please." But it wasn't for himself that he wanted that second piece of cake. It was for one of the less fortunate. Not a minute later, he was out of his chair with a string of fellow first-worlders behind him on their way to the second- and third-world sections of the gym. His gesture of kindness had a domino effect on everyone around him, and within minutes the plates of chocolate cake were sitting on the bare tables in second world and taking the place of the rice bowls in third.

Having been prepared for this, the parents were waiting with plates of cake for everyone and were soon passing them out to each of the students who'd not been so lucky earlier in the meal. Smiles were finding their way back to the once poverty-stricken faces.

By evening we'd all be filling our bellies once again with family dinners, going about our carefree lives as fortunate children, forgetting about the hunger in the world or the hunger some of us had experienced earlier that afternoon. But for that hour in the gym at our Third World Banquet, we understood, even though it was only for a brief time, what it felt like to be hungry, because we had eaten only rice or because we'd witnessed our friends with nothing. I still think about that humbling afternoon, and how Tyler's one small action made such a great difference.

~Andrea Fecik

Thanks Giving

I feel a very unusual sensation — if it is not indigestion, I think
it must be gratitude.
~Benjamin Disraeli

I shivered with cold and excitement as I scuffed through the yellow maple leaves that blanketed my backyard. The next day was Thanksgiving, my favorite holiday, and I was looking forward to seeing my whole family. Even though my three older sisters were married now, I was sure we'd all get together to eat turkey, relax, reminisce, and watch home movies.

I walked into the house expecting to smell pumpkin pie baking and willing to help my mom get ready for our company. I was surprised to find there wasn't any sign of holiday preparations.

What was going on? Mom must have been planning to start baking after dinner.

At the dinner table, I found I couldn't have been more wrong. "Listen, everyone, I have something to tell you about tomorrow," my dad announced.

Four pairs of eyes looked at him expectantly.

"Your older sisters all have other plans this year for Thanksgiving...."

"But it's a tradition to come here," I interrupted.

"Teresa, you have to realize that once you're married, you have two sets of parents to spend the holidays with. Your sisters can't always be here," my mom explained.

"Anyway," Dad said, "I've decided to give your mom a much-deserved break this year. I'm taking everyone to dinner at the Harvest Cafeteria tomorrow."

Dad's announcement was met with stony silence.

"You're kidding, aren't you?" I was the first to speak.

My dad shook his head.

He was immediately greeted with a chorus of: "But, Dad, that's a terrible idea!" "But, Dad, I don't want to go out to eat!" "But Dad, a cafeteria?"

"Dad," I said, presenting what seemed to me to be the perfect argument, "the pilgrims would never have celebrated Thanksgiving anywhere but at home."

"Teresa," my dad replied, "after nearly starving, the pilgrims were happy just to have food. I don't think it mattered to them if that food was served in their homes or at a restaurant down the street."

I could tell it was no use arguing. As the sound of his proclamation died away, so did my dreams of a homespun Thanksgiving holiday complete with turkey and all the trimmings.

As I lay in bed that night, I wanted to cry, but the tears wouldn't come. "Maybe it's silly to be so upset," I said talking to God through the canopy of my bed, "but how would you like it if someone ruined Your favorite holiday?"

When I awoke the next morning, there was no smell of turkey roasting in the oven. Instead I was greeted by the smell of coffee and burned toast. I burrowed back under the covers. There was no reason to get up.

The day dragged by. At five o'clock, we headed for Harvest Cafeteria. "You could have picked a better place to eat," I grumbled under my breath.

"Enough," my dad warned. "Just enjoy your evening."

Enjoy my evening. Right!

I wasn't surprised that the restaurant wasn't crowded. Normal people have Thanksgiving dinner at home, I wanted to say as I slid my tray down the metal runners, but I remembered my dad's warning and kept silent.

"Turkey or ham?" the lady behind the counter asked.

"Turkey," I mumbled. I chose very little, then followed my family to a table by the window.

As Dad said the blessing, I looked out the window. Instead of sitting at home looking at a backyard full of brilliantly colored leaves, I'm looking at an old black-topped parking lot. This isn't what Thanksgiving is all about.

Throughout the meal, my parents made attempts to lighten my mood. Finally, they gave up and let me sulk.

By the time dinner was finished, none of us seemed to have the holiday spirit. There was no lingering for another piece of pie or a second cup of coffee. We put on our coats and headed home.

Once there, Dad started outside to get firewood. When he saw me heading for my room, he called me back. "I want us to spend some time together as a family." My brother, Marty, was pulling some DVDs of our family's home movies out of the cabinet.

"Do we have to watch these?" I asked. I thought it couldn't be any fun without the whole family together.

"We do," Dad replied.

So I sat and watched my family history pass before my eyes. There were scenes from when we were babies, scenes of the whole family at the park, even scenes from Thanksgivings past. I smiled at pictures of my mom pulling the turkey from the oven and my dad carving it. It felt good to see the whole family around the dinner table. That's what Thanksgiving is really all about, I thought.

As the projector continued rolling, I saw another dimension to our family life. I saw how hard my parents worked to care for seven children. I saw the plain meals we ate. I saw the tired, but happy, looks on my parents' faces as they were surrounded by their children.

I remembered my earlier comment about going to dinner at a better restaurant and winced. Maybe Harvest Cafeteria was what we could afford.

I also thought about how hard my mom worked with four kids still at home. Maybe dinner out was a special treat for her—a break from a tradition that meant hours of cooking and preparation.

As I sat in the dark, the tears I'd wanted to cry last night finally flowed. All these things I have to be thankful for, and all I can do is complain.

I got out of my chair and went to sit at my dad's feet. I laid my head against his knee. "Dad, I appreciate you and mom working so hard to take care of our family," I told him.

If my out-of-the-blue comment surprised my dad, he didn't let on. "You're welcome," he said, stroking my hair.

"I'm sorry for spoiling everyone's Thanksgiving," I continued.

"You didn't spoil it, Hon. You just took longer than the rest of us to get used to the idea of celebrating Thanksgiving in a different way."

As the projector whirred on, I relaxed against my dad, content at last. I'd finally found out just what Thanksgiving was all about.

"Be joyful always; pray continually; give thanks in all circumstances, for this is God's will for you in Christ Jesus" (1 Thessalonians 5:16-18).

~Teresa Cleary

The Adventure of Change

Change always comes bearing gifts.
~Price Pritchett

'm a military brat. When my father was a marine officer, we moved twelve times in fourteen years. When people hear this, they say, "That must have been hard on you."

I disagree. Each move was an adventure, an opportunity that contributed to who I am as an adult.

At family meetings, my parents would announce, "We're being transferred." Then the map would come out and we'd go into a huddle.

"This is where we are. This is where we are going." My father's fingers landed on our current home state and with the other hand, he pinpointed our next home.

I might have been sad to leave behind a favorite hiding place but I looked forward to finding a new one at the next place. I was exposed to the different seasons when we moved from the East to the West Coast. In school I learned the history of more than one state, something I wouldn't have been exposed to if we hadn't moved. My brothers and I got to visit many amusement parks and museums across the country as we traveled. These experiences were only some of the common threads among military families.

As my family ticked off the trip miles, my mother engaged us in a plethora of games, including my favorite — listing state license plates we saw. I was fascinated to see the variety. I'd wonder where the other families were headed. Were they moving too? Were they headed to Grandma's house or were they out for a local trip?

If we hadn't moved across this great country, I wouldn't have spotted a Kaibab squirrel, admired the petroglyphs of Zion National Park, or wondered at the hoodoos of Bryce Canyon. I wouldn't have giggled as we dipped deep in the water on a river float, screeched as I reeled in a trout from a babbling creek, or gazed in wonder at the Atlantic and Pacific Oceans. Although I love my Tex-Mex, the taste of true Cajun food and fresh seafood gave me a desire for a variety of cuisines. I doubt I would have tried chicken shawarma if I hadn't tried an assortment of dishes as a child.

Although the distances seemed vast when my dad would show us the map, some of my fondest memories involved the miles we covered. Our longest trek? From North Carolina to California in the summer of 1970. My parents broke each trip into segments. As an adult, I surmised it was easier on them to shoo four kids out of the car to run off energy at frequent stops. But as children, we delighted in the adventure of each break.

My parents scoped out the national and state parks along the route, and researched the hotel and camping options. Camping usually won out. With six of us, I suspect it was the cheaper solution. This led to memories such as crawling into a tent on a clear evening in the Rocky Mountains and waking up to more than eight inches of pristine snow blanketing our tents, the ground and picnic tables. When we opened the flaps of our tents, we stared in wonder at the crystal white of the landscape and then huddled back into cozy, flannel sleeping bags for a late start that morning.

Breakfast over a Coleman gas grill always tasted better than a meal cooked on a kitchen stove. Camping meant more effort for my parents than for my brothers and me. We'd clamor out of the car, help unload a few things, and leave our parents to do the real camp setup. For my brothers and me there were critters to chase and a half-hearted attempt to gather kindling for a fire. With the smell of pine needles in the Rockies, or the squish of sand between our toes on a beach, we'd be off and return as mealtime approached.

As Dad announced, "Just a little farther," we always became antsy. Would it be a big house? Would it have a bedroom for each of us? Would the back yard have enough room to toss a ball? When we pulled into our new home's driveway, I remember the excitement of solving those mysteries. My brothers and I ran from one bedroom to the next, discussing which room belonged to whom. I don't remember any arguments. It seemed as if each house was made just for our family and specific bedrooms fit our needs and personalities. Once we'd staked our claims, we'd run out the back door to see what was there. Each varied environment influenced me.

One of my favorite homes in Camp Lejeune, North Carolina, gave me a tremendous love of nature. I remember gasping when I went out the back door. Woods! Not twenty feet from the back porch, a forest of pine, beech and ash served as the property line. It didn't take the four of us long to disappear into the trees with the promise to stick together and not go too far. We spent many afternoons discovering birds, lizards and other critters among the leaves of that forest floor. By the time we'd moved away a year later, we could each explore without getting lost.

From the stops along the route to the mysteries awaiting us at the end of our journey, our military life provided opportunities that serve me well as an adult. I'm never bored, always curious to learn, and usually look at any change as an opportunity to grow. Military brats can't say, "I've lived in this house for twenty years," but we can brag about the different states we've explored and the friends and adventures we've experienced.

~Gail Molsbee Morris

Under One Roof

Christmas waves a magic wand over this world, and behold,
everything is softer and more beautiful.
~Norman Vincent Peale

On the day of my fourteenth birthday, in late October 2013, a huge winter storm rolled in as if from thin air. So instead of celebrating outside around our backyard fire pit the way we'd done the year before I had to move my party inside our small Toronto bungalow. Then, on the heels of the chill that disrupted my birthday came a frost that covered the lawns in early November. It was our first sign of the long, cold winter ahead. By mid-November, snow already covered the porches and driveways of Toronto homes. Although it was early, I was absolutely delighted because I loved snow. It was already starting to feel like Christmas!

I was in my first year of high school, majoring in vocal at a special school for the performing arts. It was now mid-December, and our annual Christmas Concert was finally finished. This followed weeks of high tension and struggles simply getting to, and especially home from late rehearsals because of the intense early winter weather, and the continuous, large quantities of snow. Every morning I would wake up surprised to find it had snowed yet again. The holiday season was finally in full gear, and everyone in my family was ready for the Christmas break.

Despite the excitement of Christmas fast approaching, people around me were getting edgy. As the presents and parties grew in numbers, so did the fears that a power outage could occur at any time. Short summer outages in Toronto aren't uncommon, but losing power in the summer seemed more of an inconvenience than a hardship. A day or two of barbequing was fun, and my family found it was a good excuse to go camping at Sauble Beach!

This time it was different. The snow was piling up, the thermometer showed negative numbers, and worst of all was the biting wind chill. With all this non-stop snow the possibility of losing electricity was becoming a real concern. A power outage in winter meant no heat, no lights, no cooking — and often no hot water. And there would definitely be no barbequing outside, or going camping to escape. I began reconsidering my thoughts about snow and how much I loved it.

It was the Saturday before Christmas when the freezing rain started. I woke up to a cold house and an eerie silence. My dad is an electrician and a sound engineer, so our home is filled with electronic devices that announce things — like the house is at the right temperature. But the house was silent… and cold. It had finally happened.

When my parents told me that most of Toronto was without power and covered in ice, I had no clue what to do. So, being a lazy teenager, I decided to just sleep through it. I figured it would last an hour at most. Hopefully by the time I woke up from my nap the lights and the heat would be back on. Surely people wouldn't be able to last long without heat in these temperatures. I just assumed the city was already doing everything they could to restore the electricity. Like everyone else I could only hope.

Miraculously, in our home, that hope was fulfilled! Suddenly, after only a few hours, the electricity in six houses on my street, including ours, came back on, bringing this small strip of neighbourhood back to life. We were so thankful to once again have power, and along with it lights and heat, and the ability to take a hot shower and cook a meal. Unfortunately, this wasn't the case for everyone.

When I tried to keep in touch with my friends I discovered their cellphones and laptops were all dying. One friend told me that recharging his phone meant going to a mall (or someplace else with power) and sitting on a wet floor. After three days the freezing rain finally stopped, but the streets were now littered with fallen trees and broken branches all coated with ice. And they continued to fall. Then the temperatures plummeted, causing everything to freeze solid. Then it started snowing again on top of the ice, making driving and walking conditions even more treacherous.

Over the days leading up to Christmas Eve many people came in and out of our home to find shelter from the bitter cold for a few hours, or just hang around to charge their phones. Their own homes were still cold, and without lights or hot water. My family was more than thrilled with all the company.

By the time Christmas Eve arrived on Wednesday, our small bungalow was packed with at least fifteen people from four different families, along with friends of mine and two of my sister's classmates. Their homes had now been dark and cold for five days. Again, the snow fell heavily that night. Desperate for relief, friends and neighbours streamed into our home seeking refuge—and my folks welcomed them all.

In our small living room we all shared stories over cups of coffee and hot chocolate. Children ran around and, after bringing their presents from their own homes, they set them under our Christmas tree hoping that even though they weren't at home Santa would still find them. Late Christmas Eve my house turned into a motel, with people sleeping on anything that looked relatively comfortable. Despite the reason, it felt so intimate spending Christmas Eve with so many people in such a compact space. When everyone was finally settled, beds, couches, even padded chairs were covered with balls of comforters. It was just one big sleepover!

I gave up my double bed to a couple who hadn't slept well in days. One of my sister's classmates slept in the second bed in her room, and I slept on the floor between them. Knowing that everyone in the house was snug and warm for the first time in many days allowed me to do that with a lot more acceptance. I hadn't had to deal with the cold and discomfort that they had.

I woke up early that Christmas morning to a house full of happy faces from a proper night of sleep in a warm house. Someone had brought a real evergreen wreath and the fragrance permeated the room. There was heat, and light, and water to wash sleepy faces. The huge breakfast made by the combined efforts of all the parents filled everyone with laughter and joy. Christmas morning is always magical, but opening my presents that morning with other teens and younger kids and everyone still in their pyjamas made Christmas seem more magical than ever. My mom had backup gifts on hand, which she gave to my sister's classmates so they had something to open as well. With everybody warm and full and laughing and hugging, overnight my family had turned from four people into fifteen. I don't remember ever before having such a heart-warming feeling. It was extraordinary!

That experience was a real turning point for me. Before this I hadn't really thought about Christmas in such an intimate way. And even though this amazing experience came out of hardship and misfortune, it renewed for me, and still does, the magic of Christmas that I'd had as a small child. Whenever I think of Christmas now, it includes the memory of the smell of sweet evergreen, hot chocolate, piles of snow and the laughter of many — all under one roof. This experience brought me face to face with the true spirit of Christmas.

~Alexa Danielle Patino

My Story

*The journey in between what you once were and who you are
now becoming is where the dance of life really takes place.*
~Barbara De Angelis

never thought about killing myself; it just became a condition.
Kind of like catching a cold. One minute you are fine, and the
next minute you are sick. Whenever people would talk about
suicide, I would think to myself, "I would never do that." Why
would someone want to do something so final, so stupid?

For me, I just wanted the pain to stop. And it got to the point
where I was willing to do whatever it took to make that happen. It
started with the usual stuff....

I am 16. I spend the summer with my mom and during the school
year I live with my dad. I feel like an inconvenience to both of them.
At my mom's I have no room. My mom isn't there for me when I need
her because she always has something more important to do. At least,
that is how it feels.

I was having trouble with my friends. The ones I had not lost
already to "different lifestyles" were unable to help me. In their own
words, my problems were "too much" for them. The intensity of my
pain scared them, like it did me.

Oh, yeah… did I mention my boyfriend, John, had dumped me
that day? My first boyfriend had left me, too. He said I had become
impossible to love and now John was gone, too. And it wasn't that I

would be without him that mattered… it was me. What was wrong with me? Why is it so hard to love me and why is it that when it gets hard, everyone bails?

I was alone. All I had were the voices in my head telling me I blew it, I was too needy, I was never going to be loved once someone really got to know me. I felt that I wasn't even good enough to be loved by my own parents.

You know how, when you are really hurting, you feel like you can just call the person (the boyfriend, the friend) and tell him or her how much it hurts and they'll say, "Oh, I am so sorry; I didn't mean to hurt you; hang on, I will be right there"? Well, I called and I was crying, and I said it hurts too much, please come talk to me. He said he couldn't help me… and he hung up.

I went into my mom's bathroom and took a bottle of Tylenol PM, some tranquilizers and a couple pain pills I had left from an injury. Soon the pain would be over.

I will spare you the gruesome details of what followed. It was a whole new kind of pain. Physically, I puked until I couldn't move. Emotionally, I was more scared than I have ever been. I did not want to die. (Statistics show that immediately after "attempting" suicide, the person desperately wants to live… not die, which makes it even sadder to think about those who do succeed.) Luckily for me, I did not die. But I hurt my body (my stomach still aches). And I scared and hurt a lot of people. I scared myself, but I didn't die and I can't even begin to tell you how happy I am about that.

I cringe every time someone else finds out. I did not want to write this story, but I did want to help anyone else who might be thinking about it or who is in a lot of pain.

It has been a month since that night. I have laughed at least 500 times, many of those real "pee your pants" kind of laughing. I have a therapist who really cares about me, and we are making real progress in building up my confidence. She is also helping my mom and dad be "better parents." I have realized that they really do care and that they are doing the best that they can. I have a new friend who has gone through some hard stuff herself. My intense feelings do not scare her, and we know what it means to "be there" for someone you care about. I have worked things out with some of my old friends and we are closer than ever. I have earned $500 and spent it all on myself... without guilt (well, maybe a little). And I am starting to forgive myself.

Oh, yeah... I met a guy. He is really sweet and he knows "my story." We have agreed to take things really slow.

These are only a few of the things I would have missed. Life gets really hard sometimes and really painful. For me, I couldn't feel everyone else's love because I had forgotten how to love myself. I'm learning now — learning how to accept, forgive and love myself. And I'm learning that things change. Pain *does* go away, and happiness is the other side. Although the pain comes back, so does the happiness. It is like waves in the ocean coming and going... coming and going... breathing in and breathing out.

~Lia Gay

The Old Green Coat

*It's difficult to decide whether growing pains are something
teenagers have — or are.*
~Author Unknown

C hildren learn a great deal from their parents through
the years, from the basics of walking and talking, to the
more complex concepts of beliefs and values. Some of this
information is taught through words, but most is simply
learned by example. Occasionally, a lesson remains so vivid in your
memory, that it dramatically influences your life. My mother's old green
coat had that impact on me.

My mother and I never had one of those cutesy, "dress in matching
mother-daughter clothes" relationships. But it was good — until my
teenage years when my mother became my opponent in a battle of
wills. In the confused, uncertain mind of a teenager, this translated to,
"She doesn't care, understand or love me." As a matter of fact, I was
quite sure that she had no idea what love was really all about. While
she was mopping the floors, cooking meals, helping my father with
their business and raising five children, I was listening to the music,
reading poetry and experiencing the excitement of love.

As the winter of my sixteenth year approached, the tension
between us grew. Looking back now, I realize that I took every opportunity to lash out at her in an effort to soothe my own insecurity. And
that is exactly what I did when she unpacked that old green coat of

hers. Well-worn and out of style, I bluntly told her that I could not believe she would wear it for another season. She began to say something about not having the money for a new coat, but I was already spouting phrases like, "When I'm older, I will have a beautiful coat, a rich-looking coat. I wouldn't be caught dead wearing a rag like that." She hung the coat in the closet and said nothing.

Christmas morning was always an exciting time in our house, and that year was no exception. The sound of laughter, kids yelling and paper ripping filled the living room. Though I tried to maintain what I thought was a sense of maturity, I was anxious to see what "Santa" had brought. One box way in the back caught my attention. It was large, brightly wrapped and it had my name on it. I quickly tore it open and lifted the lid. Inside was the most beautiful coat I had ever seen. Brown suede with a white fur collar, it was nicer than anything I had ever dreamed of owning.

Looking up, I caught my mother's eyes. I thought of the old green coat and, instantly, I realized how precious this gift really was. She knew what a coat like this would mean to me, and she was willing to make do with her old coat so that I could have it. And what was even more profound was what I saw in her eyes. They did not reflect resentment from her having made this sacrifice, but instead they gleamed with joy, as if it were she who had received the very best gift. Suddenly the true meaning of love was clear to me.

I wish I could tell you that our relationship magically changed into a loving and giving one after that day, but that only happens in the movies. We still fought and found fault with each other, but I always held a special place in my heart where I loved her and I knew that she loved me.

Eventually, the teenage years ended and mutual love, respect and friendship grew between us, and has remained there since. I now have children of my own and I love them with an intensity they cannot yet understand. It's the love my mother taught me the year she wore her old green coat — and I began to grow up.

~Kathy Smith Solarino

A Visit with My Parents

Two of the greatest gifts we can give our children are roots and wings.

~Hodding Carter

While I was serving as a Peace Corps volunteer in the Philippines, my parents came to visit me. They arrived three days before my birthday. We rested one day in the capital city of Manila before embarking on the twenty-four-hour boat ride to the small island of Sibuyan where I was assigned.

The heat was intense inside the ship's cabin. Rows of bunk beds with vinyl mats filled the small space, and every bed had at least one body. I had advised my parents to dress conservatively in below-the-knee attire to adhere to the cultural norms. Dad, who is claustrophobic by nature, sweated miserably in his pants and collared shirt; Mom fared little better in culottes and a T-shirt.

I lay on my bunk, accustomed to the discomfort and worried about how they would do once we actually arrived on the island. I lived in an eight-by-ten-foot hut by the ocean, without electricity, plumbing, beds or window screens.

Upon our arrival, we traveled to my host family's house in a 1970s vintage motorcycle with a creatively welded sidecar. There waiting for us were my host mother Nanay, father Tatay, two sisters Gina and Nene, and brother Bindel. Like the timid first meeting of spouses in a prearranged marriage, my two families stared inquisitively at each other as we sat together in the bamboo rest house.

Both had been anticipating this in-person assembly. After the initial introductions were complete, my mother with wavering voice tried to express in broken and simple English the gratitude she felt toward my Filipino hosts for taking care of me as one of their own. In her eyes and in her words, I could sense all of the worries that she had harbored for me in this place so far from home, so foreign. Nanay looked into my mother's eyes and smiled knowingly. She is the mother of six children.

We washed up at the river, then walked the half-mile through groves of mango and coconut trees, across the swamp outlet, and finally along the seashore to my hut. Mom and Nanay walked together.

As I watched them, I was struck with the awareness of my good fortune. These two amazing women are mine to learn from, to lean on, to love and to be loved by. Nanay possesses an enduring strength and peacefulness much like my own mother. It shows in the way she winnows rice in the wind until her arms won't raise up any more, in the tender way she holds her first grandchild, and in the way she spoke to me of love, family and the responsibilities of women.

Approaching my little hut, my parents grew quiet as they took in the seemingly impoverished human condition of island life — my life.

Dad stood on the bamboo platform under my roof and cast his eyes seaward. His shoulders bespoke the sad and amazed bewilderment that his eyes would not show me. I had already been living on the island for over a year and was not prepared for how this lifestyle might appear to a "more comfortable" mind, especially my father's.

He was farm-raised on the ideal that hard work will get you somewhere. When we visited my host father at work, Dad stood solemnly watching as Tatay, clucking and grunting, trudged through the thick mud of his rice field.

He guided a handmade plow with one hand, while wound around the other was a rope leading to the nose of the water buffalo straining against the plow. Tatay has toiled that way all of his sixty-seven years, and he will continue to do so until his body won't let him. Tatay and Nanay know hard work. Tatay and Nanay have lived hand-to-mouth every day of their lives.

While celebrating my birthday with coworkers from the Philippine Department of Environment and Natural Resources, we unwittingly ended up taking part in the confiscation and seizure of an illegal fisherman's boat. It was full of dynamite that the fisherman would have used to blast a school of fish, consequently destroying the already damaged corals.

There was some shooting and a boat chase, and the birthday party was over when our group was forced to flee — confiscated boat in tow — for fear of retaliation.

My parents were not comforted in the least by this display of my work environment. I tried to ease their fears and my own threadbare nerves by explaining repeatedly that this was not a normal day on the job.

At night, we retired to the comforts of my bamboo floor and the darkness, where Mom and Dad cringed in horror at the sounds of rats and mice scuttling, lizards chuckling, palm-sized spiders leaping, and carnivorous cockroaches gnawing just beyond the flimsy mesh barriers of their mosquito nets. While I slept soundly, my parents had an altogether different experience. In my mother's words, "It seemed as if dawn would never come."

When dawn did arrive, we were up at the crack of it. And I was the one, this time, cracking the whip. Chore time! Water needed to be fetched, food scavenged for, laundry soaked and scrubbed, and a fire started to heat the day's cooking and drinking water.

The day before my parents departed from the Philippines, we had lunch at a hotel overlooking the island's shore. As we finished eating, I glanced over at Dad and the look on his face stilled me. I saw tears where I hadn't seen them in years.

I asked him what was wrong. He shook his head and, looking deeply at my mother, he said, "We've seen so little of the world, other people, other customs, other ways of living." He paused before continuing, "Thank you, Leah, thank you for opening our eyes."

~Leah Burgess

My Epiphany

With the past, I have nothing to do; nor with the future. I live
now.
~Ralph Waldo Emerson

t seems that when something awful happens to me, my mind just
shuts down. These things change the way I think for a period
of time after they happen. Somehow, I find a way to keep it all
together by reverting to my "one day at a time" motto, but really,
inside, I'm freaking out. Sometimes I'm freaking out and I don't even
realize it yet. I've discovered lately that moving on from those difficult
times really is a process.

These days, I am in the final stages of my long battle with osteosar-
coma, a bone cancer, which made its appearance when I was fourteen
years old, claimed one of my lower legs and a lung along the way, and
recently spread to my brain. The doctors found three or four new
tumors in my brain. This news was a terrible blow since it meant two
huge things. It meant that one, along with the nodules that I already
had in my single lung, the Thalidomide I have been trying isn't doing
a single thing for me. And secondly it officially marked me as terminal.
The doctors told us that they thought I probably had less than a month
to live.

It has now been longer than a month, and I am still here and still
feeling well. Nothing has truly changed about my situation. I am still
taking medication for the headaches, and sometimes my breathing

is a lot more strained than it used to be. Although I do have a cold, which could be part of it, it's most likely that the cancer *is* progressing. There is nothing in my situation that has changed. I know that I probably won't make it, still. But there is something different now about the way I look at things. I *feel* different. I feel inspired! I feel invigorated! I don't feel like I'm just sitting around waiting to die anymore. I feel infused with life. There's a reason I have already beaten the odds. There's a reason it's not time yet.

I don't know what came first — the changes to my daily routine, or the changes to my perspective. But somehow they're working together to be just what I needed. During the past week or so we've been making small changes to my medications since I've been doing so well. The first thing we did was drop the nausea medicine I'd been taking on a schedule with the pain medication. It turns out that I don't really need it at all, since I haven't had any nausea since. We also started weaning me off the steroid I'd been taking to control swelling, which makes me eat everything in sight and makes me swell up like a balloon. Somehow, and the only thing I can think to attribute it to, is that by getting rid of those two medications, I am feeling a little more like myself. I haven't had to take a nap in ages! My eyes, which had been blurry and unfocused, are doing so well that I finished a book that I was reading... on my Kindle! My computer screen no longer tries to flip letters around. But that's not all — a few days ago Mom convinced me to put my prosthetic leg on for a while. It didn't take too much cajoling, since it was something I'd been meaning to try since I have been feeling better. It doesn't quite fit right because I haven't worn it in a month. Right now because I haven't been wearing it, I have no leg muscle to even hardly hold it up. But I can kind of walk on it, with my crutches, and I have hope and faith that before long I'll be able to use it again for a short time. :)

I'm not sure where it came from, this sudden epiphany I've had. But something inside me has clicked. It reminds me of a story my pastor told me when he came by for a visit, about a man who was pronounced terminal. Another person asked him, "What are you doing right now?" And the man who was dying answered, "Well I'm terminal, I'm dying." The first man either asked him again what he was doing right now or informed him somehow that he was wrong. The man who was terminal wasn't dying just then, just at that moment he was living. And as long as he was breathing he would be living. That's the epiphany I've had. Right now, regardless of the things to come, I'm living! I'm not sitting around waiting to die. My entire perspective has changed. I'm alive right now. I'm living.

So, today I leave you with this message, one that I can hardly believe that I went this far without. Cherish every single day. It is one of those things that is easier said than done. The way that something feels is all about perspective. Sometimes our hearts don't need a miracle. Sometimes there just aren't any miracles and the world around us feels like there can never be any happiness in it again. I know how that feels. I have had some dark days these last few months. I won't lie. It's difficult to know that eventually I won't feel good. It's hard to know that essentially I'm just sitting around waiting for the cancer to progress.

I can't think like that anymore. I have to think about the things that I can do. The life that I can live. I may not be able to go on the ski trip this month, but I'm still doing better than expected. I'm still here. I'm still living. Life is precious, whether you have a straight road stretched before you as far as the eye can see, or whether, like most people, your road turns and bends into the undergrowth and you have no idea where it leads. Follow that bend, and your heart, no matter where it goes. Mine may go on, to places unmentionable, but everyone's does, eventually. All roads lead to the same bend, and although we can't see around the corner, I know there are people who have gone before me that will help me when I get there. But for now, I'm not there yet. Today I'm living, and my heart sings with joy for the days that follow.

For anyone going through a difficult time, I want to pass on the list of ten steps that I composed. These steps have helped me move forward in the past. I'm not a professional and I have no claim to fame, but these steps have helped me and I want to share them with other people.

Here are my Ten Steps to Moving Forward:

1. Cry, Yell, and Grieve: The first step can make you feel like you are taking a few steps back, but it is necessary. I think when something happens that reroutes your entire life and the direction you were going previously, it is normal to grieve and be sad. Because I believe that whenever you go through a difficult time, it changes you. It changes the way you think and perceive things, and the first step to acceptance of the new reality, whatever it is, is to mourn the past and the person you used to be. So, let yourself grieve for as long as you need to, and when you're able, you'll find the next step.

2. Talk When You're Ready: Sometimes you feel like talking things through and sometimes you don't. When you're ready to talk, find someone who you can talk to as an equal and whose opinion you value, and pour your heart out. Sometimes, just having someone who cares and who is there for you, no matter what, gives you the boost you need to move on from the first step (even though you may feel still the need to grieve from time to time).

3. Escape When You Need To: But not too often. Sometimes life just takes a dump on you, and your heart and mind are too full to process things in a healthy way. In these moments, escape is essential; watch a TV show or movie, read a book, or veg out on the Internet. Take a break from the things that are weighing you down, and come back to them later with a fresh outlook. But I caution you on escaping too often, because escaping never makes your problems go away, and you always have to deal with them eventually.

4. Start Small: If the big things are too overwhelming at any given moment, start small. Instead of worrying about a huge appointment next week that you're afraid might hold bad news (perhaps similar to where you just were) try to focus on smaller more attainable goals. Rather than brooding about the appointment, focus on your exercises, your chores, or even your homework assignments. You'll get there in the same amount of time, whether or not you worry about it.

5. Find Your Muse: Your muse is the source of your inspiration.

Find the thing, or things, that inspire you the most, and absorb them into your world. These could be anything. For some, it could be their children, others music or nature, and for people like me, poetry or literature.

6. Reach Out: Interaction is an important thing in any person's life. Reaching out doesn't necessarily mean telling everyone about your struggles, rather it means finding people you enjoy, and spending time with them. It can mean laughing and teasing each other, but it also means support. Maybe not support like that of step two, but support that lets you know that they care and that they're thinking of you. This kind of support is a bulwark that can bolster you through any storm. These are the people who know how to cheer you on, when you're going through a hard time.

7. Channel Your Nervous Energy: Often you may find yourself stressing out and worrying. The best way to prevent this is to throw yourself headlong into another project, albeit a more relaxing one. For me, this usually means writing, scrapbooking, or artwork of some kind. I actually find that some of my best poetry is written when I'm trying not to freak out.

8. Help Someone Else: Helping someone else is actually a great way to help you deal with tough things that are going on your own life. It may sound selfish, in an ironic way. But not only does helping someone through their problems distract you, it also fills you with a pleasant satisfaction. Plain and simple; it feels good to help someone else out.

9. Focus on the Good Things: If you go through life with a "woe is me" attitude, things can seem harder than they really are. Granted, I'm finding that optimism comes more easily to me than most, but I cannot help but feel that some optimism is imperative to dealing with any situation. By focusing on the good things in your life, you can muster up enough strength to hope. And I believe that hope is ultimately what allows you to move on.

10. Take One Day At a Time: We spend so much time worrying about things that are far in the future that we miss the things that are happening in the moment. Even if the moment you are in seems difficult, and there are things on the horizon that seem even more difficult, it is important to focus on the moment you are in. We can't worry about things that haven't happened yet, or that may or may not happen. If you must worry, worry about the day you are in, and worry about tomorrow, well, tomorrow. But remember also, no matter what you're going through, that you will get through. No matter how hard it seems in that moment, or how bleak the future looks, time will move you forward against your will. Eventually you'll find that things don't seem as hard, or hurt as bad, and life will take on a new routine. And you'll be okay. Or... at least that's the way it's been for me.

~Angela Sayers

Editor's note: Angie Sayers died on July 15, 2011, before her story was published in *Chicken Soup for the Soul: Find Your Happiness*, the book in which this story originally appeared. She was thrilled that it was going to be published.

Meet Our Authors

Amy Newmark was a writer, speaker, Wall Street analyst and business executive in the worlds of finance and telecommunications for more than thirty years. Today she is publisher, editor-in-chief and coauthor of the Chicken Soup for the Soul book series. By curating and editing inspirational true stories from ordinary people who have had extraordinary experiences, Amy has kept the twenty-one-year-old Chicken Soup for the Soul brand fresh and relevant, and still part of the social zeitgeist.

Amy graduated *magna cum laude* from Harvard University where she majored in Portuguese and minored in French. She wrote her thesis about popular, spoken-word poetry in Brazil, which involved traveling throughout Brazil and meeting with poets and writers to collect their stories. She is delighted to have come full circle in her writing career — from collecting poetry "from the people" in Brazil as a twenty-year-old to, three decades later, collecting stories and poems "from the people" for Chicken Soup for the Soul.

Amy has a national syndicated newspaper column and is a frequent radio and TV guest, passing along the real-life lessons and useful tips she has picked up from reading and editing thousands of Chicken Soup for the Soul stories.

She and her husband are the proud parents of four grown children and in her limited spare time, Amy enjoys visiting them, hiking, and reading books that she did not have to edit.

Dr. Milton Boniuk has practiced ophthalmology for nearly sixty years, and is The Caroline F. Elles Chair of Ophthalmology and Professor of Ophthalmology at Baylor College of Medicine in Houston, Texas. A native of Nova Scotia, Dr. Boniuk attended medical school at Dalhousie University in Halifax, Nova Scotia before moving to the United States for his residency at Wills Eye Hospital in Philadelphia, followed by a fellowship at the Armed Forces Institute of Pathology in Washington, D.C.

Dr. Boniuk and his wife Laurie live near their children and grandchildren in Houston. The Boniuk family has a strong commitment to philanthropy and a vision for change. Their belief that the world can be made a better place guides the work of The Boniuk Foundation, which sponsored this collection of Chicken Soup for the Soul stories. The Foundation believes that all religions, cultures, and ethnicities have a unique contribution to share with the world, and that differences among individuals are to be celebrated and not feared. Thus, the values of compassion, tolerance, and respect must be instilled in our young people, and this volume is designed to do that in an entertaining and accessible way.

Dr. Boniuk and his wife Laurie have also funded The Boniuk Institute for the Study and Advancement of Religious Tolerance at Rice University, with the mission of promoting research, education, outreach, and better parenting to foster religious tolerance by using innovative methods to reach young people, their parents, and their grandparents. The Institute's logo is seen on the cover of this book, with its three key words — Tolerance, Respect, and Compassion — surrounded by the symbols of many of the world's major religions.

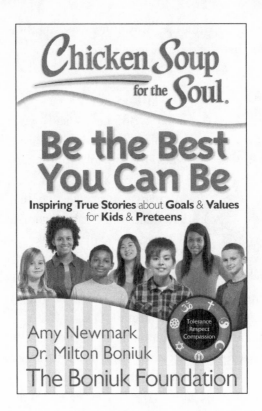

Chicken Soup
for the Soul.

Be the Best You Can Be

Inspiring True Stories about **Goals** & **Values** for **Kids** & **Preteens**

Amy Newmark
Dr. Milton Boniuk
The Boniuk Foundation

Tolerance
Respect
Compassion

Self-esteem, tolerance, good values—these are gifts that will last children a lifetime and help them become successful adults. This book, a joint project of Chicken Soup for the Soul and The Boniuk Foundation, harnesses the power of storytelling to inspire and teach kids about working together to promote tolerance, respect, and compassion. The stories, about embracing differences, rejecting stereotypes, and making good choices, are great for kids to discuss with each other and the adults in their lives. It's part of a larger effort that includes additional books for teens, college students, parents, and grandparents, as well as a family television show every Saturday morning starting in October.

978-1-942649-00-7

More great advice

Chicken Soup for the Soul.

Raising Great Kids

101 Stories about Sharing Values from
Generation to Generation

Amy Newmark
Dr. Milton Boniuk
The Boniuk Foundation

Tolerance, respect, compassion and other values start at home, in healthy, strong relationships between the generations. These stories provide practical, insightful tips for parents and grandparents looking to strengthen their families and raise successful children. The personal stories in this collection not only show adult readers how to be their best selves, but also offer great advice on how to raise resilient, confident, upstanding kids — kids who exhibit all the qualities of acceptance, courage, and inner strength. These stories provide practical, insightful tips for parents and grandparents.

978-1-942649-04-5

and inspiration!

The Boniuk Foundation
www.theboniukfoundation.org

For moments that become stories™
www.chickensoup.com